It's Our Movement Now

UNIVERSITY PRESS OF FLORIDA

Florida A&M University, Tallahassee
Florida Atlantic University, Boca Raton
Florida Gulf Coast University, Ft. Myers
Florida International University, Miami
Florida State University, Tallahassee
New College of Florida, Sarasota
University of Central Florida, Orlando
University of Florida, Gainesville
University of North Florida, Jacksonville
University of South Florida, Tampa
University of West Florida, Pensacola

IT'S OUR MOVEMENT NOW

Black Women's Politics and the
1977 National Women's Conference

Edited by Laura L. Lovett,
Rachel Jessica Daniel, and Kelly N. Giles

Featuring the photographs of Diana Mara Henry

UNIVERSITY PRESS OF FLORIDA

Gainesville / Tallahassee / Tampa / Boca Raton
Pensacola / Orlando / Miami / Jacksonville / Ft. Myers / Sarasota

Publication of this work made possible by a Sustaining the Humanities through the American Rescue Plan grant from the National Endowment for the Humanities.

27 26 25 24 23 22   6 5 4 3 2 1

Library of Congress Control Number: 2022944403
ISBN 978-0-8130-6948-7 (cloth)
ISBN 978-0-8130-6881-7 (paper)

The University Press of Florida is the scholarly publishing agency for the State University System of Florida, comprising Florida A&M University, Florida Atlantic University, Florida Gulf Coast University, Florida International University, Florida State University, New College of Florida, University of Central Florida, University of Florida, University of North Florida, University of South Florida, and University of West Florida.

University Press of Florida
2046 NE Waldo Road
Suite 2100
Gainesville, FL 32609
http://upress.ufl.edu

Contents

Figures

Acknowledgments

THIS PROJECT EMERGED from Diana Mara Henry's generous donation of her photographic archive to the University of Massachusetts' Special Collections and University Archives. As the official photographer for the 1977 National Women's Conference, Diana was uniquely situated to document this historically significant event. While her photographs have been widely reprinted, sometimes without permission as Diana will tell you, we realized that we had an opportunity to use them as pieces of historical evidence as we sought to craft narratives that captured the experiences of a selected group of African American women leaders who were present in Houston for the 1977 conference. We are extremely grateful for Diana's support of this project, and for her generous permission to use her photographs. Rob Cox and Danielle Kovacs at the University of Massachusetts' Special Collections and University Archives have also provided invaluable support, including extensive photograph digitization. Carole Connare at the W.E.B. Du Bois Library was a source of continuous encouragement.

We are extremely grateful to the Women's Fund of the University of Massachusetts for their generous support. A grant from the Women's Fund supported a workshop at the University of Massachusetts where our contributors met to discuss each other's drafts and the framing of this project.

Introduction

Beyond the Minority Plank

**LAURA L. LOVETT, RACHEL JESSICA DANIEL,
AND KELLY N. GILES**

IN NOVEMBER 1977, over 20,000 women gathered in Houston to set a plan of action for the nation. The National Women's Conference has been depicted by historians and some participants as the culminating moment of the women's movement.[1] Gloria Steinem described it as profoundly transformational as delegates worked through controversial topics that had previously divided them.[2] Ironically, the National Women's Conference is now widely recognized, not for its unity, but for its division as it provided a national stage for the opponents to the feminist agenda being crafted inside the conference hall.[3]

We seek to recover a different history of the National Women's Conference (NWC). A history that grapples with the incredible diversity of the women in Houston. A history that makes visible the leadership and presence of Black women who made the meeting possible. A history that recognizes the NWC as the place where the phrase "women of color" became a means of representing that diversity and leadership. Most importantly, we seek a history that makes a wide range of Black women's political action visible.[4]

Feminism never spoke with a single voice, even when countering its most vociferous opponents. Some histories of the women's movement have been criticized for portraying a middle-class, white movement, overlooking the African American women who were active participants locally, nationally, and internationally.[5] We join other contemporary scholars who value the many ways in which Black women took the lead in the women's movement and used it as a means to address crucial issues in their communities and their lives. Historians seeking to understand Black feminism have focused on the Combahee River Collective, the National Black Feminist Organization, the National Alliance of Black Feminists, Black Women Organized for Action, and the Third

World Women's Alliance, all Black radical feminist groups, among other Black feminist organizations that existed at the time.[6] These histories are focused and powerful. We have chosen a different strategy for making Black women's agency visible.

The lives that are depicted in these pages speak to Black women's politics at a critical juncture of the women's movement. Where other collections, such as Dayo F. Gore, Jeanne Theoharis, and Komozi Woodard's *Want to Start a Revolution?* and Bettye Collier-Thomas and V. P. Franklin's *Sisters in the Struggle*, provide histories of African American women in the Civil Rights Movement and radical politics, *It's Our Movement Now* focuses on Black women's activism in relation to the women's movement in different terms.[7] We are focused on African American women's political action either in the women's movement or as informed by the women's movement. Of course, we have left important stories untold and meaningful lives unexplored in this slim collection, but we believe that our selection of women significantly expands the history of Black women's political action.

The NWC was an unprecedented political gathering of women both in terms of its size and its diversity. Inspired by Diana Mara Henry's photographs of Black women at the conference, we use the NWC as a means to make visible Black women's presence, the range of Black women's feminism, their political action and experiences, and the range of their leadership. We are using photographs, even some that may be familiar, to acknowledge an invisible past.

The popular narrative of the mainstream second wave feminist movement prioritizes the voices of white women. This book challenges the notion that Black women were on the sidelines for any aspect of the women's movement. By moving Black women's activism from "margin to center," we offer a new perspective on the scholarly discussion of the 1977 National Women's Conference. The women in this volume may not have all identified as feminist; however, as bell hooks reminds us, "we can act in feminist resistance without ever using the word feminism."[8] Participating in the 1977 National Women's Conference was an act of feminist resistance for the women whose lives we explore in this volume.

When Diana Mara Henry went to the National Women's Conference as its official photographer, she was not tasked with taking photos of anyone in particular. Nevertheless, in the hundreds of images she made in Houston, a remarkable record of Black women's activism emerges and is made visible. Drawing from this visual record, we consider how Black women were rendered visible and invisible in American activism in the late twentieth century using the NWC as a focal event. In eighteen profiles of Black women *It's Our Move-*

ment Now does not tell a singular story of the National Women's Conference or sketch a singular legacy. Rather our goal is to engage with a spectrum of Black women and their experiences. We chose to profile Black women rather than all of the Women of Color represented at the Houston Conference, because we want to resist any reductive sense in which Black women can be said to have a simple shared experience as defined by their race. Sketching the different paths of Black women through Houston reveals a diversity of experiences and perspectives that constituted Black women's activism.

The International Road to Houston

In July 1975, the United Nations sponsored the World Conference of the International Women's Year and adopted the Declaration of Mexico on the Equality of Women and Their Contribution to Development and Peace. From the beginning, the political context for the first UN Women's Conference was embroiled in Cold War politics and global conflict. The International Women's Year originated with the Women's International Democratic Federation, an organization that sought to improve the status of women and children, support anti-fascism, world peace and decolonization after World War II. In the bifurcated Cold War–era world that pitted the US against the USSR, the proposal only went forward through the Economic and Social Council of the United Nations because the Soviet Union abstained from the vote. The Cold War context thwarted the plans of the US International Women's Year Commission executive director, Mildred Marcy, to have First Lady Betty Ford occupy the dais with Congresswoman Barbara Jordan when the US National Security Council denied Ford's personal request to represent the United States. The high-profile meeting was becoming a site for international conflicts over racism, Zionism, and international development [9] In what can only be called a serious misunderstanding of gender politics, Daniel Parker, the head of the US Agency for International Development was initially appointed to lead the US Delegation to Mexico City, instead of Ford.[10] Only later was Patricia Hutar, a leader of the Republican National Committee, appointed to cochair the delegation when the problem of gender representation was realized by the Ford administration.

The dynamics at the Mexico City Conference were complicated to say the least. Because geopolitics was seen as competing with women's issues, many countries sent men to represent them at the conference. A separate space for the nongovernmental organizations, called the Tribune, offered an alternative site for the conference's discussion. Unlike the formal conference, the Tribune would not issue a report. Nevertheless, the NGO Tribune became a site for negotiating not only the content and process of recognizing women's issues but also a site for negotiating what participatory democracy looked like.[11] Jill Ruckelshaus, the presiding officer of the US Commission on the Observance of International Women's Year, noted that many Americans attended only the NGO Tribune, which was five miles away from the official conference site, and challenged the validity of the US Official Delegation.

The tension between the members of the US Formal Delegation and the NGO Tribune echoed tensions among members of the conference with what was called the World Plan of Action, which had been circulated in advance. The conference, however, saw two different committees convened to propose the World Plan of Action, one to merely focus on the introductory rationalizations and the other to discuss the sixty proposed resolutions.[12] The debate over the inclusion of the term "sexism" in the document, offered by American Rita Johnston, became a site for contention, when she suggested that it be listed among the obstacles to women's equality, alongside "alien and colonial domination, foreign occupation, racial discrimination, apartheid, and neo-colonialism in all its forms."[13] Dorothy Height (chapter 4), a leader in the American Civil Rights Movement who attended the NGO Tribune on behalf of the YWCA, affirmed this linkage between sexism and racism.[14]

As a result of the conflict between official delegates and Tribune participants, Patricia Hutar, the official cochair of the US delegation, organized a three-hour-long session at the American Embassy to help clear the air.[15] In her article "Who Shall Speak for Our Nation's Women," Jill Ruckelshaus describes the meeting at the US Embassy attended by hundreds of women. Ruckelshaus notes that Jewel LaFontant was the first delegate to speak, "As she began to talk forcefully and eloquently of her involvement in the Civil Rights Movement of the 1960s, the room quieted down." LaFontant is reported to have declared that racism was "still very much a problem in the United States . . . but I am going to do my job," meaning that she was going to support the position of the official US delegation.[16] LaFontant had seconded Richard Nixon's run for the presidency at the 1960 Republican National Convention. According to Ruckelshaus, "People were listening. They were feeling some wonder at the variety of experiences, some respect for those women whose lives had been stories of the underdog who eventually won."[17] This spirit of solidarity was captured by "an eloquent Black woman," who "in language that would have graced the most distinguished pulpit, appealed for unity and love among all women."[18] The play here is to bring forward African American women, loading Jewel LaFontant as the voice of the Civil Rights Movement and an unidentified Black woman as an expression of women's unity. Ruckelhaus does not say that all the differences were resolved at this meeting, but she deploys Black women as a means of making unity visible but at the same time allowing the US color line to stand in for numerous and complex differences that are not openly addressed. Just as it does in Ruckelshaus's "Who Shall Speak for Our Nation's Women?," the visibility and simultaneous invisibility of Black women runs through many dimensions of the international and national women's conferences.[19]

Despite the geopolitical struggle, as historian Jocelyn Olcott notes, the International Women's Year (IWY) meeting not only created powerful networks of organizers on behalf of women's advancement through the Tribune, it also created institutional structures and influenced both governmental and UN officials to better consider women's issues as complex and foundational.

The National Context

The World Plan of Action was intended to inspire National Plans of Action. In her report on the Mexico meeting, Jill Ruckelshaus documented the struggles over the World Plan of Action and disparaged efforts "to bring purely political matters into the report."[20] From her perspective, conflict at the IWY was rooted in a connection between women's inequality and underdevelopment made by seventy-seven of the 133 attending countries. This made the "existing inequitable system of international economic relations" the focal issue of the meeting.[21] When it came to the US Plan of Action, Ruckelshaus instead wanted to focus on "the barriers to the full participation of women in our Nation's life."[22]

As a starting point, the US National Commission identified concrete policy recommendations from a series of fourteen committees, ranging from Arts and Humanities to Child Development, Media, Homemakers, the Equal Rights Amendment, Enforcement of Laws, Women in Employment, and Power. Discussion of economic issues connected to the International Convention's conversations about "underdevelopment" was relegated to the twelfth section identifying special problems. This is also the place when race is first addressed in terms of the "Minority Women's Employment and Training Program," where it is made part of a larger discussion of the need to expand Social Security benefits. There is no discussion of the exclusion of Blacks from entitlements because of their type of employment. It is the only place where any form of historical redress for discrimination was proposed. Because the commission included a number of separate constituencies, the US Plan was broken out into formal planks that addressed those constituencies, including planks addressing "Older Women," "Women Offenders," and

"Physical and Mental Health of Women." This initial plan formed the starting place for a national discussion.

To facilitate the National Women's Conference, every state and territory held local conferences with the twin goals of electing delegates for Houston and articulating the issues to be addressed as planks at the national meeting.[23] The question of "Who Shall Speak?" also framed the representation of the state and territorial meetings. The International Women's Year Commission insisted that delegates to the national meeting be elected at state or territorial meetings to which every resident over age 16 who registered in advance was eligible. They put a special emphasis on racial, ethnic, and economic diversity among commission members, state organizers, and delegates to Houston, offering travel expenses for anyone "who did not have the money for a trip away from home."[24] Indeed, the commission report celebrated the lengths to which various locales went to diversify the attendance, noting, "From Eskimo villages to the Florida keys, every woman living under the American flag during the summer of 1977 had a chance to make her voice heard."[25]

The fifty-six meetings, attended by more than 150,000 people, used the sixteen resolutions proposed in the 1976 Report (*"To Form a More Perfect Union"*) along with guidelines for workshop discussions and background discussions as a common starting point but reiterated that these "core" recommendations were merely suggestions. Meetings were intended to reflect the interests of the attendees. The organizers' hope, that everyone attending these meetings would be persuaded by a feminist vision for change, met with stark reality when about halfway through the meetings opponents of the Equal Rights Amendment (ERA) and opponents of the right to abortion focused on taking over the state meetings.[26] Of course, the ERA and abortion had become deeply divisive topics in the 1970s. The ERA had been sent to states for ratification in 1972 and by 1977 it had received support from 35 of the 38 states needed. Like abortion, the ERA was used as means of political organization. Both issues would profoundly influence party politics and the electoral landscape in the United States.[27]

The commission report focuses nearly four of the dozen or so pages on the state meetings discussing the first meeting held in Vermont in May of that year.[28] While seven of the eight states holding meetings in early June both backed what were called the "core resolutions" and elected delegates "committed to equality for women," the tide began to turn with the Missouri State Meeting.[29] Storming the conference at the last minute, a coalition of Missouri anti-ERA and pro-life groups, nominated a slate of delegates who represented what they called "New Suffragists," which the Commissioner Report described as "anti-change."[30] Opponents organizing in Utah, most of them urged on by the Church of Latter Day Saints' Relief Society, contributed to the largest state meeting at 14,000 participants, where they voted NO on every proposed resolution and even proposed a resolution calling for the repeal of women's right to vote, despite the fact that Utah was one of the first territories to allow female suffrage in 1870.[31]

This was not to say that state and territorial meetings, prior to this shift in political organizing had been without disputes. Indeed, the Minnesota meeting, where the IWY commissioner had proclaimed as keynote speaker, "This is the only revolution in history financed by the Federal Government!" While the majority of attendees voted for wages for housework, they met with complaints by "minority" activists for ignoring "their problems."[32] Yet, when prodded by conservatives to join them in a protest walk-out, historian Marjorie Spruill notes, "one African American woman told the assembly she had waited far too long for such an opportunity to discuss the concerns of women and minorities" to consider walking out.[33]

Southern states with large percentages of Blacks met with expressly racist opposition to their representation. For example, in South Carolina, where James Clyburn attended the state meeting, the governor stayed away for fear of provoking political repercussions, after promising to give opening remarks. Opponents could not make a dent on the support for the Core Resolutions. Nevertheless, South Carolina state representative Norma Russell held a press conference condemning the "well-heeled leaders of the conference" for exploiting the poor and minorities, busing them into the meetings, to get their votes, promising them "a 'sugar daddy' from the cradle to the grave."[34] Sometimes these attacks turned to physical violence, as described in Spruill's account of the physical attack of an Black Alabaman college student, Mary Carstarphen, by a white Eagle Forum (Phyllis Schlafly's group) member, who shouted, "God is going to punish you" and slapped her across the face when she rose to speak at a microphone in favor of the right to abortion.[35] Mississippi sent twenty-nine delegates to the national conference. The only Black delegate from Mississippi, however, resigned in protest, so the entire delegation was white, including the wife of a Ku Klux Klan Grand Wizard, adding their endorsement to the "anti-change forces."[36]

Nevertheless, as a group, the delegates from across the country formed an incredibly diverse assembly.[37] This was in part a result of President Jimmy Carter's restructuring of the National Commission in 1977, which doubled the percentage of commissioners who were women of color.[38] Of the 100,000 women and men who participated in the preparatory conferences, the fact that

35.5 percent of the selected delegates were racial or ethnic minorities and that sixty of the 2,000 delegates openly identified as lesbian made this the most diverse federal conference ever held in the United States.[39] According to the Minority Caucus report, the diversity of the conference was "the most remarkable and distinguishing characteristic of the delegate body."[40]

Black Women and the Women's Movement

To be a Black woman who supported the Women's Movement was to build a connection with white women who, at the very least, did not understand how Black women were impacted by both racism and sexism, and at the worst, excluded them from their organizations. Black women who supported the Women's Movement also faced the danger of being ostracized from their communities because some imagined feminism to be antithetical to Black Nationalism.[41] Historian Paula Giddings notes that, "Before 1973, virtually the only Black women who acknowledged the value of feminism were those ensconced in the women's movement itself." Giddings points out that Kathleen Cleaver, a member of the Black Panther Party, is the "exception, who argued that 'in order for women to obtain liberation, the struggles are going to have to be united on the basis of being women, not on the basis of being Black women or White women' . . . still, she did not believe that Black and White women could work toward liberation within the same organization."[42]

As the women's movement gained momentum in the early 1970s, Black women authors reflected on the fraught relationship. In 1970, Toni Cade Bambara wrote for and edited *The Black Woman,* an anthology that collected essays, poetry, and prose from writers, critics, scholars about the complexities of being a Black woman; Morrison's article picks up the conversation and articulates with precision the deep distrust that Black women had of white women at the time. She writes, Black women "look at White women and see the enemy, for they know that racism is not confined to white men and that there are more white women than men in this country."[43] In 1971, Toni Morrison expanded on this theme posing the question: "What do black women feel about Women's Lib?" Her answer, delivered in an article published in the *New York Times,* was "Distrust." For Morrison, "liberating movements in the Black world have been catalysts for white feminism," yet women's lib didn't pay "much attention to the problems of most Black women."[44] Morrison's article continued a critical conversation that was happening within the African American community around the role of Black women in public activism.

In this context, Black, Chicana, and white feminists on the Left organized themselves by both race and class in parallel movements.[45] Black women, some of whom were wary of both white feminists and Black liberation organizations, developed their own groups where they articulated the complexity of their experiences through a lens that took into consideration their overlapping identities. They collectively developed theories, shared resources, and partnered with mainly white feminist organizations when their interests aligned. In *Living for the Revolution,* historian Kimberly Springer argues that, "Black feminists' voices and visions fell between the cracks of the civil rights and women's movements, so they created formal organizations to speak on behalf of Black women with an explicitly feminist consciousness."[46] By conducting "politics within the cracks," or interstitial politics, where Black women both fit their activism into their daily life, and found a way to articulate the experiences that mainly white, mainstream feminist organizations could not understand, Black feminists provided a blueprint for organizing social movements that centered their intersecting identities.

Despite their long-standing distrust of the Women's Movement, Black women actively participated in the 1977 National Women's Conference. Perhaps they saw an opportunity to shape the national conversation around African American women's issues in a way that would challenge, if not stretch, the social perspective on who they truly are and what they aspire to for their lives, families, and communities. Black women understood the need to develop their own agenda before the 1977 conference. Springer writes, "Black women are, historically, the first activists in the United States to theorize and act upon the intersections of race, gender, and class." This agenda provided other Women of Color the platform to articulate their own experiences. In this way, we agree with Springer that, "black feminist activists, through their theorizing and organizations, broadened the scope of the women's movement by challenging Eurocentric and classist interpretations of women's issues." The Black Women's Agenda was the "politics in the cracks" that provided other Women of Color the opportunity to amend the Minority Plank to reflect their lived experiences. Black feminists provided an intellectual framework that benefited Women of Color, a phrase generated at the NWC from this interaction.

Consider how the lived experience of Black women was being represented by the federal government in the controversial impact of the 1965 original study, *The Negro Family: The Case for National Action,* generally referred to as the "Moynihan Report" because it was authored by Daniel P. Moynihan, American sociologist and assistant secretary of labor under President Lyndon B. Johnson.[47] The Moynihan Report arguably depicted Black life, particularly Black women and their relationship to family, labor, and sexuality as deviant—

a pathologized narrative rife with economic insecurity in fatherless homes where traditional ideals of gender weren't valued or practiced. According to Moynihan, this pathology complicated Black women's ability and the Black family's ability overall to maintain and uphold traditional American values. With this narrative looming in the shadows, impeding their reality from being seen, the 1977 conference served as a necessary platform to give voice, share truth, and seek justice through sharing their stories and challenges, while working to bring about equitable transformation in the US political landscape.

Black women are, however, not a monolithic group: with varied political opinions and beliefs, each woman ultimately chose to support the cause that best reflected her needs and those of her community. For example, Deborah Gray White notes that "the Black women of the [National Welfare Rights Organization] identified their poverty, not their race or sex, as the most determining feature of their lives. Their Blackness and femaleness was understood within the context of their status as welfare recipients."[48] While we have tried to find some connecting threads among the eighteen women profiled here, their political individuality is as important as their commonalities.

Defining a Black Women's Agenda

Of course, Black women were organizing well before they came to Houston. As states and territories organized in 1976 and 1977, they addressed the absence of minority issues from the commission documents sent to them by proposing 164 recommendations regarding minority women's issues.[49] The national commissioners then had to decide how to address these ideas. The Ad Hoc Committee appointed to craft recommendations on minority women included Gloria Steinem, Jean O'Leary, Koryne Hornbal, Audrey Rowe Colom, Rhea Mojica Hammer, and Jeffalyn Johnson. Their idea was to insert a brief placeholder resolution in the Plan of Action concerning minority women and then to invite minority women to craft a more substantive plank that could be substituted into the Plan of Action at the National Conference.[50] Audrey Rowe Colom and Jeffalyn Johnson, the Black women on the Ad Hoc Committee, created the "Group of Ten," drawing in Elizabeth Abramowitz, Amy Billingsley, Bernadine Denning, Ersa Poston, Elizabeth Stone, Ruth Sykes, Lynnette Taylor, and Ethyl Adams to draft the Black Women's Action Plan. This "Group of Ten" became the Black Women's Agenda, which, after the Houston Conference, took its mission to be the national implementation of the Black Women's Action Plan.[51]

Perhaps because it was articulated to remedy their exclusion, the Black

Women's Action Plan makes it clear that the women's movement had to include all women. In their words, "An ethnocentric women's movement which minimizes, misconstrues, or demonstrates no serious regard for the interests and views of other disadvantaged groups and minorities sows the seeds of its own destruction, in the wake, eventually, of decreasing allies and mounting hostility."[52] The importance of Black women was further reinforced by their numerical representation at the conference. In 1977, Black women made up 10.4 percent of the United States' population. At the conference, 17.4 percent of the elected delegates (247 out of 1,417) were Black women.[53] At the time, there were more Black women serving as mayors, state legislators, and representatives in Congress than there were white women in the same roles.[54] As the Minority Plank notes, "Black women have been diligent in their quest for self-determination and equal opportunity, working towards destruction of vestiges of race, sex, and social-economic class discrimination. Their political experience has often put them at the forefront of the many struggles for individual justice."[55] The Black Women's Action Plan and the resulting portions of the Minority Plank stake Black women's claims to leadership within national activism, including the women's movement.

Discussion of the various proposed planks was intense and often controversial. Nevertheless, the conference passed a plan that included recognition of lesbian rights, reproductive rights, and the importance of a range of what they called "minority rights." For the women who organized the Black Women's Plan of Action, the inclusion of a Minority Plank in the list of twenty-six planks, like its predecessor in the 1976 Report by the National Commission, was rooted in biased assumptions about "minorities." Many of the Black delegates worked diligently to refine the conference's "Minority Plank."[56]

At the conference, other delegates felt the keen need to resist a singular Minority Plank confinement and worked with Black women to re-envision their role in the plan for American women. Resisting the political language of referring to smaller groups as a "minority," a term rooted in the idea of legal disenfranchisement, and in the conference setting, of being ignored for their role in organizing for women's concerns from the very beginning, the group coined a new phrase to refer to themselves. Recognizing that they did not want to be identified by the de facto concerns of white women, they described themselves as "Women of Color," the first use of this phrase.[57]

Women of Color signifies, first and foremost, that they are women, their concerns are those of all women. But unlike the power structures that allow white women to imagine themselves as unmarked, these individuals noted that their experiences with racism and discrimination marked them, "of Color."

They brought a long history of organizing in particular contexts, developing specific skills and resources together. In this collection, we recognize the importance of the varied experiences that framed the women who bravely identified as Women of Color in this setting. The phrase, "It's Our Movement Now," celebrated the ownership that Black women, in collaboration with their partners of Latinx, Native American, and Asian identities, felt about their activism of the 1970s. Nevertheless, this sense of ownership has been fraught and complicated by both debates within the Women's Movement at the time and by how its history has been recorded.

Women from "minority" races and ethnicities were given a single resolution: the Minority Plank. Unsurprisingly, finding consensus among very different constituencies was difficult. Nevertheless, on Sunday, November 20, 1977, a coalition of Women of Color read an amended version of the Minority Women's Plank during the National Women's Conference. Maxine Waters, then an assemblywoman, read the introduction. Collectively, the Women of Color "declared that minority women suffered discrimination based on both race and sex." Coretta Scott King, by then very well known as both a human rights activist and the widow of Dr. Martin Luther King Jr., read the needs of Black women, which emphasized the necessity for better employment opportunities. She ended by stating, "we will never be divided again!" The Minority Women's Plank was accepted. Afterward, "[n]early all the 2,000 delegates joined hands and sang "We Shall Overcome." Women of all racial backgrounds said that this moment was the most exciting one for them from the conference.

The Legacies of the National Women's Conference

Among historians, the NWC is best known as an organizing catalyst for the opposition to the women's movement.[58] This opposition, which emerged both in some of the floor fights over the "Agenda" or National Plan, but also outside the conference, set the stage for American politics for the next few decades. Though they did not join the opposition staged by Phyllis Schlafly, religious opponents, such as Tim and Beverly LeHaye and James Dobson, would go on to create the lobbying group Focus on the Family as a direct response to the women's conference. Indeed, the Christian Right's emergence as a political force within the Republican Party became crystal clear in 1980 when Ronald Reagan denigrated Mary Crisp, the highest-ranking Republican woman and cochair of the RNC, for her role in the 1977 National Women's Conference and in NARAL. This opposition narrative focuses our attention on political polarization, instead of the broad range of women's political action, especially African American women's action at and after the conference. Certainly, the events in Houston were dramatic and had a profound impact on women in the United States, but our focus centers the remarkable diversity of the conference and on how Black women activists, politicians, and delegates profoundly influenced the national agenda for women that resulted. The result is a more complex narrative that highlights the broad range of Black women's political action.

Narratives of division have dominated the historiography concerning the conference in part because there was not a legislative or policy legacy that emerged from the meeting. The National Plan of Action crafted and approved in Houston was submitted to Congress in 1978. Yet, President Jimmy Carter's support was limited and as a result the conference had little legislative effect.[59] According to historians Doreen Mattingly and Jessica Nare, "the most significant impact of the IWY Conference was not in policy but in consciousness-raising and networking." Indeed, Mattingly and Nare cite a 1978 article in *Ms.* magazine which claimed that the conference provided "members of minority and special-interest groups . . . not only an endorsement of their visibility from other feminists, but the beginnings of national networks."[60] While some national groups certainly began and gained a significant boost in their national profile, many African American women came to the conference as leaders of their own national organizations.

A New Legacy: Recovering Black Women's Leadership

This collection deliberately seeks to expand the range of sources and voices considered with regard to the history of Black feminism and African American participation in the women's movement by focusing on African American women's involvement in the 1977 National Women's Conference in Houston. Instead of exploring the usual narratives of opposition that see Black feminism as emerging in response to its exclusion from the women's movement, we offer a narrative approach grounded in individual women's experiences and activism—in how they each brought their particular experiences and understandings of race, gender, class, and sexuality to their forms of political action both within and beyond the women's movement.

In this collection, we recover Black women's leadership through the stories of eighteen African American women who participated in the conference. We have selected women who were renowned activists and leaders: some held elected office and others were prominent journalists, movement leaders, and community organizers. Some were young and new to activism of the women's movement; others were internationally recognized figures with years of experience. They represent a sample of African American women, some of whom had a profound impact on mainstream politics, the Civil Rights Movement, and the women's movement.[61] That said, the NWC wasn't necessarily transformative for the women we consider. Some of the women profiled here left Houston relatively unchanged, such as Yvonne Burke. Some, like Melba Tolliver, were there for work. It would be too simple to assume that women had the same experience of the conference or that the conference should be understood as a site of change for all. Instead, we treat the conference as a historical opportunity where an unprecedented number of women gathered and offer to the historian a chance to consider the incredible diversity of women activist at a moment in time.

Our selection of women to profile began with the photographic collection of Diana Mara Henry. As the official photographer of the conference, Henry had unlimited access while other photographers rotated in and out of the meeting. Henry did not set out to photograph Black women. As her essay concluding this collection makes clear, she was equally intent on capturing the luminaries on stage and lesser-known delegates without using race as a reference. Yet, her photographs create a record that documents the presence and leadership of African American women at this national event. From Henry's photographs, we formed a list of Black women to feature and then sought scholars who could document their lives and contributions. We could not successfully recruit scholars to write on every figure. Audrey Colom, for instance, played an important role in the NWC, but is not featured in a chapter of her own. In the process, we added three women whom Henry had not photographed, but whom we felt we were important to include. So, the chapter on Barbara Smith, for instance, contains a portrait from another photographer as do the chapters on Flo Kennedy and Maxine Waters. Indeed, the photograph of Waters at the conference was one that she posted herself on Twitter in 2017.

Our Plan of Action

We have placed the women profiled here into five thematic groups: symbols of sisterhood, sisters in action, activist organizers, the politicians, and communicating change. We do not intend for these to be rigid or defining categories. Certainly, they are not mutually exclusive. Rather we use them as a way of bringing individual chapters into conversation with each other.

The Houston Conference was rich in symbolism. The event was meant to convey the national political importance of women's issues. In part I, we highlight two women of particular symbolic significance, Coretta Scott King and

Michelle Cearcy. Beginning with the decision to feature Coretta Scott King on the platform of the conference for its opening session, the conference organizers sought to make clear that the women's movement was inclusive. Yet, as Rachel Jessica Daniel's chapter explores, the decision to feature Scott King, as an emblematic "first lady of Civil Rights" was not something in which she allowed herself to participate. Because she had been exploited in this way throughout her life, she resisted the cooptation of her image for the conference. Amira Rose Davis's discussion of Michelle Cearcy, likewise explores the way in which her participation in the relay torch run from Seneca Falls to Houston, while used to symbolize the "inclusiveness" of the event in images of her with Sylvia Ortiz and Peggy Kokernot, really did not truly include her. Indeed Cearcy and Sylvia Ortiz were even cropped out of a photo used *Time* magazine for its December 5, 1977, cover, leaving only Peggy Kokernot, a white woman. This section explores what it means to be selected to symbolize a movement and what a critical reading of the media's process of selection reveals to historians who wish to write a more representative narrative of the women's movement.

Where part I begins with a critique of how famous or symbolic Black women were represented, the second section allows us to understand just how important Black women's networks, like sororities, were to the project of organizing for change. Sometimes overlooked by contemporary scholars, the women in this section were particularly active in political organizing in the 1960s, building on their work from earlier movements as sorority members. Janine Fondon's discussion of Gloria Scott recovers the woman who opened the conference, just as she had helped to open up the Girl Scouts of the USA to Black girls. Hailing from Houston, Scott not only worked with the local committee organizing the NWC but, as the only member of the International Women's Year National Commission from the hosting city, she was designated as the perfect person to open up the entire conference. Her own work with the National Education Institute and the Girl Scouts immediately connected with the vision of the conference as a model for the future. Julie Gallagher's authoritative discussion of renowned organizer Dorothy Height reminds us of Height's important work crafting the Minority Plank through the Black Women's Plan of Action in the many months before the meeting. Height's skills at the behind-the-scenes work of political organizing were honed and encouraged as a leader of Delta Sigma Theta, a socially engaged African American sorority that also introduced Gloria Scott to political action as part of the Civil Rights Movement. In a similar fashion, Freddie Groomes learned to become a community leader as a member of Alpha Kappa Alpha. As Johanna Ortner's profile of Groomes demonstrates, Black sororities formed vital networks for Black women's political action, indeed if Alpha Kappa Alpha had not sponsored Groomes, she would not have been able to attend the Houston Conference. All of these women were incredible organizers with gifts for bringing people together for a cause. Lindsay Amaral's discussion of Jeffalyn Johnson helps us remember an organizer whose experience combined her interests with the power of representation, education and community connection, linking, for example, her interest in the Black Arts Movement and the creation of Ethnic Studies departments with her expertise on the effects of workplace discrimination. She saw the connections between the cultural study of successful productions with a clear-eyed assessment of the obstacles for women not only in the United States but in Africa as well. She held a globally informed vision about the role activists played in removing barriers and identifying positive models of change.

The activists in part III brought with them rich histories organizing around issues such as childcare, education, sexual orientation, labor conditions, and of course civil rights. None of them could be characterized as *only* women's movement activists. Like Flo Kennedy, they were advocates for women, but, as Kirsten Leng shows, Kennedy's feminist advocacy was mediated through an array of political causes, styles, and organizations. As Crystal Webster shows, Georgia McMurray was one of the few women in a wheelchair in Houston. Indeed, her image was featured alongside the plank on disability in *The Spirit of Houston,* the official book describing the conference. Barbara Smith, an organizer of the Black lesbian group that authored the Combahee River Collective Statement in 1976, argued "that the major systems of oppression are interlocking." Julie de Chantal's essay describes how this statement calling for the development of integrated analysis that would facilitate the simultaneous struggle against "racial, sexual, heterosexual, and class oppression" cast her as the activist to introduce the plank advocating for the elimination of discrimination around "sexual preference." Laura Lovett's essay on Johnnie Tillmon describes her trajectory as a welfare activist. As a leader of the National Welfare Rights Organization, Tillmon was an internationally recognized activist who joined a coalition of like-minded women in Houston to bring issues of class and poverty to inform their intersectionality. Marcia Walker-McWilliams describes how Addie Wyatt's experience as a labor leader helped her play a significant role as an organizer in the National Advisory Committee for Women. As with many of the Black women we profile here, these women were politically active before Houston and remained so throughout their lives.

Part IV's focus on politicians features women who held state and national office including Barbara Jordan, C. Delores Tucker, Shirley Chisholm, Yvonne Burke, and Maxine Waters. Whether as Secretary of State for Pennsylvania or as nationally recognized congresswomen, these politicians brought a different kind of visibility and gravitas to the conference. Camesha Scruggs's profile of Congresswoman Barbara Jordan's opening speech reveals its powerful impact, as the Houston native and elected representative ushered in a new national agenda. The NWC was organized in Congresswoman Barbara Jordan's Harris County home district. Houston had elected her as the first African American to serve in the Texas Senate since Reconstruction and the first Black US Senator from the South in 1972. Her political pull and the support she could marshal in a city, and even state, with a vibrant women's movement, helped to determine the locale for the event. As she had put it when she was running for office, "Women officeholders can sometimes bring a compassion to a situation that men are incapable of bringing, by the simple fact that we are women."[62] She was not alone. The year 1972 saw the largest number of women elected to Congress in history, joining Democrats Yvonne Burke from California, Elizabeth Holtzman from New York, Patricia Schroeder from Colorado, and Republican Marjorie Holt from Maryland.[63] In her public appearances, on the eve of her election to the US House, Jordan predicted political change, especially of the Democratic Party, resulting from the "growing political consciousness of both Blacks and women."[64] The very year that Jordan ran for Congress, Shirley Chisholm ran for president. By the time of the International Women's Year Conference, women in the United States, and especially African American women, were ready to make their mark politically. At the NWC, Congresswoman Shirley Chisholm did not have the stage time of her peers, but, as Zinga Fraser argues, her quiet but remarkable presence was understood and appreciated especially by other African American women at the meeting. Sabina Peck's analysis of C. Delores Tucker highlights her deliberate shift from grassroots organizing to more "top-down" political action as an elected official. Tucker's public denouncement of the Mississippi delegation's lack of racial diversity was typical of her activism, which prioritized race and the intersection of race and gender. For California congresswoman Yvonne Burke, the Houston meeting was not a watershed, but, as Sarah Rowley shows, it represented another step in a long struggle for equality and political change. In contrast, Carlyn Ferrari suggests that California congresswoman Maxine Waters's appearance at the conference was integral to the role on the national stage for decades to come.

Our final section features women who understood the power of media as a vehicle for communicating political change. As groundbreaking media leaders, Melba Tolliver and Clara McLaughlin both understood the powerful symbolism of Black women anchoring the news, as Tolliver did in New York City, and the power of women owning television stations, as McLaughlin did in Texas.

Journalists, like Tolliver, were crucial conduits for communicating Black women's issues to the public, while McLaughlin used her position to fundamentally alter how African Americans were depicted on the local features produced by her station.

We end this collection with Diana Mara Henry's reflections on her experience as photographer. After considering how Diana's images allow us to create a dialogue with the past, we felt it was fitting to engage in a dialogue with Diana. Her recollections of how she became a photographer, her relationship with the women's movement, and her approach to photographing the conference offer yet another way to contextualize these historic images.

Diana Mara Henry's photographs offer striking visual evidence of Black women's presence in the women's movement. In the hands of the scholars assembled for this volume, these images act as a catalyst for eighteen microhistories that make Black a range of women's activism, leadership, and work visible. Instead of being present, but unseen and unremarked, the essays in *It's Our Movement Now* bring the diversity of Black women's political activism into sharp focus. Rooted in the richness and difference of their lived experiences, Black women's activism expanded beyond a single plank or a single agenda. As Maxine Waters remarked, "There is a Black perspective in all the feminist issues in the National Plan."[65] We hope this book begins to make visible some of those perspectives and issues.

Notes

1. Marjorie J. Spruill, *Divided We Stand: The Battle over Women's Rights and Family Values That Polarized American Politics* (New York: Bloomsbury Press, 2017); Jocelyn Olcott, *International Women's Year: The Greatest Consciousness-Raising Event in History* (New York: Oxford University Press, 2017); Shelah Gilbert Leader and Patricia Rusch Hyatt, *American Women on the Move: The Inside Story of the National Women's Conference, 1977* (New York: Lexington Books, 2016); Doreen J. Mattingly and Jessica L. Nare, "'A Rainbow of Women': Diversity and Unity at the 1977 International Women's Year Conference," *Journal of Women's History* 26 (2014), 88–112.

2. Lauren Schiller, "Gloria Steinem Explains Why Feminism Reached a Critical Turning Point in 2015," *Fortune* (December 22, 2015). Steinem was "the token" white woman in the Minority Plank meetings in Houston.

3. Spruill, *Divided We Stand*.

4. In this text, we will use the terms Black and African American interchangeably. While we recognize that each term has a particular historical context for its accepted usage, we are writing at a time when both are being used and referencing a different historical moment when Black was the primary term. Following current practice, we will also be capitalizing the word Black.

5. Benita Roth addresses the exclusion of Black feminists by early historians of the women's movement in her "Second Wave Black Feminism in the African Diaspora: News from New Scholarship," *Agenda: Empowering Women for Gender Equity,* no. 58 (2003): 46–58. She refers to histories such as Maren Lockwood Carden, *The New Feminist Movement* (New York: Russel Sage Foundation, 1974); Jo Freeman, *The Politics Of Women's Liberation: A Case Study of an Emerging Social Movement and Its Relation to the Policy Process* (New York: Longman, 1975); and Judith Hole and Ellen Levine, *Rebirth of Feminism* (New York: Quadrangle/New York Times Books, 1976). For other critical appraisals of the history of race and the women's movement, see Dayo F. Gore, Jeanne Theoharis, and Komozi Woodard, eds., *Want to Start a Revolution? Radical Women in the Black Freedom Struggle* (New York: New York University Press, 2009); bell hooks, *Feminist Theory: From Margin to Center* (New York: Routledge, 1984); Benita Roth, *Separate Roads To Feminism: Black, Chicana, and White Feminist Movements in America's Second Wave* (Cambridge: Cambridge University Press, 2004); Kimberly Springer, *Living for the Revolution: Black Feminist Organizations, 1968–1980* (Durham, NC: Duke University Press, 2005); Winifred Breines, *The Trouble Between Us: An Uneasy History of White and Black Women in the Feminist Movement* (Oxford: Oxford University Press, 2008); and Laura Lovett, *With Her Fist Raised: Dorothy Pitman Hughes and the Transformative Power of Black Community Activism* (Boston: Beacon Press, 2020).

6. Sherie M. Randolph, *Florynce "Flo" Kennedy: The Life of a Black Feminist Radical* (Chapel Hill: University of North Carolina Press, 2015); Springer, *Living for the Revolution.*

7. Gore, Theoharis, and Woodard, eds. *Want to Start a Revolution?*; Bettye Collier-Thomas and V. P. Franklin, eds., *Sisters in the Struggle: African American Women in the Civil Rights-Black Power Movement* (New York: New York University Press, 2001).

8. Kristen Ghodess, *Second World, Second Sex: Socialist Women's Activism and Global Solidarity during the Cold War* (Durham, NC: Duke University Press, 2018), 139.

9. Spruill, *Divided We Stand*, 52.

10. Ghodess, *Second World*, 142–43.

11. Olcott, *International Women's Year*, 63, 165–7.

12. Olcott, *International Women's Year*, 195.

13. Olcott, *International Women's Year*, 195.

14. Olcott, *International Women's Year*, 196.

15. Spruill, *Divided We Stand*, 53.

16. Jill Ruckelshaus, "Who Shall Speak for Our Nation's Women? An American Dialogue," *Redbook Magazine*, March 1976, 47, 49–50, reprinted in United States, National Commission on the Observance of International Women's Year, "*. . . To Form a More Perfect Union . . .*": *Justice for American Women: Report of the National Commission on the Observance of International Women's Year*, 365–67.

17. Ruckelshaus, "Who Shall Speak," 50.

18. Ruckelshaus, "Who Shall Speak."

19. Leah Wright Rigueur, *The Loneliness of the Black Republican: Pragmatic Politics and the Pursuit of Power* (Princeton, NJ: Princeton University Press, 2014), 36–37.

20. "World Plan of Action: A Decade for Women and Development," United States, National Commission on the Observance of International Women's Year, "*. . . To Form a More Perfect Union . . .*": *Justice for American Women: Report of the National Commission on the Observance of International Women's Year*, 363.

21. United Nations, World Conference of the International Women's Year, Declaration of Mexico on the Equality of Women and Their Contribution to Development and Peace, July 2, 1975, 2.

22. United States, National Commission on the Observance of International Women's Year, "... To Form a More Perfect Union ...": Justice for American Women: Report of the National Commission on the Observance of International Women's Year, 363.

23. Mattingly and Nare, "'A Rainbow of Women'"; Spruill, Divided We Stand; Leader and Hyatt, American Women on the Move.

24. Spruill, Divided We Stand, 139, 141; quotation from National Commission on the Observance of International Women's Year, The Spirit of Houston: The First National Women's Conference; An Official Report to the President, the Congress and the People of the United States (Washington, DC: US Government Printing Office, 1978), 99.

25. National Commission on the Observance of International Women's Year, The Spirit of Houston, 99.

26. Spruill, Divided We Stand.

27. Ruth Rosen, The World Split Open: How the Modern Women's Movement Changed America (New York: Penguin Books, 2006); Jennifer Nelson, Women of Color and the Reproductive Rights Movement (New York: New York University Press, 2003).

28. Spruill, Divided We Stand, 99–103.

29. Spruill, Divided We Stand, 104.

30. Spruill, Divided We Stand, 104, 152.

31. Leader and Hyatt, American Women on the Move, 49; National Commission on the Observance of International Women's Year, The Spirit of Houston, 109; Spruill, Divided We Stand, 170.

32. Spruill, Divided We Stand, 151.

33. Spruill, Divided We Stand, 151.

34. Quotation taken from Spruill, Divided We Stand, 159.

35. Quotation taken from Spruill, Divided We Stand, 183.

36. Leader and Hyatt, American Women on the Move, 55; National Commission on the Observance of International Women's Year, The Spirit of Houston, 109

37. Demographic and diversity data for the participants are presented in Alice S. Rossi, Feminists in Politics: A Panel Analysis of the First National Women's Conference (New York: Academic Press, 1982).

38. Spruill, Divided We Stand, and Leader and Hyatt, American Women on the Move, have published two histories of the 1977 National Women's Conference. While Spruill describes the process of articulating the Minority Plank, Mattingly and Nare's article, "'A Rainbow of Women'" offers the only extended discussion of African American women at the meeting.

39. Mattingely and Nare, "'A Rainbow of Women,'" 88.

40. "The Minority Caucus: 'It's Our Movement Now,'" in National Commission on the Observance of International Women's Year, The Spirit of Houston, 156–57. See discussions in Mattingly and Nare, "'A Rainbow of Women'"; Sara Evans, Tidal Wave: How Women Changed America at Century's End (New York: Free Press, 2003), 139–42; and Winifred D. Wandersee, On the Move: American Women in the 1970s (Boston: Twayne Publishers, 1988), 175–202.

41. Deborah Gray White, Too Heavy a Load: Black Women in Defense of Themselves 1894–1994 (New York: Norton, 1999).

42. Paula Giddings, *When and Where I Enter: The Impact of Black Women on Race and Sex in America* (New York: Harper Collins, 1984).

43. Toni Morrison, "What the Black Woman Thinks about Women's Lib," *New York Times*, August 22, 1971.

44. Morrison, "What the Black Woman Thinks."

45. Roth, *Separate Roads to Feminism*.

46. Springer, *Living for the Revolution*.

47. Daniel Patrick Moynihan, *The Negro Family: The Case for National Action* (Washington, DC: United States Department of Labor, Office of Planning and Research, 1965).

48. White, *Too Heavy a Load*.

49. Mattingly and Nare, "'A Rainbow of Women.'"

50. Mattingly and Nare, "'A Rainbow of Women.'"

51. Black Women's Agenda. http://www.bwa-inc.org/about.html. Accessed September 2, 2018.

52. "Black Women's Plan of Action," in National Commission on the Observance of International Women's Year, *The Spirit of Houston*, 272–77.

53. Rossi, *Feminists in Politics*, 32.

54. Linda Faye Williams, "The Civil Rights-Black Power Legacy: Black Women Elected Officials at the Local, State, and National Levels," in Collier-Thomas and Franklin, *Sisters in the Struggle*, 306–32, 310.

55. "Plank 17: Minority Women," in National Commission on the Observance of International Women's Year, *The Spirit of Houston*, 70–75.

56. Caroline Bird, *What Women Want: From the Official Report to the President, the Congress, and the People of the United States* (New York: Simon and Schuster, 1979), 24–25.

57. Interview with Janine Fondon and Gloria Scott, December 22, 2020. Interview with Laura Lovett and Loretta Ross, n.d.

58. Spruill, *Divided We Stand*; Leader and Hyatt, *American Women on the Move*.

59. Mattingly and Nare, "'A Rainbow of Women.'"

60. "The Houston Coalition Lives On," *Ms.* magazine, August 1, 1978, 82.

61. Alice Rossi tried to assess the impact of the conference on women's political involvement in her 1982 study of the conference delegates. Rossi took a quantitative sociological approach, however, that looked at trends rather than at particular experiences. In contrast, we seek to create a thematic microhistory through collective historical narratives of eighteen participants. While our sample is not as extensive as Rossi's, we believe our narrative approach offers a richer representation of the participants' experiences.

62. "The Politics of Compassion: Opening the Door for Women: Barbara Jordan," *Washington Post*, December 15, 1971, A12.

63. Spruill, *Divided We Stand*, 29; Leandra Zarnow, *Battling Bella: The Protest Politics of Bella Abzug* (Cambridge, MA: Harvard University Press, 2019), 212.

64. "Senator Jordan Predicts Change," *New Journal and Guide*, January 8, 1972, 9.

65. Bird, *What Women Want*, 24–25.

1

Symbols of Sisterhood

SYMBOLS ARE DEVOID of life, yet they can inspire you to engage and act. Symbols in and of themselves do not matter nearly as much as the inspiration, motivation, and trust that they evoke. We can see them. We can feel them. But, what about when the symbol is also a person? Do they matter? Do they get a say?

Coretta Scott King understood the value of the visible and iconic, knowing its intricacies and secrets, which allowed her to navigate its terrain using those invisible qualities of presence, compassion, and grace to leave a legacy rooted in humanity and justice.

While the "Spirit of Houston" rested in the hands of Michelle Cearcy, a young Black woman representing her home and her people, she never considered how her power, her presence as a symbol of hope, could be tainted by the throes of racism. She too found strength in knowing that her visibility mattered and contributed to an agenda built to inform and transform, whether you saw her or not.

1

Coretta Scott King

Icon as Activist

RACHEL JESSICA DANIEL

Figure 1.1. Coretta Scott King, member of the President's Commission on the Observance of International Women's Year, applauds Barbara Jordan's keynote address at the First National Women's Conference in Houston, Texas, in 1977. Diana Mara Henry Papers (PH 51). Special Collections and University Archives, University of Massachusetts Amherst Libraries. Copyright © Diana Mara Henry / dianamarahenry.com.

TO CORETTA SCOTT KING, the 1977 National Women's Conference (NWC) was a footnote in a lifelong journey of human rights activism. By the time she was selected by President Carter to be the commissioner of the International Women's Year Conference, she already spent her college years as an activist; worked alongside her husband, Dr. Martin Luther King Jr.; raised money for the Southern Christian Leadership Conference with her freedom concerts; and, after she was widowed, spent time fighting for peace abroad, for labor rights at home, and for politicians who would at least promise to uphold the vision that her husband introduced to the world. Her respectful nonchalance about the National Women's Conference is reflected in the few sentences she dedicates in her memoir. She writes, "I was honored when President Carter also appointed me to serve as commissioner of the International Women's Year Conference. The appointment gave me the opportunity to be a key organizer and participant in the National Women's Conference."[1] Yet, her presence at the National Women's Conference was an important one. At this point, Coretta Scott King was widely considered a global icon of peace and justice. For some audience members, Scott King could have represented a tangible connection between the Civil Rights Movement, which led to the Civil Rights Act of 1964, and the women's liberation movement. After all, the Civil Rights Act included gender in its mandate and enabled complaints based on gender discrimination. While Scott King is often depicted as a cooperative icon rather than an activist with her own political agenda, before, during, and after the 1977 conference, she strategically used her image as a First Lady of the Civil Rights Movement to advance radical political causes.

This chapter joins a growing body of work about Black women who were visible icons of the Civil Rights Movement, but whose contributions to the Movement were largely invisible to the public. Rosa Parks and Coretta Scott King are twin icons of the Civil Rights Movement. Both were recognized as First Ladies of Civil Rights—Rosa Parks was declared the "First Lady of Civil Rights" by Congress; Coretta Scott King's obituaries and a children's book also recognize her as a "First Lady of Civil Rights," citing her identities as an activist, and the wife of Dr. Martin Luther King, who was, at the time of his assassination, a pastor at Ebenezer Baptist Church. Parks and Scott King are known for fixed images: Parks, seated on a bus, and Scott King, seated and veiled at her husband's funeral. As Katharina M. Fackler writes, Parks has been subject to a sanitized memory; her image falls within a "visual grammar of respectability" that "restrained the public understanding and the potential political impact of Parks, Black women leaders, and the Civil Rights Movement in general."[2] Jeanne Theoharis notes that Rosa Parks and Coretta Scott King were, in death, "stripped of their long histories of activism and continuing critique of American injustice."[3] Scott King's contributions to multiple, overlapping political movements were important. However, her careful protection of her legacy means it is challenging to read her outside of her connection to her husband, her children, and to the partnerships that she developed as she worked toward global peace and economic justice.

The Civil Rights Movement era, and the propagation of the politics of respectability within Black church culture, meant that Black women leaders had to be strategic as they negotiated the sexism of the time period. Powerful women were seen, but not always heard in rooms crowded with men. Coretta Scott King's visibility increased in the wake of her husband's assassination; however, rather than abandon Martin Luther King Jr. after he died, Scott King leveraged her identity as a widow in order to build upon and expand the dream that they both shared, but that he articulated. In *I May Not Get There With You*, Dyson writes, "Coretta is mocked as 'My husband' behind her back, a nod to how she sows influence and opens doors with the magic wand of King's golden name . . . [i]t may be argued that she is still in death tethered to King in an unhealthy manner—that she is posthumously codependent on an image that still binds and exploits her."[4] Scott King provided a consistent, public performance that protected her respectability as the widow of Martin Luther King Jr. Her position as widow, along with her deeply held convictions, provided her with the power she needed to do the political and spiritual work to which she was called. This served her well at the NWC, where she advocated for unity among women.

Photographing an Icon

Coretta Scott King was not only a part of the Civil Rights Movement; she helped to record and shape its narrative, as well as the King family image through her careful curation of memorabilia. In her memoir, *My Life, My Love, My Legacy*, Scott King wrote: "I remember telling myself that the life Martin and I were living was important and that, just maybe, people might someday want to know what was said and done. I knew I could not depend upon most of the mainstream press to record these events accurately; I often agonized over the ways they mangled the truth. So, beginning with Martin's first mass address, which officially launched the Montgomery Bus Boycott, I started saving his speeches, his papers, and all other memorabilia." Scott King understood how media could tell a story and was careful to project images that would tell her vision of historical moments; the documents she collected were the beginning of the Martin Luther King Jr. Center for Non-violent Social Change.[5]

Scott King's control of her image was even more visible in the aftermath of her husband's assassination. On April 9, 1968, Coretta Scott King, flanked by thousands of people, paid her last respects to her husband, who had been assassinated five days earlier. Moneta Sleet Jr., a photojournalist who developed a strong relationship with the King family after years of photographing Martin Luther King Jr. during key moments of his activism, was denied access to the funeral. "When Mrs. King discovered that the press pool covering her husband's funeral included no Black photographers, she sent word: If Sleet wasn't allowed into the church, there would be no photographers, period."[6] Scott King's insistence allowed Moneta Sleet access to the funeral, where he took the now well-known photo of Coretta Scott King holding her daughter Bernice. In 1969, Sleet was awarded the Pulitzer Prize for this photo; he was the first African American man to win a Pulitzer.[7] Scott King trusted Moneta Sleet to tell a visual story of the funeral in a way that honored her family.

This kind of control of her image continued with the writing of her memoir, *My Life, My Love, My Legacy.* Scott King carefully selected Reverend Dr. Barbara Reynolds to write her memoir. Reynolds first interviewed her in 1975, and afterward, their professional relationship turned into a friendship, with Scott King inviting Reynolds to events. Reynolds writes, "I wish I could say I knew she was grooming me for the task of working on her memoir. I didn't know. And that tells you something about who she was. . . . [S]he could help people and events evolve without anyone understanding the dynamics of the change until it was done."[8] Scott King's approach of working behind the scenes to create change or stepping into the public light to invoke her husband's memory, means that most know her as Martin Luther King's widow rather than an activist in her own right. Within the national imagination, we read her as a supporting cast member in the civil rights, labor, and women's movements, rather than someone who successfully steered these political movements. Yet, it was in the invocation of his name and memory that Scott King was able to gain access to political platforms where she could effect change.

In Diana Mara Henry's collection of photographs, there are seven images of Coretta Scott King. In them, she is often in a supportive role. In a few, she celebrates with other large groups of women, or listens attentively as they speak. In others, she grips the arms of First Lady Rosalynn Carter, smiles alongside Bella Abzug, and applauds for congresswoman and keynote speaker Barbara Jordan (see Figure 1.1). Arguably, Scott King's most substantial contribution to the 1977 National Women's Conference is her reading of the Minority Plank. It was such an inspired reading that the audience erupted into "We Shall Overcome" at its end. National newspapers reference this moment, yet there are few recordings that capture Scott King's voice.[9] Current critical scholarship about Scott King, and her posthumously published memoir, *My Life, My Love, My Legacy,* serve as a corrective to this erasure or relegation to a supporting role.[10] At the time of the National Women's Conference, only nine years after her husband's assassination, Scott King was considered a civil rights icon whose considerable loss was representative of the cost of fighting for equality.

The Making of an Icon

Scott King was born on April 27, 1927, in Heiberger, Alabama, a state that would become well known for its mistreatment of African Americans. Her parents, Berniece Murray-Scott and Obadiah Scott, were socially progressive and unafraid of the white people who tormented them. For Scott King, negotiating racism and discrimination with dignity became routine. Along with the institutional barriers to getting a good education, and the daily challenges of not being treated equally in social interactions with white people, Scott King's childhood home was deliberately burned down in a racial attack when she was fifteen years old. Scott King's parents owned their land, and the house was built by her father in 1920. Of her home, Scott King writes, "the house was simple and plain, but we felt fortunate to have it. We knew scores of Black sharecroppers around us who were not living on their own land, and some of their homes were little more than shacks." Obadiah Scott also owned a truck and transported lumber. His independence infuriated white men in his neighborhood, who routinely threatened him by pulling their guns out on him while he was traveling. After the fire, he bought more land, built a new home, and owned his own lumber mill. The mill was also burned down. After that, he opened up a grocery store and gas station.[11]

From her parents, Coretta Scott King inherited an incredible determination to continue working toward a just world even when under attack. Learning how to live with the fear of racist violence, as well as how to forgive, prepared Coretta Scott King for her future as a human rights activist. She writes, "Our burned-out home served as a primer, a prelude, an introduction. The postcard from hell was my first taste of evil, the kind that shows up at your door in such a way that you can never forget its smell, its taste, its sting."[12] This event was a foreshadowing of the house bombing Coretta Scott King endured fourteen years later in Montgomery, Alabama.[13]

Long before Scott King met Martin Luther King Jr., she became an activist in her own right. As a student, she joined the "Antioch NAACP, a race relations committee . . . a civil liberties committee, as well as with the peace movement, an organized group that aimed to bring about peace in the world." Scott King became a pacifist in college, and credits the end of World War II, as well as her own Christian belief in "loving thy neighbor as thyself," with her position. As an active member in the Progressive Party, she served as a student delegate at the party's national convention in Philadelphia in 1948. The platform "sought to end segregation, support voting rights for Blacks, and provide national health insurance." Scott King's presence there foreshadowed her role in the NWC in general, and the Minority Plank specifically. She writes of her early experiences, "although I had a gentle manner, I was beginning to suspect that I had a warrior's spirit. I was not the kind of person who was content leaving hurt or harm unchanged."[14]

Growing up, Scott King quickly developed the capacity for responding to injustice with dignity and grace. Scott King called out the administration of Antioch College when she faced discrimination there. As an elementary education major at Antioch, she faced a problem fulfilling her requirements. Scott King was supposed to teach for a year in the Yellow Springs, Ohio, school system, which, at that time, had no Black teachers. Instead, she was forced to travel nine miles to teach in a segregated school. Scott King did not quietly accept this, however: she spoke to her supervisor, the president of Antioch College, the local school board, attempted to get fellow students to help her, and finally, wrote a letter to the administration. In the letter, she states plainly, "I was rejected because I happened to be the wrong color. This kind of injustice which I experienced is mild compared to what Negroes are facing all of the time in our society. Do you then wonder why America as a leader among nations in the world cannot command more respect among the common people who make up the majority of the citizens of the world?"[15] Although Scott King spent her life witnessing or experiencing racist actions, this was one of the first moments when Scott King attempted to strategically dismantle the segregation system. Her letter is powerful because it situates the racism she faced in a local, national, and global context. That framework served her well later during her work in the Civil Rights Movement and other movements for labor and human rights. I see this incident as indicating her ability to act independently in response to injustice, something that becomes obscured in most of the narratives about her.

Scott King continued her education at the New England Conservatory of Music in 1951. By the time she met Martin Luther King Jr. on a blind date in Boston, Scott King already developed the political and spiritual philosophies that would inform her activism. She says, "when Martin and I were tossing around ideas, I saw that my views were more global and pacifist, while his were more focused on direct action to change the oppressive structures of Black America."[16] During their twelve year marriage, Coretta Scott King gave birth to and raised their children, Martin Luther King III, Yolanda, Dexter, and Bernice while actively supporting her husband, oftentimes strategically coaching him about his public image and mission. However, she also found her own way to participate as an activist. Through her concerts, Scott King raised money for the Montgomery Improvement Association and the Southern Christian Leadership Conference.[17] Scott King was also invited to be part of the Women for Peace delegation to Switzerland. The Women's Strike for Peace was founded in 1961 by Bella Abzug and Dagmar Wilson. The delegation's goal was to "join the international effort to influence the atomic ban talks being held in [Switzerland] by the United Nations Committee on Disarmament."[18] Bella Abzug and Scott King would work together again as Commissioners of the National Women's Conference. Scott King's work toward global peace impacted Martin Luther King Jr., who personally opposed the Vietnam War, but initially was publicly silent about the war. Scott King participated in a protest against the Vietnam War at Madison Square Garden and "was the only woman and one of only two Black people invited to speak." Her husband opted not to attend.[19]

After Martin Luther King Jr.'s assassination, Scott King continued her work. While newspaper articles argued that she was "continuing Martin Luther King's dream," she resisted this characterization, instead saying that they had been partners in the struggle, and that she always fought for human rights. As she continued to carve out her own identity, she fought for labor rights and global peace, movements that she started alongside Martin while he was still alive.[20] She was often invited to be involved in political and activist endeavors because of her marriage to King. She wrote "I began to understand the power and the ministry of presence. Sometimes we win just by showing up." Harry Belafonte, a prominent singer, actor, and fellow activist, helped her understand her power, telling her, "Coretta, I don't know what your public plans are, but you have more power just sitting in a room than most people. You don't even have to say much. It's your presence that carries so much weight."[21] She did more than show up though. She thoughtfully strategized how to attain political goals, such as raising $20 million to create and direct the King Center, or lobbying for Martin Luther King Jr.'s birthday to become a national holiday. Scott King was, unlike Martin, involved in local politics and she endorsed candidates in Atlanta and other local elections. She was one of the influential Black leaders who often helped select and support politicians who would be progressive. However, she also began to shape national elections and policy.

In 1974, three years before the National Women's Conference, Scott King founded and cochaired both the National Committee for Full Employment and the Full Employment Action Council."[22] The goal of both groups was to advocate "for the federal government to provide jobs for all unemployed people."[23] Scott King's attention to employment and economic opportunity was not new. It grew from the Poor People's Campaign that had been the focus of the SCLC in the late 1960s. In the 1970s, Scott King's activism did not allow dreams of economic equity be deferred. In 1976, then-presidential hopeful Jimmy Carter understood Coretta Scott King's political power. Carter was not well known nationally and his relationship with the King family helped him win crucial votes. Scott King, aware of the power she wielded, withheld her endorsement of Carter until he promised support of the Humphrey Hawkins Bill for Full Employment.[24]

At Carter's request, Scott King gave her first speech at the Democratic National Convention. In her speech, Scott King deploys her power as a widow of the Civil Rights Movement and uses it to ask that the Democratic Party focus their efforts on human rights. In her short address, Scott King begins and ends with direct quotes from Martin Luther King Jr.'s "I Have a Dream" speech, strategically leveraging her identity to ask the Democratic Party to carry out her vision of a future America: one that would focus more on human rights globally, thus restoring the American reputation abroad, as well as nationally, thus supporting the "millions of Americans" who have been treated with "benign neglect."[25] Scott King understood that the audience might receive this criticism best through the lens of Martin Luther King Jr.'s memory, but she prioritized her ideas. Scott King's speech provided her with a platform to advance human rights; however, she also knew that her support of Carter would get him votes, and thus allow her to advance a political agenda for full employment.

In a speech to commemorate the fiftieth anniversary of the March on Washington, Carter attributes his presidential win to the King family, writing, "I was really grateful when the King family adopted me as their presidential candidate in 1976. Every handshake from Dr. King, from Daddy King, every hug from Coretta got me a million Yankee votes. Daddy King prayed at the Democratic Convention—for quite a while, I might say—and Coretta was in the hotel room with Rosalynn and me when I was elected president."[26] Carter was clearly grateful for their support, but the language of his speech again relegates Scott King to a supportive role: Scott here is someone who hugged him, and perhaps someone who was a confidant to the Carters; however, he doesn't remind the audience that she spoke at the Democratic Convention in the same way that he emphasizes Daddy King's prayer. Though Carter may not have acknowledged

Coretta Scott King's leadership abilities in this speech, he did reward her for the support she offered him during the election.

In March 1977, President Carter announced that he would choose forty-two citizens to form the National Commission behind the National Women's Conference (NWC); Coretta Scott King was among them. As an easily recognizable figure, Scott King's presence, alongside that of other leaders, such as poet Maya Angelou, may have signaled to African American women that their concerns would be represented and carefully considered. According to a 1978 article, although Scott King was involved in women's rights, she was "skeptical about the sensitivity of the general membership of the modern feminists. She didn't think they really understood infant mortality and involuntary sterilization."[27] However, Scott King agreed to participate as a commissioner for the National Women's Conference.

As a commissioner, she participated in meetings to help determine "the barriers that prevent women from participating fully and equally in all aspects of national life."[28] The commission had only seven months to select recommendations on issues, plan the procedures for statewide conferences, and plan the national conference. Scott King's previous activism during the Civil Rights Movement and work with other women's organizations likely prepared her for contentious discussions and rigorous debates. She had worked with Bella Abzug previously and she knew how to appeal to women of different backgrounds, as she demonstrated during a passionate speech to convince women in Chicago to support a strike for wage equality in 1963.[29]

King's name, which was often a part of headlines about the commission, was used to attract women to the conference. While STOP ERA, organized by Phyllis Schlafly, used the Bible and other sacred texts to justify their opposition to the Equal Rights Amendment and the conference, Coretta Scott King was a publicly recognized Christian whose spirituality was wedded to her activism. Commissioners were not asked for their personal opinions on issues before they were chosen for the commission; yet the combination of Scott King's radical activism and her involvement in Black Baptist churches indicates that she may have offered a spiritual perspective. Phyllis Schlafly and Coretta Scott King were both public Christians; yet they were on opposing sides of a rigorous debate about race, women's roles, and the role the federal government should play in creating a country where women are equal citizens and have the same rights as men. As symbols, they both represented different struggles as well: Schlafly faced barriers to being involved in a political debate about foreign policy; Scott King struggled with poverty.[30] Scott King knew what it meant to lose a husband, a breadwinner, and to be a single mother with four children to feed. It makes sense, therefore, that Scott King would fight for labor rights for women and Black youth, and actively prioritize economic equality over the women's movement.

Minority Plank

On November 18, 1977, the conference began. Coretta Scott King was on the stage, alongside current First Lady Rosalynn Carter, former First Ladies Lady Bird Johnson and Betty Ford, and poet Maya Angelou. Although there were many other influential African American women who were a part of the conference and were publicly recognized, it is likely conference organizers thought Scott King's presence would indicate the racial diversity of the conference to the media, as well as advance the idea that the conference would be on the right side of history when it came to the fight for civil rights. The image of the First Ladies of America, as well as Scott King, a former First Lady of Ebenezer Baptist Church and widow of the Civil Rights Movement, and Angelou, a radical poet and speaker, pledging allegiance to the American flag, is an indication of their willingness to fight for justice as a patriotic endeavor. This image refuted the idea that Schlafly and the emerging Christian Right had circulated—that the conference was anti-American. The image also differentiated them from more radical feminists who were publicly aligned with third world nations in recognition of how women of color were systematically disempowered globally.

The reading and acceptance of the Minority Plank was one of the most celebrated aspects of the conference. Assemblywoman Maxine Waters spoke first, sharing an overview of the revisions to the Minority Plank. Then, three women read their racial and ethnic group's section of the Minority Plank: Billie Nave Masters, who represented American Indian/Alaskan Native women, Mariko Tse, who represented Asian Pacific American women, and Sandy Serrano Sewell, who represented Hispanic women. However, the organizers may have placed Coretta Scott King and the Black Women's Agenda last because of her significance as an activist. A description of the Minority Plank reads, "Coretta Scott King reads the statement regarding Black women last, placed out of alphabetical order to honor the symbolism of her presence."[31] The organizers of the conference understood the impact that Coretta Scott King would have in reading this statement last. And Coretta Scott King's reading reflected the importance of the moment: her reading of the Minority Plank was passionate, slow, and deliberate.

According to Steinem, Scott King focused on "the unemployment rate for young Black women that was even higher than that for young Black men, as well as housing bias against Black families, Black children in need of adoption, and more."[32] During and after the Civil Rights Movement, Scott King was heavily invested in labor and housing crisis among African American women and children. It is likely that she lobbied and agreed with other Black women leaders to make these issues central in their part of the Minority Plank. Her last words were especially impactful, however. She stated, "Let this message go forth from Houston and spread all over this land. There is a new force, a new understanding, a new sisterhood against all injustice that has been born here. We will not be divided and defeated again!"[33] For people familiar with Christian tradition, it sounds like a benediction. She first states, "let this message go forth," which echoes the call for Christians to "spread the Gospel." Next, she discusses a "new force, a new understanding, a new sisterhood against all injustice." While the term "sister" was used frequently by Black women, and by feminists during this time period, it is also used heavily in the Christian faith. The use of familial term closes gaps over potential disagreements. "Sisters" indicates that you are deeply connected with other women who are not related to you by blood, but related to you because of a commitment to shared beliefs, ideals, and goals. Scott King's words could also be read as an acknowledgment of her close attention to the historical struggles between groups of women who were divided by politics, race, class, sexuality, and other identities. Her statement, "we will never be divided and defeated again," briefly references and at once dismisses those divisions. Scott King is the only person who could have delivered this specific message. In a three-sentence statement, Scott King addresses past divisions; acknowledges the members of the conference as a collective, bound by a familial duty to be loyal to each other and to the mission at hand; and she urges everyone to move forward in fighting for equality. Her rhetoric and style of speaking no doubt reminded the audience of Dr. King's famous "I Have a Dream" speech, given only fourteen years earlier. His speeches too, worked to unite disparate communities under a common goal of "justice for all." However, Scott King was aware of future challenges. After singing "We Shall Overcome," she said, "We have come a long way. We still have a long way to go."[34]

Steinem writes that the acceptance of the Minority Plank was, "the high point of the conference. I was as proud of my facilitating role as anything I had ever done in my life."[35] The acceptance of the Minority Plank symbolically represented a shift in the feminist movement. The reading of the plank demonstrated the willingness for women of color to share multiple, intersecting oppressions, as well as to offer best solutions to counteract them. The unanimous acceptance of the Minority Plank indicated that the white women at the conference acknowledged the challenges that women of color faced. It also represented a symbolic willingness to fight with them in that struggle for true equality.

Beyond the 1977 Conference

While Coretta Scott King's reading of the Minority Plank was a highlight for Gloria Steinem and audience members at the 1977 National Women's Conference, her memoir focuses more on her fight to close the unemployment gap. Coretta Scott King's participation in the 1977 National Women's Conference was strategic; it provided her with a national platform to highlight the need to close the unemployment gap, which she addresses in her short reading of the Minority Plank. Scholar David Klein notes, "King saw tackling issues of poverty and unemployment as the key to composing political alliances across divisions."[36] The Humphrey Hawkins Bill passed in 1978, four years after she cofounded and chaired the National Committee for Full Employment and the Full Employment Action Council, and one year after the National Women's Conference.

Scott King continued her work for equal rights until her death in Mexico in 2006. Four presidents attended her funeral and spoke about her influence.[37] Oftentimes, people wonder what would have happened if great Civil Rights leaders were still alive. The assumption is that leaders such as Martin Luther King Jr. and Malcolm X would be aggrieved to see our lack of progress, or that if they were here, our reality would look different. This line of thinking ignores the critical work that Scott King did throughout her life. Her participation in the 1977 National Women's Conference gave voice to the demands of Black women and children for equitable pay and housing at a time when negative stereotypes of Black womanhood as matriarchs and welfare queens were beginning to gain traction in the national imagination.[38] She used her image of respectability to advance the causes of Black women and to rally women of all races to fight for justice together.

In February 2017, Senator Elizabeth Warren, a Democrat, opposed the nomination of Jeff Sessions to be Attorney General of the United States.[39] This was not the first time Jeff Sessions was nominated for a federal position; Coretta Scott King wrote a nine-page letter to Congress opposing his nomination to federal judge in 1986. Scott King asserted that, if Jeff Sessions was allowed a place on the federal bench, it would "irreparably damage the work of [her] husband." Scott King continued, "Mr. Sessions has used his awesome powers of his office in a shabby attempt to intimidate and frighten elderly Black voters. For this reprehensible conduct, he should not be rewarded with a federal judgeship."[40]

Warren attempted to read this letter to oppose Jeff Sessions' nomination; however, Scott King's influence and words were so threatening to Sessions that Warren was silenced. In a press conference, Senator Mitch McConnell tried to justify silencing Warren. He stated, "She was warned. She was given an explanation. Nevertheless, she persisted."[41] In response, "nevertheless she persisted" became a new political slogan at a time when women seemed to, yet again, be politically devalued and rendered invisible. Jeff Sessions served as attorney general; however, he resigned at President Trump's request after only a year of service.[42]

Though she passed away eleven years before her letter was read, Scott King's words reached from beyond the grave to breathe life into the current political moment. Furthermore, the fact that Scott King understood Sessions's power, and was an eloquent writer, was a reminder to many that, in all of the discussions about Martin Luther King Jr. we haven't properly considered Coretta Scott King, the woman who married him because they had a shared mission, the woman who kept his memory alive, and the woman who courageously fought for equal rights for the rest of her life. Coretta Scott King, far from a silent icon, was a political activist with a voice, presence, and power that transformed the United States.

Notes

1. Coretta Scott King and Barbara A. Reynolds, *My Life, My Love, My Legacy* (New York: Henry Holt and Company, 2017).

2. Katharina M. Fackler, "Ambivalent Frames: Rosa Parks and the Visual Grammar of Respectability," *Souls* 18 (2016): 2–4, 271–82.

3. Jeanne Theoharis, *A More Beautiful and Terrible History: The Uses and Misuses of Civil Rights History* (Boston: Beacon Press, 2018).

4. Michael Eric Dyson, *I May Not Get There With You: The True Martin Luther King* (Washington, DC: The Free Press, 2000).

5. Scott King and Reynolds, *My Life*.

6. Sharon Shahid, "A Prized Photo Fit for a King," Newseum, September 9, 2016. Accessed June 27, 2019. http://www.newseum.org/2016/09/09/a-prized-photo-fit-for-a-king/.

7. "Moneta Sleet Jr. of *Ebony Magazine*." The Pulitzer Prizes. Accessed June 27, 2019. https://www.pulitzer.org/winners/moneta-sleet-jr.

8. Scott King and Reynolds, *My Life*.

9. Anna Quindlen, "Women's Conference Approves Planks On Abortion and Rights for Homosexuals," *New York Times*, November 21, 1977. Accessed June 27, 2019. http://www.nytimes.com/1977/11/21/archives/womens-conference-approves-planks-on-abortion-and-rights-for.html?_r=0. On March 19, 2015, Senator Maxine Waters posted a photograph of

Coretta Scott King reading the Minority Plank on Facebook, flanked by herself and other women who were members of the Minority Caucus. Maxine Waters. (n.d.). Retrieved September 7, 2017, from Facebook.

10. David P. Stein, "'This Nation Has Never Honestly Dealt with the Question of a Peacetime Economy': Coretta Scott King and the Struggle for a Nonviolent Economy in the 1970s," *Souls* 18, no. 1 (2016): 80–105. doi:10.1080/10999949.2016.1162570.

11. Scott King and Reynolds, *My Life*.

12. Scott King and Reynolds, *My Life*.

13. "King's Home Bombed." The Martin Luther King, Jr., Research and Education Institute. April 5, 2018. Accessed June 27, 2019. https://kinginstitute.stanford.edu/encyclopedia/kings-home-bombed.

14. Scott King and Reynolds, *My Life*.

15. Scott King and Reynolds, *My Life*.

16. Scott King and Reynolds, *My Life*.

17. "Coretta Scott King: Remembering a Georgia Hero." Georgia.gov. October 17, 2017. Accessed June 27, 2019. https://georgia.gov/blog/2017–04–27/coretta-scott-king-remembering-georgia-hero.

18. Scott King and Reynolds, *My Life*.

19. Scott King and Reynolds, *My Life*.

20. Scott King and Reynolds, *My Life*.

21. Scott King and Reynolds, *My Life*.

22. "About Mrs. King." The King Center, www.thekingcenter.org/about-mrs-king.

23. David Klein, "The King Who Carried on the Fight for Economic Justice." *Washington Post*, April 4, 2018. https://www.washingtonpost.com/news/made-by-history/wp/2018/04/04/the-king-who-carried-on-the-fight-for-economic-justice/

24. Jacqueline Trescott, "The New Coretta Scott King: Emerging From the Legacy," *Washington Post*, Jan. 15, 1978, www.washingtonpost.com/archive/lifestyle/1978/01/15/the-new-coretta-scott-king-emerging-from-the-legacy/4af10528-7ba3-45cb-b91f-f8bbdad317c6/?utm_term=.44503003eb94.

25. "Excerpts from Some of the Major Addresses Delivered at Democratic National Convention," *New York Times*, 1976, 26.

26. Jimmy Carter, "Former U.S. President Jimmy Carter's Remarks at the 50th Anniversary of the Civil Rights March on Washington for Jobs and Freedom and Martin Luther King Jr.'s 'I Have a Dream Speech.'" The Carter Center. Accessed June 27, 2019. https://www.cartercenter.org/news/editorials_speeches/jc-march-on-washington-50-anniversary.html.

27. Trescott, "The New Coretta Scott King."

28. National Commission on the Observance of International Women's Year. (n.d.). *Background on the National Women's Conference and the IWY Commission* [Press release]. Retrieved July 21, 2019, from The Commission's task was to adopt recommendations aimed at eliminating barriers to equality for women.

29. Scott King and Reynolds, *My Life*.

30. Nicole Hemmer, Jarrett Blanc, and Jeff Greenfield, "What Phyllis Schlafly Owes Feminism," *POLITICO Magazine*, September 6, 2016. Accessed June 27, 2019. http://www.politico.com/magazine/story/2016/09/phyllis-schlafly-death-housewife-activism-feminism-214213. Trescott, "The New Coretta Scott King."

31. Admin. "Minority Women." *Women on the Move*, January 5, 2018. https://www.womenonthemovetx.com/minority-women/.

32. Gloria Steinem, *My Life on the Road* (Carlton, Victoria, Canada: Black Books, 2017).

33. Quindlen, "Women's Conference Approves Planks."

34. Steinem, *My Life.*

35. Klein, "The King Who Carried On."

36. Maria Newman, "Four Presidents Join Mourners at Funeral of Coretta Scott King." *New York Times,* February 7, 2006. www.nytimes.com/2006/02/07/national/four-presidents-join-mourners-at-funeral-of-coretta-scott-king.html.

37. "'Welfare Queen' Becomes Issue in Reagan Campaign," *New York Times*, February 14, 1976. timesmachine.nytimes.com/timesmachine/1976/02/15/113445299.pdf.

38. Leigh Ann Caldwell, et al., "Elizabeth Warren Barred from Senate Debate for 'Impugning' Jeff Sessions." *NBCNews.com* www.nbcnews.com/politics/congress/sen-elizabeth-warren-barred-speaking-impugning-sen-jeff-sessions-n718166.

39. Wesley Lowery, "Read the Letter Coretta Scott King Wrote Opposing Sessions's 1986 Federal Nomination," *Washington Post,* January 10, 2017, www.washingtonpost.com/news/powerpost/wp/2017/01/10/read-the-letter-coretta-scott-king-wrote-opposing-sessionss-1986-federal-nomination/?utm_term=.367e5824e00d.

40. Amy B. Wang, "'Nevertheless, She Persisted' Becomes New Battle Cry after McConnell Silences Elizabeth Warren," *Washington Post,* February 8, 2017. www.washingtonpost.com/news/the-fix/wp/2017/02/08/nevertheless-she-persisted-becomes-new-battle-cry-after-mcconnell-silences-elizabeth-warren/?utm_term=.05aa99f22f71.

41. Devlin Barrett, et al., "Jeff Sessions Forced out as Attorney General," *Washington Post,* November 7, 2018. www.washingtonpost.com/world/national-security/attorney-general-jeff-sessions-resigns-at-trumps-request/2018/11/07/d1b7a214-e144-11e8-ab2c-b31dcd53ca6b_story.html?utm_term=.6fde92451751.

2

Michelle Cearcy

Carrying the "Torch of Equality"

AMIRA ROSE DAVIS

Figure 2.1. Last Mile to Houston. Billie Jean King, Susan B. Anthony, Bella Abzug, Sylvia Ortiz, Peggy Kokernot, Michelle Cearcy, and Betty Friedan carry the torch into Houston, 1977. Diana Mara Henry Papers (PH 51) Special Collections and University Archives, University of Massachusetts Amherst. Copyright © Diana Mara Henry / dianamarahenry.com.

DIANA MARA HENRY'S PHOTO captures Michelle Cearcy smiling wide in light rain, standing under a sea of American flags. She is slightly off-center with one hand interlocked with Betty Friedan and the other hand outstretched, firmly grasping a bronzed torch. Cearcy, along with her fellow torchbearers, Sylvia Ortiz and Peggy Kokernot, carry the "torch of equality" as they lead an enthusiastic throng of people through downtown Houston. The multiracial torchbearers were completing the final leg of the 2,000-mile, six-week-long relay from Seneca Falls, New York, to the 1977 National Women's Conference in Houston, Texas.[1] The images of Cearcy, Ortiz, and Kokernot with their arms interlocked as they hoisted the torch high among waving flags, would become some of the most widely circulated images of the historic conference.

For many observers, the image of Cearcy and her fellow runners represented the diversity and energy of the women's conference in Houston that fall.[2] Conference organizers and reporters used images of the diverse torch relay to celebrate the entire conference while newscasters looped the grainy footage of Cearcy, Ortiz, and Kokernot carrying the torch together into the packed convention floor. When the editors of *Time* magazine selected a cover photo for its issue on the conference they also looked toward the torchbearers to represent the historic gathering. Yet, *Time* chose to solely feature Peggy Kokernot, the white runner, on their cover, leaving out Cearcy and Ortiz entirely.[3] The presence, visibility, and *invisibility* of Michelle Cearcy informs a larger discussion about the experiences of Black women who went to Houston in 1977. Indeed, considering the ways in which the images of Cearcy and her fellow torchbearers were used helps to illuminate the larger politics of racial representation, visibility and symbolism at the NWC.

The idea for a torch relay was first suggested by Sey Chassler, editor of *Redbook* magazine and one of the few male IWY commissioners. Chassler initially proposed the torch relay as a way to "add sports to the conference in a meaningful way."[4] The National Commission on the International Women's Year collaborated with the National Association of Girls and Women in Sport to organize the massive relay. With additional support from *Women-Sports* magazine, the Road Runners Club of America, and the President's Council on Physical Fitness and Health, the torch relay grew into a well-publicized event that drew attention to the conference itself. Corporate sponsors also threw their support behind the relay. Colgate-Palmolive made bright blue "Women on the Move" t-shirts for every runner, while Ford donated a $13,000 matching bright blue Lincoln so that relay organizers could pace the runners.[5] As the relay garnered more attention IWY commissioners seized the opportunity to demonstrate that the conference had wide-ranging support from a variety of women.[6]

The commission decided the torch would begin in Seneca Falls, the site of the 1848 women's rights convention. From there it would travel roughly 2,600 miles over a span of six weeks, as more than 2,000 volunteers organized to collectively run the torch to Houston.[7] The volunteers were an intentionally diverse group aimed to underscore the array of conference participants and the larger support for a movement for women's rights. As the *Breakthrough* recounted there were "local and national celebrities, mayors, governors, athletes, homemakers, students, grandparents, mothers, nurses, secretaries, teachers, farm women, rural women, city women, IWY commissioners and some men."[8] Accompanying the torch was a declaration about vibrancy and resiliency of American womanhood written by poet Maya Angelou. Each volunteer was to add their name to the document after they completed their part of the relay. While some notable athletes and celebrities ran parts of the relay, the race organizers hoped to showcase "ordinary women."[9] The relay was originally planned to end with a celebrity mile featuring former Olympians Wilma Rudolph and Donna de Varona among others. However, relay coordinator, Pat Kerry, along with other members of the IWY Commission ultimately decided it would be more symbolic to select a multiracial group of local Houston athletes to be the official torchbearers for the last mile.[10]

First, the IWY Relay coordinators selected Peggy Kokernot, a white woman who was a local marathon participant and former college track star. Kokernot was tapped by a local relay committee member who was looking for a long-distance runner to fill in as a torchbearer in Alabama. The Ku Klux Klan as well as ERA opponent Phyllis Schlafly and her organized group of supporters called the Eagles, had effectively mobilized in Alabama to discourage women from running with the IWY.[11] There was a sixteen-mile gap in Alabama where there was no one to run with the torch. The solution was to fly Kokernot, who was in the middle of training for the upcoming Houston Marathon, to Alabama where she ran the torch sixteen miles out of Alabama to the next relay checkpoint. After her relay-saving run, Kokernot was asked to be one of the official "last milers."[12] Next the relay committee tapped Sylvia Ortiz, a Latina and a University of Houston student who played volleyball and badminton. Lastly, the committee chose a local Black high school athlete—Michelle Cearcy.[13]

Michelle Cearcy's formative years occurred upon a backdrop of national and local upheaval. Born at the beginning of the 1960s, Cearcy's childhood coincided with increasingly visible Civil Rights struggles, student protests, and antiwar demonstrations that were sweeping the nation. And within her own neighborhood it was a period of much transition. At the time of the conference Cearcy was a junior at Phillis Wheatley High School in Houston's Fifth Ward. Both the school and neighborhood had once been vibrant epicenters of Black life in

Houston. Phillis Wheatley High School boasted a long and influential alumni list including US congresswoman and fellow NWC participant Barbara Jordan. However, in the two decades between when Jordan attended Phillis Wheatley and when Cearcy did, desegregation and all its discontent had hit Houston.[14]

In the late 1960s and early 1970s the geopolitical landscape of the Fifth Ward was rapidly changing. The construction of Interstate 10 and US Highway 59 cut directly through the formally bustling "Afro-American downtown" area. As one historian describes it, the highways "literally crucified the area by creating large freeways in a cross pattern through its heart."[15] The highway decimated large swaths of the community and cut off access to Black businesses. Class stratification within the Black community became more pronounced as Black business owners and middle-class families begin to move to Houston's Third Ward. While Wheatley High School remained a central institution in the Fifth Ward, the larger instability of the area was starting to have consequences the historic school as well.

Despite the *Brown v. Board* decisions in 1954, it took Houston most of the 1960s and countless local protests to actually adhere to its ruling. When Cearcy arrived at the high school, Wheatley was beginning to lose Black teachers and middle-class Black students to neighboring and newly integrated schools that offered magnet programs and more resources. As one former principal observed, "We [Houston Public Schools] desegregated but we never integrated."[16] Wheatley High School reflects the reality of many Black institutions who bore the costs of integration.[17] Despite these changes Wheatley's athletic department remained a dominant player in high school sports. Cearcy found a plethora of athletic opportunities available to her in high school. She ran track, played volleyball, and took up cheerleading. Cearcy was a part of the first generation of high school girls to come up after the passage of Title IX. While the landmark act radically changed the landscape of girls and women's sports nationwide, at Wheatley the effects of the legislation were much less discernible as a result of the long history of sporting opportunities for girls within Black secondary schools.[18] Given her local profile as a high school athlete the IWY Relay Commission approached Cearcy to serve as a torchbearer. After gaining approval from her mother to participate—Cearcy agreed, despite "not knowing much about the conference" or "the impact it would have on [her] life."[19]

When Cearcy and her fellow torchbearers gathered in Tranquility Park to complete the final miles of the relay, the intended symbolism of their run was on full display. Besides being evidence of a multiracial women's coalition, the commissioners wanted the final torchbearers to represent the youth and the future of the women's movement.[20] The selection of a recent college graduate, a current college student and a high school student represented the youthful energy and next generation of the movement. The relay had moved the torch from the hands of the descendants of suffragettes in upstate New York to the diverse and interlinked hands of the rising leaders of the next wave of the women's movement coming down those Houston streets.

As Cearcy, Ortiz, and Kokernot made their way from the park to the conference site they slowed the pace to a walk and were joined by conference organizers, celebrities, and a large group of women chanting "E-R-A" while "The Yellow Rose of Texas" played in the background.[21] The images of Cearcy linking arms with her fellow torchbearers Betty Friedan, Bella Abzug, Billie Jean King, and Susan B. Anthony Jr. would be splashed on front pages of local and national newspapers in the coming weeks. The image was used as evidence to describe the "Kaleidoscope of American Womanhood" that had gathered in Houston.[22] The captions under the images of the "kaleidoscope" of women along with the broadcasts of the culmination of the torch relay reveal that reporters and newscasters sometimes struggled to identify Cearcy. Some newspapers misspelled her name, while others failed to include it at all. However, the most notable misidentification was when newscasters and reporters called her Wilma Rudolph,[23] even though the torchbearers including Cearcy had been announced ahead of time.[24] Moreover, the Houston teenager did not resemble the thirty-seven-year-old former Olympian. The subtle mix-up reveals the interchangeability of Cearcy's Black body. The individual identity of the third torchbearer was less important than the fact that it was a Black woman who could help construct the collective identity of the movement. Ironically Cearcy's symbolic value as a Black women athlete fit a larger history, that included earlier athletes such as Rudolph, whose Black female and athletic bodies were used by institutions, organizations, and state apparatuses to further various political and social goals.[25] As one article illustrated in the wake of their run, it mattered little who Cearcy, Ortiz, and Kokernot were because above all they were "ordinary women"—"a Black, a Chicano and a white."[26] The IWY Commission noted this symbolic importance when it described the last mile of the torch relay in its official report. In describing the "striking image" of the "dramatic last mile," the reports noted that the "bronzed torch" was held by the "pale arm of Peggy Kokernot . . . the golden arm of Sylvia Ortiz . . . and the dark-skinned arm of 16-year-old high school track star Michelle Cearcy."[27]

The description of the image by the IWY Commission reveals the intended symbolic significance of the chosen torchbearers. However, their positionality in most of the pictures subtly reveals the larger tensions around the racial politics of the women's convention. While the bodies of Cearcy, Ortiz, and

Figure 2.2. Sylvia Ortiz, Peggy Kokernot, and Michelle Cearcy with the American flag, November 19, 1977. Diana Mara Henry Papers (PH 51) Special Collections and University Archives, University of Massachusetts Amherst. Copyright © Diana Mara Henry / dianamarahenry.com.

Kokernot were used to transmit messages of inclusion and diversity, the placement of Ortiz and Cearcy flanking Kokernot in the middle signified that while the convention was a multiracial coalition it remained centered—both organizationally and politically—on the voices and experiences of white middle-class women. Such lingering tensions are why the other iconic multiracial images of conference-women of color uniting to present the Minority Plank were necessary. Cearcy was present at a conference that witnessed women of color attempting to centralize themselves within the women's movement.

The collected demographics of participants reveal a large presence of women of color—including 17 percent of attendees identifying as Black women.[28] Yet numerical presence did not always result in increased visibility or attention. Even the multiracial, oft-celebrated image of Cearcy and the other torchbearers would experience an erasure. Two weeks after their celebrated run, Peggy Kokernot would be featured alone on the cover of *Time*, effectively rendering Cearcy and Ortiz invisible and whitewashing the IWY Conference and the women's movement.[29] The week before, Wilma Rudolph was speaking about the plight of Black women athletes when she offered a prophetic statement. "Black women athletes are on the bottom of the ladder. White women, Billie Jean King, Chris Evert, Donna de Varona . . . they make it on the front cover of magazines. . . . The Wilma Rudolphs of the world don't."[30]

By the time Cearcy carried the torch into the Houston Conference, the relay had grown significantly in scope and symbol. Yet the relay still served its original purpose as well—highlighting women in sport. The event itself was a challenge to prevailing ideas about women's ability to run distances. The appearance of Cearcy and her fellow runners with short shorts, flowing hair, and shining earrings pushed back on lingering charges that sports was inherently masculine. The relay had boosted many former women athletes, from Kathrine Switzer to Billie Jean King. Moreover, it had featured the next generation of women athletes in the form of girl's track teams and women's college athletic departments who also ran with the torch.[31] The generations of girls and women who would grow up with more access thanks to the recently passed Title IX Education Act.[32]

Despite the symbolic use of her body and the age at which she participated, Cearcy recalls the 1977 IWY Conference with fondness. The energy, experience, and connections made were a part of a formative moment that meant a lot to the local teenager. It was as if the world had come to Houston with new and invigorating ideas and understandings about modern womanhood. Cearcy reflected on the impact of her experience noting that "after [the conference] I remained a woman on the move."[33] After touring with USVBA Cearcy returned to Houston to work for the City of Houston Parks and Recreation Department.

The image of Cearcy, as one part of a multiracial torch-bearing trio, tells the idyllic story of an energetic and diverse women's movement. The erasure of the women of color from the *Time* cover and the positioning of their bodies in the widely circulated pictures makes it evident that for Black women there was still work to be done. For Cearcy, however, it was the experience behind the images that remained with her. The moments left uncaptured and where she wasn't preforming a symbolic gesture, but was a teenager soaking in a historic moment and inspired by what she saw.

Notes

1. Karen Malnory, "Women on the Move," *Daily Breakthrough*, November 19, 1977, 14. Houston and Texas Feminist and Lesbian Newsletters, Special Collections, University of Houston Libraries (HTFLN-UHL).

2. A picture of the three runners appeared as the cover of the official conference report, *The Spirit of Houston,* sent to President Jimmy Carter. The image of the last mile of the torch relay also appeared in national and local newspapers including the lower half of the front page of the *New York Times*. National Commission on the Observance of International Women's Year, *The Spirit of Houston: The First National Women's Conference; An Official Report to the President, the Congress and the People of the United States* (Washington, DC: US Government Printing Office, 1978) cover; *New York Times,* November 19, 1977; *Los Angeles Times,* November 19, 1977, 13; *Houston Chronicle,* November 19, 1977; *In These Times,* Dec. 6–12, 1977, 1. More recently the image has been used on the front cover of books, films, and magazine articles about the 1977 conference. See the covers of: Marjorie Spruill, *Divided We Stand: The Battle over Women's Rights and Family Values That Polarized American Politics* (New York: Bloomsbury USA, 2017); and *Sisters of '77,* film, dir. Cynthia Salzman Mondell and Allen Mondell, IVTS-*Independent Lens,* Public Broadcasting Company, 2005.

3. *Time* magazine, December 5, 1977, cover.

4. Karey Bresenhan and Beverly Hebert, "Seneca Falls Relay," *Daily Breakthrough*, November 18, 1977, 7 (HTFLN-UHL).

5. Bresenhan and Hebert, "Seneca Falls Relay," 7–8.

6. National Commission on the Observance of the International Women's Year, *The Spirit of Houston,* 196.

7. Update on the State Women's Meetings and The National IWY Conference, National Commission on the Observance of International Women's Year, July 25, 1977, 10. Marjorie Randal National Women's Conference Collection, Special Collections, University of Houston Libraries (MRNWC-UHL); Bresenhan and Hebert, "Seneca Falls Relay," 7.

8. Bresenhan and Hebert, "Seneca Falls Relay," 7.

9. Edith Herman, "Ordinary People Keep the Women's Movement Running," *Chicago Tribune,* November 19, 1977.

10. International Women's Year Conference Houston Information Packet—Celebrity Mile, National Commission on the Observance of International Women's Year, nd, 1977. (MRNWC-UHL).

11. The Eagles drew their name from the Eagle Forum, a conservative interest group founded by Schlafly in 1972. The Forum had begun as a political trust fund in 1967 after Schlafly had begun receiving donations to champion conservative causes. In 1972 Schlafly formally founded the group "STOP ERA" which was subsequently renamed Eagle Forum in 1975. Today the Eagle Forum is the parent organization for both the Eagle Forum Education and Legal Defense Fund and the Eagle Forum PAC. For more on Schlafly and the Eagles see: Donald T. Critchlow, *Phyllis Schlafly and Grassroots Conservatism: A Women's Crusade*

(Princeton, NJ: Princeton University Press, 2005); "A Relay for Women's Rights Runs into Southern Chivalry," *New York Times,* November 4, 1977.

12. For more on the torch relay see: Spruill, *Divided We Stand,* chapter 10; Shelah Gilbert Leader and Patricia Rusch Hyatt, *American Women on the Move: The Inside Story of the National Women's Conference, 1977* (New York: Lexington Books, 2016), 60–61; Alyssa A. Samek, "Mobility, Citizenship, and 'American women on the move' in the 1977 International Women's Year Torch Relay," *Quarterly Journal of Speech* 103, no. 3 (2017).

13. Bresenhan and Hebert, "Seneca Falls Relay," 7–8; *Houstonian* Yearbook—Sports, University of Houston, 1975. Special Collections, UHL.

14. Michael Berryhill, "What's Wrong with Wheatley?," *Houston Press,* April 17, 1997.

15. Patricia Pando, "In The Nickel, Houston's Fifth Ward," *Houston History Magazine* (Summer, 2011), 33.

16. Berryhill, "What's Wrong with Wheatley?"

17. For more on the cost of desegregation on Black schools see: Adam Fairclough, *A Class of Their Own: Black Teachers in the Segregated South* (Cambridge, MA: Harvard University Press, 2009).

18. For more on the history of Black girls and sport see: Susan K. Cahn, *Coming on Strong: Gender and Sexuality In Women's Sport* (Urbana: University of Illinois Press, 1995); for a specific discussion of the history of Black girl's athletic and recreational opportunities see: Amira Rose Davis, "'Watch What We Do': The Politics and Possibilities of Black Women's Athletics, 1910–1970," PhD dissertation, Johns Hopkins University, 2016.

19. Michelle Cearcy letter to Diana Mara Henry, October 30, 2012.

20. Bresenhan and Hebert, "Seneca Falls Relay," 7–8.

21. "Feminists Greet Symbolic Torch," *Los Angeles Times,* November 19, 1977, A1. The ERA chants refer to the Equal Rights Amendment, once of the most fiercely contested issues of the decade and a focal point of the convention.

22. Judy Kelmesrud, "At Houston Meeting, A 'Kaleidoscope of American Womanhood,'" *New York Times,* November 19, 1977.

23. Ethel Taylor, "The Women Have a Plan," *Philadelphia Inquirer,* November 30, 1977, 13.

24. "Billie J. King, Wilma Rudolph to Complete IYY Torch Relay," *Atlanta Daily World,* November 18, 1977; Herman, "Ordinary People Keep the Women's Movement Running." One publication cropped Cearcy out completely: *In These Times,* Dec. 6–12, 1977, 1.

25. Davis, "'Watch What We Do'"; Rita Liberti and Maureen Smith, *(Re)Presenting Wilma Rudolph* (Syracuse, NY: Syracuse University Press, 2015).

26. Herman, "Ordinary People Keep the Women's Movement Running."

27. National Commission on the Observance of the International Women's Year, *The Spirit of Houston,* 128.

28. National Commission on the Observance of the International Women's Year, *The Spirit of Houston,* 128.

29. *Time* magazine, December 5, 1977, cover.

30. "Wilma Rudolph Moving into the Spotlight Again," *Philadelphia Inquirer,* November 28, 1977, 7-C.

31. Herman, "Ordinary People Keep the Women's Movement Running"; Bresenhan and Hebert, "Seneca Falls Relay."

32. Title IX refers a section of the 1972 Educational Amendments signed into law by Presi-

dent Richard Nixon. The section held that no person shall be discriminated on the basis of sex from an educational program or activity receiving federal financial assistance. While not specific to athletics the amendment had a severe impact on high school and college athletics for girls. Realizing the implications of the law many sporting organizations and athletic departments, including the National College Athletic Association (NCAA), attempted to change Title IX in court. These highly publicized challenges helped shape public knowledge of Title IX and led to widespread association of the amendments with sports. Title IX has also been used to address campus sexual assault and the handling of sexual harassment cases. The very public legal battles of sexual assault protection and Title IX at schools like the University of Tennessee and Baylor University have once again shifted public association with the amendment some fifty years after its passage. Deborah L. Blake, *Getting in the Game: Title IX and the Women's Sporting Revolution* (New York: New York University Press, 2012).

33. Michelle Cearcy letter to Diana Mara Henry, October 30, 2012.

II

Sisters in Action

THE FIGHT FOR equity, liberation, and freedom is not meant for the weary. However, we all get weary sometimes. Which is why help, community, and support are critical to one's survival. No one person accomplishes anything on their own. Nor can accomplishments sustain without sharing and being willing to pay it forward.

Sisters in Action is a testimony to the intergenerational impact that advocacy and activism can have on one's life. In addition, it highlights the unwavering support that Black women are willing to extend to ensure that we all have a chance to not simply survive, but to live, thrive and excel. Whether the championing is being done through national organizations such the Girl Scouts of the USA, service clubs, sororities, labor unions, or institutions of higher learning, Black women have and continue to serve as change-agents within their homes, communities, cities, states, nation, and beyond. For Gloria Scott, Dorothy Height, Freddie Groomes-McLendon, Addie Wyatt, or Jeffalyn Johnson, all aspects of their lives were oriented toward change.

3

Dr. Gloria Dean Randle Scott

Raising the Gavel with Hope for All Women

JANINE FONDON

Figure 3.1. Dr. Gloria Scott at the podium, 1977. Diana Mara Henry Papers (PH 51). Special Collections and University Archives, University of Massachusetts Amherst Libraries. Copyright © Diana Mara Henry / dianamarahenry.com.

WHEN DR. GLORIA DEAN RANDLE SCOTT raised the gavel to open the 1977 National Women's Conference (NWC), she was coming home to Houston's Third Ward that had nurtured her and a place that had inspired her to fight for profound change in one of the country's most important youth organizations, the Girl Scouts of the USA. The NWC brought women of all backgrounds together to create change in a world where women from different cultures, races, and classes rarely shared the same stage and platform. In her speech, Scott set in motion a call to action for conference attendees to find common ground through dialogue, debate, and discussion—all to set a new path for women to stand united—not divided. She raised the gavel at the conference to demonstrate her will that women become inclusive leaders: "leaders for all people, and not just some."[1]

Scott's path to Houston took her from the Third Ward to Black sorority membership at Indiana University, where she learned the power of social activism and how to lead as a Black woman. These early lessons were translated into national leadership roles in the Girl Scouts, at Bennett College, and, of course, at the NWC. Scott was the only woman from Houston named to the National Commission on the Observance of International Women's Year. Scott's leadership was shaped by the Civil Rights Movement and the women's movement, but reflected an overarching commitment to inclusivity premised on the idea that empowering all women required the inclusion and empowerment of Black women.

Rooted in Houston

Scott stepped onto to conference platform stage as a daughter of Houston's Third Ward, who was born in 1938 to Juanita Bell, a part-time nurse, and Freeman Randle, a cook. Houston's predominantly African American, poverty-stricken, socially segregated Third Ward was home to a long line of African Americans who became leaders, educators, and business owners. It was known as the place where "many African American judges, elected, and appointed public officials have traditionally resided."[2]

The Third Ward was rooted in Scott's every step—and she was proud to carry the powerful legacy of Houston's Third Ward. As she put it, "I was born in Jefferson Davis Hospital in Houston, Texas on April 14, 1938. I attended Fourth Missionary Baptist Church Kindergarten from September 1941 when I was three years old until May 1943 when I graduated as the valedictorian of my class. I went on to attend Blackshear Elementary School (which was two blocks from my house) and Jack Yates High School."[3] Blackshear and Yates were segregated schools, but like the rest of the Third Ward institutions, attending them added determination, strength, and perseverance to Scott's upbringing.

In 1953, when she was fifteen years old, she signed up with the "Girl Scouts in Troop 155 at Jack Yates Secondary School." Girl Scouts of the USA had made concessions to local laws and practices for years by not allowing Black girls to join and then only allowing membership in segregated troops. While the first troop for Mexican American girls had been organized in Houston in 1922, the first troop for African American girls was not officially recognized by the Girl Scouts of America until 1942.[4] Despite this context, Scott was attracted to activities that seemed to encourage girls to develop skills.[5]

She left Houston to attend college only two years after joining Troop 155—but never forgot the Girl Scouts or Houston's Third Ward. In the organization's own account of her role, "Her love of Girl Scouting blossomed through her involvement as a Girl Scout Junior in Troop #155, and in spite of the segregation her troop experienced, she learned unique leadership skills that would later propel her into her larger leadership roles."[6] Those skills would be honed at Indiana University, where she was a member of historical African American Greek-letter organization Delta Sigma Theta, Inc. (DST).

Finding Her Voice at Indiana University

Scott left Houston to study at Indiana University in 1955.[7] Known for educating African Americans as early as 1895, she chose Indiana because the year before had opened residence halls to Black women.[8] While Indiana University still held many challenges for African American students in the 1950s, with her Houston mindset, Scott found the mentoring and leadership she needed to succeed and survive. Through her years at the university, Scott defined herself in settings where most peers and professors didn't look like her by placing herself in the center of communities of women who were often addressing civil and women's rights.

Scott also looked beyond her campus to find inspiration in other Black women leaders like Anna Julia Cooper, whom Scott considered a role model. Scott worked with Cooper on various women's committees and civil rights activities in nearby communities during her years at Indiana University and made sure to attend meetings with Cooper whenever she could. The relationship helped Scott learn how to speak up for herself and speak out for others. As Scott put it, with heartfelt pause of admiration and deep emotion, "She is my role model. I will never forget her or her words of wisdom. I would go to see her at meetings any chance I had to get off campus."[9]

Cooper especially influenced Scott's belief the value of solidarity, unity, and inclusion. Cooper's book, *A Voice from the South*, made the case for women's solidarity arguing: "The colored woman feels that woman's cause is one and universal; and that . . . not till race, color, sex, and condition are seen as accidents, and not the substance of life; not till the universal title of humanity to life, liberty, and the pursuit of happiness is conceded to be inalienable to all, not till then is woman's lesson taught and woman's cause won—not the white woman's nor the Black woman's, not the red woman's but the cause of every man and of every woman who has writhed silently under a mighty wrong."[10] Scott took Cooper's wisdom to heart she pledged the Gamma Nu Chapter (Bloomington, Indiana) of Delta Sigma Theta, cultivating not only sisterhood but a commitment to equity and humanity rooted in Black feminist struggle.

Through sorority life, Scott found opportunities for mentorship and leadership. In 1958, she was elected the second national vice president for Delta Sigma Theta and went to their headquarters for meetings run by Jeanne Noble, the twelfth national president. Noble had earned a doctorate from Columbia University and was a leader of national renown, being "the first Black woman to serve on the National Board of the Girl Scouts USA," among other accomplishments.[11] Noble served as a mentor to Scott. She not only advised her in terms of her professional duties as part of the sorority, but also showed her how to anticipate needed actions in the community in support of civil rights and her "sisters."

Scott remembered that during one meeting, Noble interrupted the agenda with news that the "girls at Bennett" were demonstrating in Greensboro, North Carolina. Noble knew that they would need support. The Deltas had set up arrangements with white women to bail out female protesters rather than have them jailed overnight. As the Deltas swung into action to support the 600 women marching through Greensboro, Scott became seriously involved in civil rights activism. This commitment to civil rights and women's empowerment proved to become part of Scott's mission in life and continued throughout her journey.[12]

While a graduate student, Gloria married Will Scott, a sociologist with an interest in social work. In 1960, after receiving her master's degree in zoology, she became research associate in genetics and embryology at the Indiana University Institution for Psychiatric Research and started teaching biology at Marion College, becoming the first African American instructor at a predominantly white institution in Indianapolis, Indiana. While she worked at Marion College, Scott earned her PhD in education from Indiana University. With her degree in hand, Scott went on to serve as the special assistant to the president and educational research planning director at North Carolina A&T University and as senior research associate and head of post-secondary education at the National Institute of Education in Washington, DC.

In her years at Indiana University and working in the field of education after, Scott's activism in civil and women's rights grew. In each of her positions, Scott understood what it was like to be the only or one of the few African Americans at the decision-making table. She also knew that continued activism was necessary in order to create change for women and for Black communities. As her commitment matured so did her voice and influence in spaces for women like the Girl Scouts and the National Women's Conference. Delta Sigma Theta Sorority, Inc. is a historically African American national sorority. Its national motto is "Intelligence is the Torch of Wisdom."

Raising Her "Inclusive" Voice for Women at the Girl Scouts of the USA

In an environment where life for Black women and white women were divided in many ways, Scott intentionally broadened her voice to evoke change for all women and girls. During her tenure as the first African American to be elected as president of the Girl Scouts of the USA, from 1975 to 1978, she sought to bring women together to advance them all.

In 1969, the National Board of the Girl Scouts sought to move beyond token racial representatives on their National Board. Several white board members declined to be reappointed and eleven women of color were elected, Scott was among them.[13] The board assured Scott that the 1970s were going to be dedicated to diversity in the Girl Scouts under a program called Action 70. Scott was probably also encouraged to join by the presence on the board of her old mentor from Delta Sigma Theta, Jeanne Noble.

At the Triennial Meeting in Seattle later that year both Noble and Scott were dumbfounded when all of the girls chosen to participate in the opening ceremonies were, in Scott's words, "lily white." The next morning an anonymous telegram was waiting for Scott. It asked, "Why are you going to take your intellectual ability and your know-how with organizations to a racist organization?" The other women of color on the board received similar telegrams. That morning they all met to discuss diversity and pluralism in the Girls Scouts and decided to call for a conference on scouting for Black girls. At the January 1970 board meeting, their proposal met with significant resistance and the resignation of four members of the board. Nevertheless, the Girl Scouts supported the idea and later that year representatives from the sixty largest Girl Scout communities met in Atlanta.[14]

The conference on Black girls was an important call for political action in the Girl Scouts. Attendees at the meeting wanted to increase the numbers of Black girls in scouting, publicize the achievements of Black girls, and change the image of Girl Scouts to be more inclusive. Importantly, the meeting invited senior girl scouts themselves to represent their councils as voting delegates. This was the first time that girls had been allowed to vote on national Girl Scout Policy. This marked the beginning of a process of decentralization that allowed local councils and troops to be more responsive to their community needs.[15]

In 1972, Scott moved from her position as chair of the program committee and member of the Minority Task Force to serving as vice president. Her governmental experience and her long standing connection to Girls Scouts enabled her to become the national president in 1975—the first Black in the organization's history of more than sixty-five years.[16]

During this time, the Girl Scouts began an explicit turn toward feminism. In 1974, national leaders, including Scott, began to discuss two major actions: endorsing the Equal Rights Amendment and bringing Betty Friedan on to the National Board. Both proved to be very controversial.

Worried that endorsing the passage of ERA would endanger their status as a nonprofit organization, Girl Scout leaders consulted attorneys in 1974. While the attorneys did not think it would violate any laws to endorse ERA, the Girl Scouts of the USA remained silent until January 1977 when the board announced its endorsement.[17] In her defense of the endorsement, Scott noted that individuals were of course free to hold their own opinions, but that the organization's rights, duties, and responsibilities toward the 2.6 million girls in its membership led them to support women's equality. Nominating Friedan to the National Board was somewhat less controversial in that many saw her as a national figure who would bolster efforts to promote diversity and pluralism. Also, as one among fifty board members, Friedan was not seen as having too much influence within the organization. From Scott's perspective, supporting women's equality through Friedan's board membership or the endorsement of ERA was a natural extension of her efforts to promote what was best for girls, Black, white and brown.

During her tenure with the Girl Scouts, Scott agreed to chair the National Women's Conference in Houston. Her presence opening the conference was more than symbolic. She was not simply a place holder for girls as the president of the Girl Scouts. Instead, she was recognized as an African American woman leader who was changing one of the largest organizations of white women in the country—by making it more inclusive. She brought the same message of change and inclusiveness to Houston as she truly felt that women needed to stand together, and not be divided on issues deserving the attention of all women.

The Road to Raising the Gavel

Scott's leadership at the Girl Scouts brought her to the 1977 conference yet her personal commitment to women's empowerment and civil rights were with her as well. For years prior to the conference, Scott used her voice to inspire and model women's leadership. She was named to the National Conference Commission because of that voice and her influence.

Scott understood the power of creating more than a moment, but a movement of women and was a leader by example: "As a member of the IWY Commission, Scott was heavily involved in the planning and executive of the National Women's Conference. She also helped the Houston Committee, a volunteer group that conducted much of the groundwork prior to the conference. Scott was first to speak at the event."[18] Scott not only helped plan the conference by supporting the local committee and as commissioner from Houston; she even joined other women to run the torch for "last grand mile" into Houston. The torch traveled around the world and included a 51-day, 2,600-mile journey from Seneca Falls, New York, to Houston, Texas, with some 2,000 women carrying it over the journey. Scott said, "I was able to run a mile, so I did it."[19] A photo of Scott running with torch was noted in the official report of the conference: "Gloria Scott, IWY Commissioner and Girl Scout President, makes the makes the early morning mile."[20] During the official opening of the National Women's Conference, the torch was presented to the three First Ladies in attendance.

Scott understood that history would be made by the people who stood together and made it happen. Scott was a part of this new history and understood what it meant for a Black woman to be included in decision-making, planning sessions, and proposing solutions. Scott persisted to lead by not only carrying the torch but also by raising her voice and gavel for all women—and especially African American women.

Scott, as an organizer, a leader and an educator, was all too familiar with the mountain of controversy that circled the conference and people who attended. She understood that there were women who wanted to change and those who only wanted change on their own narrow terms. She understood that some 20,000 people attended the conference and 2,000 were delegates who would decide what the President and Congress should know "to help American women achieve equality with men in all aspects of American life."[21] She also understood that out of some fifty Commissioners for the National Commission on the Observance of International Women's Year, she was one of only seven Black commissioners.[22]

When she ascended the steps to the 1977 Women's Conference podium during the opening session, Scott did so as a hometown hero from the Third Ward, member of the Delta Sigma Theta Sorority and president of the Girl Scouts. Looking back, she recalls that she was "the only national IWY Commission member for Houston, so I opened the conference and Barbara [Jordan] was one of the speakers and offered the keynote address." Scott and Jordan had served on many Houston committees together over the years. When I asked her about it, she said, "I was honored to be in the company of my friend and fellow soror of Delta Sigma Theta."[23] As a sorority woman, Scott felt the impending presence of African American sorority women who would participate at the conference. With many pre-conference conversations—some more formal than others—sorority women were ready to speak and be heard across many of the sessions and planks. C. Delores Tucker, Representative Maxine Waters, Maya Angelou, and Coretta Scott King were Alpha Kappa Alpha Sorority members. Congresswoman Barbara Jordan, Dr. Gloria Scott and Dr. Dorothy Height were members of the Delta Sigma Theta Sorority.

Before opening the conference, Scott glanced at the agenda of official conference business, as shared by IWY Presiding Officer Bella Abzug, and saw her name in print as part of this historic event and noted as opening the inaugural plenary session.[24] "Even though I had worked with the Houston Committee on the event for some time, I was still amazed to be part of this great event and filled with gratitude that I was in this role," Scott said.[25]

Scott ascended to the podium at the 1977 Nation Women's Conference in Houston Texas with undisputed dignity. She stood there—5' 4"—with all of her life experiences, including the hurts of exclusion, the passion of inclusion, and the will to persist, resist, and insist. She brought to the podium the spirit of her mentor, Anna Julia Cooper. Scott opened 1977 National Women's Conference with intention as she stood firm and fully present behind the podium at the National Women's Conference, bringing the opening session to order with the pound of the gavel once used by Susan B. Anthony in 1896. She defined her presence by looking up and while staring into the rousing audience, she said, "I am Gloria Scott, member of the presidentially appointed National Commission on the Observance of International Women's Year. I am a Texan and a native Houstonian."[26] In her deepest authenticity as an African American woman, Scott was seen and heard as she looked deeper into the audience of women from all walks of life and communities. She raised the gavel with a spirit of hope and visible sign of inclusion—and especially the inclusive leadership needed to drive the difficult, uncomfortable conversations to be conducted at the conference.

At the steady hand of Scott, the historic gavel brought new meaning to its resounding pound on the podium. Her act of raising the gavel signaled that change could and would come with inclusive leadership. Women in attendance from all parts of the country, income levels, diversity, and walks of life were expected to work collectively despite historic divisions based on race, class, geographic location, sexuality, and perspectives. As Scott publicly raised this gavel, she became a bridge connecting the women's struggle in 1848 to the more current intersectional women's struggle experienced by Black women and women of color. In doing so, she stood on the right side of history and ignited a new chapter in the Women's movement built on new terms—with hopes that African American women in leadership would be seen, heard, and included this time.

When her voice was heard, her presence known and her words felt, Scott declared that she had the official power to open the meeting by saying: "It is now my official pleasure to open this meeting of American women on the move."[27] Scott's life journey of quiet strength and leadership was heartfelt as she noted in her opening speech that: "It is a sobering experience to preside over the opening ceremonies of the most significant and far-reaching event in this century. This National Women's Conference will insure that we the people of the United States of America, in order to form a more perfect union, do move closer to the possibility of what America can be."[28] Scott's speech allowed attendees to hear the resonating words bearing the need for coming together with the spirit of inclusion from an African American woman who was birthed out of struggle in Houston, fought civil rights battles over 30 years since entering school, and rose to prominence by advising the Girl Scouts of the USA on how to be more inclusive. She forged her message highlighting the need for inclusion at the conference with the following statement:

We live in a time where the rate and quality of change combine to produce a sometimes formidable combination. Increasingly, there is the request and demand for the enactment of a change in societal mores which address the true realization of a pluralistic culture in which variables that describe or define individuals have fundamental equal status. We are "in passage" and our fates are inextricably bound. The aim is the fostering of the well-being of people—not of women alone or of men apart—but a society of diverse talents. For a brief period in our lives we will deliberate across variables which might tend to isolate, stereotypes which tend to separate—yet we will share the same experiences. As we approach this delegate assembly, let us keep ever before us the concept that the unexamined issues is not worth holding on to forever.[29]

Scott officiated her first lesson in inclusion by declaring that of all the diversity in the room, the meeting engaged "American" women on the move—not just Black women or white women. Together, women of all backgrounds would be challenged to stand on the side of change or remain entrenched in old ideas. Some women were opposed to the conference's mission and others in similar camps were divided on the twenty-six planks on the National Plan of Action.

In reflecting on her experiences at the conference Scott said, "Outside of the sessions, women just came together to have conversations over lunch, and dinner—and found that we just talked about the thoughts and feelings about things said during the day. We sat with each other in small groups and talked about many things. During the conversations, people were entitled to their own opinion. If this is how you think and what you believe, then stand by it, until you come to understand or accept something different. They all seemed to accept my viewpoint on this point."[30]

After the 1977 Conference

Scott's commitment to women's empowerment and leadership as well as pursuit of civil rights kept her on the frontlines of change. She maintained her focus on mentoring women and fighting for the changes needed for their future success. Over the years after the conference, she continued to serve as an educator and administrator at various universities and always supported mentoring activities for women.

From 1987 until 2001, Dr. Scott was President of Bennett College, "While at Bennett, Scott was instrumental in founding Africa University in Zimbabwe."[31] She also founded a women's mentoring program—The National African American Women's Leadership Institute (NAAWLI) that still exists today.

Over the years of her long career, Dr. Scott has found peace in the potential of women, as change-agents and bridges to the future. She has inspired young women to make their voices heard and women of color to take their place in a world that may not see or hear them. Above all, her life journey represents a story quilt of courage that demonstrates how you empower others to change the world as you create internal change to develop your own skills, perspective, and voice. The 1977 National Women's Conference documented that Dr. Scott's life experience directed the intentional pounding of the gavel to signal a new beginning for women with inclusive leadership.

Notes

1. National Commission on the Observance of International Women's Year, *The Spirit of Houston: The First National Women's Conference; An Official Report to the President, the Congress and the People of the United States* (Washington, DC: US Government Printing Office, 1978), 2; interview with Gloria Scott by Janine Fondon, December 22, 2020.

2. Third Ward Initiative, University of Houston. https://uh.edu/third-ward/third-ward-map/

3. K. Cooper, "Meet Dr. Gloria R. Scott," *The Bend Magazine—Coastal Bend Life,* January 21, 2021. http://www.thebendmag.com/2021/01/21/343443/meet-dr-gloria-r-scott. Accessed June 30, 2021.

4. On segregation in Girl Scouts of America, see "Honoring Josephine Holloway during Black History Month," GSBlog, February 17, 2015, https://blog.girlscouts.org/2015/02/honoring-josephine-holloway-during.html, accessed July 10, 2021; and Barbara Arneil, "Gender, Diversity, and Organizational Change: The Boy Scouts vs. Girl Scouts of America," *Perspectives on Politics* 8, no. 1 (2010): 53–68, doi:10.1017/S1537592709992660. Shanise Harris, "Dr. Gloria Randle Scott: Making History," Girl Scouts of the Colonial Coast Blog, March 2020, gscccblog.blogspot.com/2020/03/gloria-randle-scott-making-history.html.

5. Harris, "Dr. Gloria Randle Scott."

6. "Girl Scouts Honors Gloria R. Scott, First Black National President," https://blog.girlscouts.org/search?q=gloria+scott, Accessed February 6, 2015.

7. "Gloria Scott," *The History Makers.* February 8, 2007. https://www.thehistorymakers.org/biography/gloria-scott-41

8. Gloria Scott Interview, June 20, 2009, Indiana University Bicentennial Oral History Project. https://oralhistory.iu.edu/collections/123/collection_resources/17179.

9. Interview with Gloria Scott by Janine Fondon, December 22, 2020.

10. Charles Lemert and Esme Bhan, eds., *The Voice of Anna Julia Cooper: Including a Voice from the South and Other Important Essays, Papers, and Letters* (Lanham, MD: Rowan and Littlefield, 1998).

11. "Dr. Jeanne Noble, Educator, and Author." *African American Registry* (n.d.), https://aaregistry.org/story/dr-jeanne-noble-educator-researcher-author-and-consultant/, retrieved July 4, 2021; "Gloria Scott," *The History Makers.*

12. Laura Michael Brown, "Remembering Silence: Bennett College Women and the 1960 Greensboro Student Sit-Ins," *Rhetoric Society Quarterly* 48, no. 1 (2018): 49–70.

13. "Girl Scout head says program is for girls," *Press and Sun-Bulletin* (Binghamton, New York), Nov. 2, 1975, 18.

14. "Gloria Scott," *The History Makers.*

15. Phyllis E. Reske, "Responding to Change: Girl Scouts, Race, and the Feminist Movement," master's thesis, Department of History, University of Wisconsin, Milwaukee, December 2018.

16. "Gloria Scott," *The History Makers.*

17. Reske, "Responding to Change," 41.

18. Texas Archive of the Moving Image. (n.d.). *Women on the Move, Gloria Scott.* http://www.womenonthemovetx.com/gloria-scott/

19. Interview with Gloria Scott by Janine Fondon, December 22, 2020.

20. National Commission on the Observance of International Women's Year, *The Spirit of Houston,* 199.

21. National Commission on the Observance of International Women's Year, *The Spirit of Houston,* 119.

22. National Commission on the Observance of International Women's Year, *The Spirit of Houston,* 124.

23. Interview with Gloria Scott by Janine Fondon, December 22, 2020.

24. Letter to Delegates and Agenda for the National Women's Conference, November 10, 1977. https://digitalcommons.unf.edu/cgi/viewcontent.cgi?article=1474&context=saffy_text.

25. Interview with Gloria Scott by Janine Fondon, December 22, 2020.

26. National Commission on the Observance of International Women's Year, *The Spirit of Houston,*217.

27. National Commission on the Observance of International Women's Year, *The Spirit of Houston,* 217.

28. National Commission on the Observance of International Women's Year, *The Spirit of Houston,*217.

29. National Commission on the Observance of International Women's Year, *The Spirit of Houston,* 217,

30. Interview with Gloria Scott by Janine Fondon, December 22, 2020.

31. Donald W. Patterson, "Bennett Group Helps Make Africa University a Reality," *News and Record,* April 19, 1994. https://greensboro.com/bennett-group-helps-make-africa-university-a-reality/article_c6f64f4a-14c3-5e71-a17d-231d8aa49894.html.

4

Human Rights on the Homefront

Dorothy Height and Spirit of Houston

JULIE A. GALLAGHER

Figure 4.1. "Dorothy Height and Maxine Waters at Minority Women press conference," in Caroline Bird, "Houston Day by Day," from National Commission on the Observance of International Women's Year, *The Spirit of Houston: The First National Women's Conference* (Washington, DC: US Government Printing Office, 1978), p. 160.

IN A CAVERNOUS HALL filled with thousands of seasoned activists as well as first-time participants, Dorothy Height, president of the National Council of Negro Women (NCNW), stood out. Born in 1912, eight years before women secured the right to vote, she had already spent forty years fighting for civil, political, economic, cultural, and social rights—human rights—for all women and for African Americans, when Commissioner Gloria Scott leveled the gavel to open the National Women's Conference. Before her death on April 20, 2010, Height would commit another thirty years to the fight for women's rights and racial justice within the US and internationally. Winner of the nation's highest awards including the Presidential Citizens Medal, the Presidential Medal of Freedom, and the Congressional Gold Medal, and referred to by President Obama as the "Godmother" of the Civil Rights Movement, Height was also decorated with the Spingarn Medal from the National Association for the Advancement of Colored People (NAACP), inducted into the National Women's Hall of Fame, and the recipient of over thirty honorary degrees. Few, if any, among the impressive crowd in Houston that gray November weekend in 1977 could claim a longer or deeper commitment to the nation's unfinished struggles for justice and equality.[1]

In attendance as a delegate-at-large representing the NCNW, Dorothy Height utilized her finely honed organizing and coalition-building skills prior to and throughout the Houston Conference to ensure that minority women's lived experiences and recommendations were concretely reflected in the final report to the President and Congress. As NCNW president, she had spearheaded the pre-Houston effort to collect the concerns of African American women across the country and to ensure they were represented in the National Plan of Action. The NCNW orchestrated the drafting of the Black Women's Action Plan, a powerful document that explained how racism had distinctly shaped the experiences of Black families, Black children, Black men, and Black women in profound and detrimental ways. It substantively informed deliberations during the Houston Conference, contributed to the Minority Plank, and shaped the resulting National Plan of Action. Significantly, it continued after Houston as the Black Women's Agenda, the only post-Houston plan to continue to the present.

Pictured with California assemblywoman Maxine Waters, Dorothy Height conveyed, through her focused countenance and posture, the moment's symbolic and material importance. The conference was at an electrifying, pivotal point for women of color. At the moment of this photograph, a group of women representing the Minority Caucus had just presented the revised Minority Women's Plank, which Height had helped craft, to thunderous, emotional approval.

Height's Path to Houston—A Life of Commitment to Freedom, Equality, and Justice

When Dorothy Height helped shepherd the Minority Plank through to its historic adoption, she had a tremendous wealth of experience and a nuanced understanding of institutional power from which to draw experience. A native of Virginia, Height was a talented student with hopes of becoming a doctor. She was accepted to Barnard College in 1929, but quickly confronted the long arm of racism when the dean informed her that "Barnard had a quota of two Negro students per year, and two others had already taken the spots."[2] Temporarily crushed, Height was immediately accepted at New York University and commenced her new life in Harlem.

Height's interest in organizational leadership and activism was bourgeoning by the time she graduated from college. During the Depression, she served as a representative of the Harlem Christian Youth Council in the Popular Front, which was an ideologically diverse coalition that worked together to support the New Deal and oppose fascism. It was the first of many times that Height demonstrated her openness to working across the political and ideological spectrum on issues of social and economic justice, and to her recognition of lessons that could be gleaned from various constituencies, including radicals.[3] She elaborated on the excitement and commitment that she felt as part of the youth movement in the 1930s. "We really believed that . . . we were building a new world."[4] And indeed she was, although the world she was helping build took far longer and faced steeper challenges than she might have imagined as an optimistic twenty-five-year-old.

Emergence of a Feminist Consciousness

In the late 1930s, Height met two pioneering civil rights activists who shaped her professional path and the legacy she would create as a civil rights and women's rights leader. Veteran activist Cecelia Cabaniss Saunders hired Height to work at Harlem's Emma Ransom House of the YWCA, which was a cornerstone of Harlem's social and cultural life. As part of the staff, Height, like Ella Baker and Anna Hedgeman, investigated the "Bronx slave markets" where African American women were hired for day-work and often horrendously exploited. From that point, Height's life mission became clear: she would fight for Black women and human rights more broadly through women's organizations.

Height made another consequential connection in the same period. Mary McLeod Bethune, founder of Bethune-Cookman College, commanding leader of President Roosevelt's Black Cabinet, and most significantly, founder and president of the National Council of Negro Women, brought Height into the organization after meeting her at a Harlem event for Eleanor Roosevelt.[5] Recounting the day in her autobiography, Height noted that Bethune, "made her fingers into a fist to illustrate for the women the significance of working together to eliminate injustice. 'The freedom gates are half ajar,' Bethune said. 'We must pry them open fully.' I have been committed to the calling ever since."[6] Height's connection to the NCNW that began in the 1930s would last into the twenty-first century.

From World War II through the 1950s, Height gained crucial professional and organizing experience. As part of the home front war effort, she worked in the nation's capital for the Defense Department's Advisory Committee on Women in the Services, struggling to eliminate racial discrimination faced by women in the armed services. When she returned to New York she resumed her work with the YWCA, and at the same time, she was elected national president of the Delta Sigma Theta Sorority, which was founded by African American college women in 1913. In an era of intense political repression in the 1950s, left-leaning activists in unions and progressive organizations including the National Negro Congress, were accused of being Communists or Communist sympathizers by the House Un-American Activities Committee (HUAC). So were members of the NCNW, an organization hardly known for radical or even progressive activism. Especially in this context, the peak of Cold War McCarthyism, Height demonstrated political courage and a savvy understanding of strategy. In an effort to challenge the repressive climate, she organized a public outreach event between the YWCA and the National Council of Jewish Women in New York City titled "Speak Up, Your Rights Are in Danger."[7] A seasoned activist by this time, she carefully engaged Cold War debates about the role of the state and human rights to paradoxically open up new conversations about racial and gender-based inequality even as the boundaries of those debates contracted dramatically in an era of intense fear-mongering. As a result, Height moved closer to the centers of political power and brought with her ideas about the ways American society should be organized.

Working through the 1960s Liberal Establishment

After the 1960 presidential election, racial discrimination and social injustices in jobs, housing, education, and politics—problems that Height had been fighting for the past three decades—were raised anew before leaders of the liberal political establishment. Invited to participate in these national conversations, Height, who was elected president of the NCNW in 1957, made important contributions on numerous fronts. One of the most relevant in terms of the role she would later play at the 1977 National Women's Conference was her participation on the President's Commission on the Status of Women (PCSW). Formally chaired by Eleanor Roosevelt, the commission had twenty-six members including five members of the president's cabinet, four members of Congress, two college presidents, labor leaders, and presidents of four national women's organizations.[8] Height was the only African American woman on the commission.

The work of the PCSW was done through seven committees. In that committee work, Height was joined by a small number of prominent African American women including Jeanne Noble, president of the Delta Sigma Theta Sorority, and Pauli Murray, legal scholar and human rights activist.[9] Together these three and a handful of other Black women sought to broaden discussions and raised matters of economic, political, and social concern to African American women, while they rigorously explored issues of significance to women of all races and classes across the nation. At the same time, recognizing the distinct history and challenges Black women faced in American society, the commission sponsored a special consultation to discuss "Problems of Negro Women." The one-day meeting in April 1963, held as the committees were finishing their work, was chaired by Height and brought together twenty African American leaders.[10] Of importance, she was the bridge between the 1963 PCSW special consultation and the 1977 National Women's Conference minority women caucus meetings. In both cases she oversaw the collection of vital data on African American women's lived experiences in work, education, politics and home life, and she helped shape them into meaningful policy statements. These included the Problems of Negro Women which was presented at the PCSW and the "Black Women's Action Plan: A Working Document for Review and Ratification," and Plank 17 on Minority Women which was adopted in Houston.[11]

In her opening statement to the 1963 day-long consultation, Height explained the commission's charge, some of its preliminary conclusions, and she elaborated on points she felt were particularly important to the consultation's work. Among them was the commission's goal to see that conditions were created across the nation to "assure the widest possible freedom of choice" to women including the right to stay at home or to work. Height stressed to her sympathetic audience, however, that, "I think for women in minority groups we are constantly aware of how little freedom of choice there often is around the things for which they care the most."[12] To underscore persistent added burdens women of color faced in the United States in comparison to white women, Height quoted Mary Church Terrell who had written about the "double handicap of race and sex," sixty years earlier.[13]

Proceeding from the assertion that "the problem of race discrimination permeates the whole life picture of the Negro," the group analyzed a number of pressing problems for African American women.[14] These included Black women's work in the waged labor force and the need for and the challenges of getting more Black women involved in local government agencies and civic organizations. They also analyzed the ways negative portrayals of African American women affected their interactions with white colleagues. The discussion on work focused on the ways racism denied Black women access to relevant job training, employment opportunities, and professional advancement.[15] If the PCSW was serious about not only collecting information about the challenges African American women faced, but also advancing solutions, the consultants gathered under Height's leadership gave them plenty to work with, even if they did not challenge traditional assumptions about gender roles or family norms.

Dorothy Height summed up some of the key themes that emerged from the day, themes that she would help surface in the Black Women's Plan of Action fourteen years later. One of the most important focused on the reality of racism and the deleterious effects it had on African American women's lives, particularly as it intersected with sexism. She stated unequivocally that African American women faced serious and at times overwhelming challenges that were different from white women's challenges in significant ways. These differences, Height stated poignantly, included "the place that we are in the body-politic and in the economy[,] the impact of the racial factor and the role that the Negro woman has within the family." The problems demanded meaningful attention from the PCSW and society at large. In her final emotional appeal she stated that the differences that Black women faced in American life, "they are not minor, they are quite major, in influencing the extent to which the sense of equitable participation in the democratic society can be realized and in which the sense of being personally fulfilled can ever be dreamed of as Negro women try to participate as members in our democratic society."[16] Height's message was as powerful as it was clear: Black women paid a terribly high and distinct price for being both Black and female in a society that distributed the psychological and material benefits of political, social, and economic citizenship most heavily to others in the social order, but especially white Americans.

Height's perspective was shaped by her painful yet clear-eyed understanding of Black women's history and current reality, at a personal as well as a societal level. She had worked on behalf of Black women at the local level in Harlem and in the Jim Crow South, and at the pinnacle of African American women's organizations and the national liberal establishment. Height carried this burden of knowledge with her fourteen years later into the National Women's Year preparatory meetings and Houston convention, determined to shape its outcomes in ways that could improve the lives of African American women and all women of color especially.

Civil Rights Activism on the Ground

Height capitalized on her experience on the PCSW and began to build relationships with the leaders of other national women's organizations. In the fall of 1963, after the momentous March on Washington as well as the devastating bombing of the 16th Street Baptist Church, she gathered a group of women together to evaluate civil rights priorities and to strategize about how women could advance them. She had found it difficult to get the male civil rights leaders "to accept the fact that the conditions affecting children, affecting youth, and affecting women," including childcare and jobs for women, "were all a part of civil rights." She was encouraged by the different response she got from the women she had called together, noting that they understood "the relationship between decent housing, schooling, and childcare, to employment, and employment to job opportunities."[17] In thinking back over the contributions the NCNW made to the struggles for racial equality, Height recalled proudly that "[M]any groups came into Mississippi. NCNW never left. . . . Whether it was carrying books and art supplies to the freedom schools during Wednesdays in Mississippi, keeping Head Start on track, setting up pig banks, or building houses, we were helping people meet their own needs, on their own terms."[18] She understood and advocated for women whose lives were shaped by the intersectional dynamics of racism and gender discrimination. Under Height's tireless leadership, the NCNW empowered poor women in substantive ways that would enable them not only to survive in an economically and socially hostile world but to also live in dignity.

As the 1960s drew to a close, Height's national reputation was solidified by her demonstrated political acumen within liberal establishment circles, remarkable skills as an organizational leader, and astute and courageous activism in the South. Not only had she led some of the nation's most prominent women's organizations including the YWCA, the Delta Sigma Theta Sorority and the NCNW but she was veteran of the civil rights struggle for racial justice. Moreover, she had a global vision of power, oppression, and resistance that was shaped by frequent travel overseas that started in the 1930s and included her participation at the United Nations International Women's Year Conference in Mexico City in 1975 (and years later at the United Nations Conference on Racism in Durban, South Africa, in 2001). The insights she gained from these myriad and diverse experiences informed Height's formative contributions to the Black Women's Plan of Action and the Minority Plank.

Houston—1977

Dorothy Height was not one of the prominently featured speakers at the Houston Conference. She was not one of the forty-seven International Women's Year (IWY) commissioners who planned the National Women's Conference. The leaders and organizers of the conference tended to be women who explicitly identified as feminists or were younger or more politically outspoken than Height. They included Bella Abzug, Maya Angelou, Eleanor Smeal, Barbara Jordan, Gloria Scott, Gloria Steinem, Addie Wyatt, Maxine Waters, and Coretta Scott King.[19] In the absence of focused media attention and in a crowd of two thousand delegates, one might overlook Height's participation. That would be a grievous mistake. She engaged the Houston Conference as she did all of her work, with an open mind to ideas from across the political spectrum, a clear and deep understanding of social, economic, and political power, a recognition of the need to engage the state to bring about lasting change in society, and a keen understanding of history.[20] By virtue of the hard-won lessons she acquired and nuanced political philosophy she honed over decades of activism, Height served as essential connecting tissue of past to present, of people to each other and to organizations, of ideas and experience to policy, in pivotal ways. Her contributions to the Houston Conference, unrecognized until now, were foundational.

• • •

Informed by prior, generally unsuccessful battles to ensure Black women's voices were heard and their challenges in American society recognized, especially during the PCSW, Height was determined to make sure the Houston Conference was different for Black women and minority women more generally. In the spring of 1963 she had worried aloud that the efforts of those who participated in the consultation on the "Problems of Negro Women" would not be reflected in the PCSW's final report and that readers would not have "much understanding of how minority groups are affected."[21] When *American Women*, the commission's final report, was released later that year, Height could argue that her concerns had been justified. There were but a handful of references woven through the document regarding the particular problems Black women faced.[22]

With the National Women's Conference one month away, Height, as president of the NCNW, wrote to friends and colleagues urging them to complete a circulated form that was designed to capture Black women's concerns. Noting the historic opportunity the conference presented, she urged that "the issues that directly affect Black Women will have to be identified and underscored." Further, Height explained, "We want to assure that there is direct and uncomplicated communication between us during the conference." Black women needed to work together and communicate with each other. Height felt strongly about that. She wanted Black women's concerns and contributions collected in advance so that "upon arriving in Houston, there is sufficient information and direction readily available that we may all 'get down to business' right away."[23]

The result of the pre-conference meetings, surveys, and conversations among African American women led to the creation of the aforementioned "Black Women's Plan of Action."[24] One can hear echoes of Height's warnings about the PCSW's negligible inclusion of Black women's perspectives in a pointed statement included in the Black Women's Plan of Action. "[W]e present this position paper—not only as a representation of our views, to be recognized by the Conference and forgotten" it maintained, "but as a proposal that these views be considered and included in the total IWY program."[25] In other words, they urged, "don't dismiss us."

The Plan of Action highlighted the impact of the double oppression African American women experienced in American society and presented compelling data on their participation in the labor force and characteristics of female-headed families. It also made concrete recommendations to increase Black women's access to jobs and equal pay, political participation, and appropriately funded social services.[26] When read together, one can also see clear connections between the Black Women's Plan of Action and the content of the revised Minority Plank (Plank 17).

The Minority Plank, which was adopted by the convention in that transformational moment, highlighted with stark data, the fact that minority women experienced the detrimental, combined effects of racism and sexism that undermined their opportunities in the labor force, in health, and in education. The plank explicitly demanded, therefore, that "every level of Government action should recognize and remedy this double discrimination and ensure the right of each individual to self-determination."[27] Here were the powerful themes that Dorothy Height had surfaced during the PCSW's special consultation on the Problems of the Negro Women in the PCSW and in the Black Women's Plan of Action. She joined now with other minority women to shape their articulation in the National Plan of Action. Many considered it at the time, and a growing number of women's historians now have come to recognize it as "the most significant event of Houston and of all that had preceded it. For the first time, minority women—many of whom had been in leadership of the women's movement precisely because of their greater political understanding of discrimination—were present in such a critical mass that they were able to define their own needs as well as to declare their stake in each women's issue."[28] Height's handiwork was essential in the conceptualization of the plank and the determination to ensure its historic resonance at the conference.

Re-imagining the Women's Movement

Height and the women of color who crafted the Minority Plank (Plank 17) helped broaden the feminist agenda in fundamental ways. They pushed for a recognition of human rights that included but was also broader than women's rights alone. In doing this, they spoke to the intersectional realities of women across the nation. The legacies of their efforts are evident everywhere today in the ways activists organize and fight for social justice across intersectional identities, in the ways organizations frame their agendas and pursue their goals, and in the ways scholars approach research and teaching. Under Height's leadership, African American women brought a vitally important, expansive view of justice and equality to the National Women's Conference. "We propose that IWY, in concern for all citizens and for the great institutions of our nation, dedicate women not to the betterment of themselves alone, but to the compelling challenge of gaining human rights in America."[29] Right up to her death in 2010, Dorothy Height was committed to that effort and remained an inspiration and a guiding voice in the struggle for justice and human rights. As she had all her life, she urged younger generations to "Keep struggling for jobs and freedom. I don't think we're going to get it by talking, and we're not going to get it just by laws. We're going to have to take the hands and make the laws work."[30]

Notes

1. Dorothy Height, *Open Wide the Freedom Gates: A Memoir* (New York: Public Affairs, 2003); Eleanor Hinton Hoytt, "Height, Dorothy Irene," *Oxford African American Studies Center*, 1 Dec. 2006, https://doi.org/10.1093/acref/9780195301731.013.44191 (accessed Wed Apr 12 14:30:52 EDT 2017); "The Life and Surprising Times of Dr. Dorothy Height," National Council Negro Women, http://www.ncnw.org/dr-dorothy-height/.

2. Height, *Open Wide the Freedom Gates*, 31.

3. Julie Gallagher, *Black Women and Politics in New York City* (Urbana: University of Illinois Press, 2012), 177.

4. Height interview, 60.

5. Height's oral history, 37, 66–67; Height, *Open Wide the Freedom Gates*, 82.

6. Height, *Open Wide the Freedom Gates*, 83.

7. Dorothy Height interview in Ruth Edmonds Hill, ed., *The Black Women Oral History*

Project: From the Arthur and Elizabeth Schlesinger Library on the History of Women in America, Radcliffe College (Westport, CT: Meckler, 1991), vol. 5 of 10, 105.

8. Background information on commission members came from *Current Biography,* Years 1944, 1947, 1949, 1955, 1956, 1958, 1959, 1961, 1962, 1964, 1965, 1967 and 1970.

9. Rosa Gragg, president of the National Association of Colored Women's Clubs served on the Committee on Home and Community; Lillian Holland Harvey, dean of the School of Nursing at Tuskegee served on the Committee on Education.

10. Transcript of PCSW meeting, April 9, 1962, 188. Box 4, folder 4, PCSW Papers, JFKL. Report on Four Consultations, PCSW, List of Participants in Consultation on Problems of Negro Women, 37. Box 3, folder 13, PCSW Papers, JFK Library. For a detailed profile on participants of the Consultation, see Duchess Harris, *Black Feminist Politics from Kennedy to Clinton* (New York: Palgrave, 2009), 72–80.

11. Statement by Dorothy Height, April 19, 1963, Transcript of the Proceedings of the Consultation of Minority Groups. Box 4, Folder 7, PCSW Papers, JFK Library, Report of Consultation on Problems of Negro Women, in *American Women: The Report of the President's Commission on the Status of Women and Other Publications of the Commission,* eds. Margaret Mead and Frances Kaplan (New York: Scribner, 1965), 220, and Report in Box 3, Folder 13, 29; National Commission on the Observance of International Women's Year, *The Spirit of Houston: The First National Women's Conference; An Official Report to the President, the Congress and the People of the United States* (Washington, DC: US Government Printing Office, 1978), 70–75, 156–157, 272–277.

12. Statement by Dorothy Height, April 19, 1963, Transcript of the Proceedings of the Consultation of Minority Groups, 12–14. Box 4, Folder 7, PCSW Papers, JFK Library.

13. Statement by Dorothy Height, Transcript of Consultation, 14.

14. Statements by Walter Davis, Ruth Whitehead Whaley, and Dorothy Height, Transcript of Consultation, 17, 24, 179. See also Report of Consultation on Problems of Negro Women, in Mead and Kaplan, *American Women,* 220 [and Report in Box 3, Folder 13, 29.]

15. Statement by Paul Rilling, Consultation Transcript, 66.

16. Statement by Dorothy Height, Transcript of Consultation, 180.

17. Dorothy Height interview in Hill, *The Black Women Oral History Project,* 173.

18. Height, *Open Wide the Freedom Gates,* 199.

19. National Commission on the Observance of International Women's Year, *The Spirit of Houston,* 6–8, 233, 243–249.

20. Height, *Open Wide the Freedom Gates,* 61–63, 149–151.

21. Statement by Dorothy Height, Transcript, 179.

22. Mead and Kaplan, *American Women,* 35.

23. Dorothy Height, letter addressed to "Dear Friends and Colleagues," 10/21/77, "IWY, 7/24/73—10/78" file, Box 16. Domestic Policy Staff, Beth Abramowitz's Files, Jimmy Carter Library.

24. National Commission on the Observance of International Women's Year, *The Spirit of Houston,* 156–157.

25. Black Women's Plan of Action, in National Commission on the Observance of International Women's Year, *The Spirit of Houston,* 272.

26. Black Women's Plan of Action, in National Commission on the Observance of International Women's Year, *The Spirit of Houston,* 274–277.

27. "Plank 17: Minority Women," in National Commission on the Observance of International Women's Year, *The Spirit of Houston*, 70.

28. "The Minority Caucus: 'It's Our Movement Now,'" in National Commission on the Observance of International Women's Year, *The Spirit of Houston*, 156.

29. "Black Women's Action Plan: A Working Document for Review and Ratification, IWY Conference, Houston 1977," ii, Commission on the IWY 2/77–3/77 file, Box 5, Records of Martha (Bunny) Mitchell, Special Assistant to the President, Jimmy Carter Library.

30. "Remembering the 'Godmother' of Civil Rights, Dorothy Height," Air Date April 20, 2010, https://highered.nbclearn.com/portal/site/HigherEd/search accessed May 3, 2017.

5

"I hope we won't turn our backs on the masses of women in Florida"

Dr. Freddie Groomes-McLendon, the Florida Commission on the Status of Women, and the Struggle over the Equal Rights Amendment

JOHANNA M. ORTNER

Figure 5.1. Dr. Freddie Groomes at the National Women's Conference. Diana Mara Henry Papers (PH 51). Special Collections and University Archives, University of Massachusetts Amherst Libraries. Copyright © Diana Mara Henry / dianamarahenry.com.

DR. FREDDIE GROOMES-MCLENDON[1] was excited to participate in the 1977 National Women's Conference in Houston, Texas. As Chair of Florida's Commission on the Status of Women, the state's Governor Reubin Askew, as well as other members of the group, thought it crucial that Groomes-McLendon would represent the commission at the national conference. By 1977 Florida had become one of the battleground states for the fight to pass the Equal Rights Amendment (ERA). Governor Askew likely figured that Groomes-McLendon's position as the Chair of the Commission would be an important representation of Florida's commitment to women's rights and would also give her the opportunity to network and discuss the fight for the ERA with other delegates and women's rights activists at the national conference. However, there was one big caveat: only women's organizations were able to nominate delegates to attend the conference and the commission was not considered one. Ultimately, Groomes-McLendon's membership and leadership in the oldest African American sorority, Alpha Kappa Alpha (AKA), made it possible for her to receive an appointment as a selected delegate to represent Florida.[2]

The image of Groomes-McLendon, taken by Diana Mara Henry, shows a confident and self-assured woman in her forties, proudly wearing the blue-ribbon badge that marked her as the chairperson of Florida's Commission for the Status of Women. Groomes-McLendon was no stranger to positions of responsibility. She served as a member of Florida's Constitutional Revision Commission and enjoyed a career as the executive assistant to Florida State University's president J. Stanley Marshall from her appointment in 1972 to her retirement in 2003. With the silk scarf and neat, professional gold earrings, Groomes-McLendon proudly displays her natural Afro, which was as much a hairstyle as it was a declaration of African American women and men's Black consciousness in the decades of the modern Civil Rights Movement. Her Pro-Plan button indicates her support for passing the ERA, a subject at the forefront of her work in Florida, which was seen as the most promising of the thirteen battleground states at a time when only three more states were needed to ratify the constitutional amendment guaranteeing "Equality of rights under the law."

Freddie Groomes-McLendon and Alpha Kappa Alpha

Groomes-McLendon was born on September 2, 1934, in Jacksonville, Florida. She was named after her father Fred, who, like his wife Lenton Lang, did not graduate from high school, but instead joined the work force at a young age to provide, first, for his siblings and later for his own family. Groomes-McLendon still remembers her mother's advice to pursue education and invest in her own future.[3] Due to her parents' insistence on securing a good education, Groomes-McLendon was motivated to follow their advice. In pursuit of her first degree, a BS in Home Economics from Florida A&M University, she learned about Alpha Kappa Alpha (AKA), a Black sorority that had a chapter at the university. AKA was founded in January 1908 by nine Black women, led by Ethel Hedgeman Lyle, and by 1913, the sorority became "the first national, incorporated Greek-letter organization for Black college women."[4] According to Deborah Elizabeth Whaley, the "chief goals for AKA were programs that would better the cultural, economic, social, and educational levels of Black women and men."[5] Groomes-McLendon became a member of AKA during her undergraduate years at Florida A&M, because she was impressed by the sorority's service-oriented focus and its commitment to take on social issues as they pertained to women and minorities.[6]

Black sororities became a crucial network for Black women college students to not only bond socially but to also unite in their fight for racial and gender equality. According to Stephanie Evans, "Black women effectively organized and coalesced for community empowerment," while at the same time focusing on their academic excellence, which was a sentiment that was mirrored by the fact that "four of the first African American women to earn PhDs were in sororities."[7] AKA was at the forefront of Black sororities' political organizing when they formed the American Council of Human Rights (ACHR), which consisted of six other Black sororities and fraternities. The ACHR was established in the 1950s to "push Congress and the federal government to enact policies and laws that improved civil rights for African Americans."[8] By 1957, the ACHR became solely a Women's Council as all fraternities had withdrawn. The sororities pushed forward with their commitment to civil rights and held workshops for undergraduate students that focused on topics such as "voting, employment, housing, and education."[9] Although the ACHR disbanded in 1963, its founding showcased the group effort that Black sororities undertook in order to come together and engage with American politics.[10]

Groomes-McLendon's membership in AKA was also what afforded her a nomination for the 1977 Women's Conference. While she attended the conference to represent the Florida Commission on the Status of Women, she was only able to attend because of her connection with her sorority, which became one of the largest Black women's organizations in the United States. According to an announcement in the *News Herald* on May 9, 1975, AKA's membership had grown to include more than 45,000 undergraduate and graduate women students nationwide. Whaley states that "in 1976, there was a national mandate from AKA headquarters for the sorority women to involve themselves locally in the fight for human rights, first-class citizenship for Black Americans, and women's rights."[11]

It is not surprising then that the sorority also took a vested interest in the 1977 Women's Conference. Groomes-McLendon still vividly remembers how her membership in AKA was the only thing that secured her participation in the conference. Without Groomes-McLendon's knowledge, a staff person of Governor Askew contacted the president of AKA, Barbara Phillips, and asked her if she could recommend Groomes-McLendon as a delegate to the conference in Houston. Phillips was quite perturbed at first that anyone would tell the sorority who to nominate as a delegate, since she did not know that Groomes-McLendon was an AKA soror. Once Groomes-McLendon learned about the phone call, she contacted Phillips herself in order to apologize for the staff person's request. During that call, Phillips asked for Groomes-McLendon's resume and once she saw that Groomes-McLendon was the president of the sorority's local chapter in Tallahassee, Phillips changed her mind and nominated Groomes-McLendon as a delegate. It was not until the conference in Houston in November 1977 that Groomes-McLendon and Phillips met in person. After their meeting at the conference, Phillips was so impressed by Groomes-McLendon that she asked her to become the national chair for AKA's Connection Committee, which was formed as the political arm of the sorority. Groomes-McLendon would hold that position from the late 1970s to the early 1980s.[12]

Commission on the Status of Women and the ERA

Groomes-McLendon's involvement with Governor Askew's Commission on the Status of Women and her subsequent work during the 1970s to get the ERA passed in Florida grew out of her appointment as executive assistant for Florida State University's president J. Stanley Marshall during the early 1970s. According to a statement in the *News Herald* on December 31, 1972, "the year 1972 on the Florida State University campus was marked by a record student enrollment, the beginning of a multi-million dollar building program and a complete university-wide study." Marshall invited Groomes-McLendon, who, at that point, had earned a master's degree in counselor education and a PhD in counseling psychology from Florida A&M University, to join the administration as both the first African American and the first woman to be a member of the university council. In her role as executive assistant, Groomes-McLendon was responsible for increasing the representation of minorities and women among faculty and students.[13]

A year later, in 1973, Governor Askew appointed her as a member of his newly reinstated Commission on the Status of Women, which she assumed was due to the fact that, by then, she was established and well known for her work regarding women and minorities at Florida State University. On June 11, 1973, the *Playground Daily News* printed Askew's statements regarding his reasoning for appointing Groomes-McLendon and other women to the commission: "We want this commission to be responsive to all women in Florida and we have searched for appointees who have the background and experience to be a representative group." Further, Groomes-McLendon's racial and educational background, as well as her professional work at Florida State University were crucial for Askew, as he, according to the newspaper article, wanted to hire women whose life experiences were influenced by "marital status, age, race, level of education or training and employment hiring and promotion practices." While Groomes-McLendon was responsible for increasing Florida State University's minority and female enrollment, in turn, her presence as a Black woman also diversified the commission and showcased an effort to model the commission into a truly representative group of Florida's women population.[14]

By 1972, the passing of the ERA had become a crucial issue for the state as it became obvious that both pro- and anti-ERA forces were well supported by respective women's organizations. This divide proved to be a difficult one for the passing of the amendment in Florida. In 1970, 51.7 percent of inhabitants living in Florida were women. According to Joan Carver, particularly after World War II, a considerable influx of non-southerners to the Sunshine State led to the creation of two different cultures within Florida, which set it apart from other southern states. Carver states that "a conservative culture in the northern part of the state, where native southerners are must numerous and old attitudes strongest, and a culture more receptive to change in the central and southern parts of the state" developed within Florida.[15] Pro- and anti-ERA organizations "wrote letters, demonstrated, lobbied, and held candlelight vigils for their respective causes."[16]

Pro-ERA organizations such as the League of Women Voters, the National Organization of Women, and the American Association of University Women pushed for the ratification of the amendment in order to finally include legal equality for women in the nation's Constitution. In the *Herald Tribune* on April 10, 1976, Miriam Perry Bell, a member of Sarasota's American Association of University Women emphasized that point when she stated that "The Equal Rights Amendment gives equality to men and women under protection of the National Constitution wherever they may live." Anti-ERA forces, on the other hand, viewed the ratification of the ERA as creating a breakdown of the traditional family unit and saw the amendment as a stepping stone to creating unisex bathrooms and legalizing homosexual marriage.[17] A letter written by Gwen Button to the editor of Sarasota's *Herald Tribune*, published on October 24, 1976, exemplified that standpoint: "I cannot see (1) forcing a wife to share equally the burden of supporting a family, (2) daughters having to register for military draft at age 18, (3) invalidation of labor laws which protect women in industry, and (4) elimination of the right of a wife to draw Social Security based on her husband's earnings, as 'advancing' anything—except complete turmoil and despair." These pro- and anti-ERA statements showcase the marked divide between women's groups in Florida regarding the amendment.

According to Groomes-McLendon, the ratification of the ERA became one of the central issues for the Commission on the Status of Women and the divisive political climate over the amendment at the time made it obvious that the goal of its passing in Florida would not be an easy undertaking. In order to meet with Floridians and discuss the issue of women's rights, the commission began to hold statewide hearings to give the public the opportunity to attend and convey their viewpoints regarding the status of women in the Sunshine State. Groomes-McLendon attended a select number of hearings, first as a member of the commission, and beginning in 1975, as the chairperson of the commission.[18] A description of one of these hearings in Pensacola, Florida, allows for a clearer understanding of this particular work. A *Playground Daily News* account from June 12, 1973, describes one of these public hearings scheduled at Cordova Mall the following day, from 3 to 7 p.m., stating that it was geared toward "women and men from all walks of life concerned with the status of women" who would discuss "unique problems or viewpoints." The meeting was divided into four sessions of forty-five minutes each, focusing on issues such as education, employment, and law and business procedures. According to the newspaper article, the information gathered at these forums would then be analyzed by the commission and a report of its findings would be sent to the governor and Florida legislators. Groomes-McLendon remembered that a combination of pro- and anti-ERA supporters were attending these hearings, which showcased the divisiveness regarding women's rights in Florida that the amendment brought to the forefront.[19]

The Year of Women's Conferences: 1977

In 1975 Governor Askew appointed Groomes-McLendon as the chairperson of the Commission on the Status of Women, underscoring his decision by saying, according to the announcement in the *Herald Tribune* on October 12, 1975, that she was "one of the most talented women in Florida." In her capacity as chairperson, Groomes-McLendon's participation in the Florida Women's Conference in July 1977 remains one of her most memorable experiences regarding the struggle over the ERA and women's rights in the state. The conference in Orlando was one of fifty-six women's conferences held in every US state and territory in order to select delegates and topics that would be addressed at the National Women's Conference in Houston in November 1977.[20] According to a news report in the *Playground Daily News* on May 29, 1977, the Florida Women's Conference, was slated to take place at the Sheraton Towers in Orlando from July 15 to July 17. The same article cited Groomes-McLendon, who stated that the conference was "an opportunity to discuss, explore and celebrate womanhood."

The Orlando conference, however, turned out to be one of the most tension-filled events that Groomes-McLendon ever attended in her role as chairperson of the Commission on the Status of Women.[21] Beginning with the inaugural session, anti-ERA organizations voiced their dismay over the conference organizers' supposed favoritism of pro-ERA supporters. Anti-ERA supporter Marilyn Lucas, the President of the Florida Right to Life Committee, complained in a letter to the editor of the *Naples Daily News* on July 22, 1977, that the conference was a fraud, stating that "the conference planners were hand-picked feminists who most certainly were not representative of all women." She went on to declare that "the meetings and workshops were rigged and totally manipulated by these feminists and every law in the book was broken to keep the session in their total control." Anti-ERA attendees' main issue focused on Friday night's session at the conference when only thirteen anti-ERA women out of forty delegates were voted to travel to Houston for the National Women's Conference. According to a *News Tribune* article on July 20, 1977, anti-ERA organizations stated that they did not get enough time to nominate more than thirteen women to represent their cause during the one-hour session and felt certain that if they would have nominated more members, a larger number of anti-ERA delegates would have been able to head to Houston. Even though Rep. Gwen Cherry from Miami stated to the *Daily Herald* on July 18, 1977, that "conference officials were only following federal guidelines at the nomination session," newspapers published multiple angry letters and accounts by anti-ERA supporters after the conference in Orlando was adjourned.

The discontent of the anti-ERA attendees at the Orlando conference was also felt during the remaining days. Groomes-McLendon remembers men and women shouting loudly and aggressively at Saturday's session, which was a two-hour debate regarding the ERA. The Texas *Sunday News-Globe* reported on July 17, 1977, that Groomes-McLendon acted as the moderator and, due to the situation becoming confrontational and hostile, "declared voting for and against the ERA a draw and said the proposal will go before the last general session scheduled for Sunday." Because the atmosphere grew antagonistic after that statement, conference organizers thought it best that police officers would escort Groomes-McLendon out of the conference room and to an area from where she was able to leave the venue. To Groomes-McLendon's knowledge, other presenters did not require a police escort. However, since she was the moderator of the workshop and the chairperson of the commission and made the statement about the draw, all the aggressiveness was focused on her.[22] One might also wonder if the fact that she was an African American woman talking about the ERA influenced the anti-ERA attendees' hostility while Groomes-McLendon was at the microphone.

On July 18, 1977, the *Daily Herald News* reported that the Orlando conference was attended by about 2,700 registered attendees, but that by the final day of the conference, more than half had left. Only about 1,310 attendees remained for the final session and the conference was adjourned, since not enough people were present to reach a quorum, which resulted in a shouting match between pro- and anti-ERA supporters. Anti-ERA supporters made it a point to state that they did not recognize the legality of the proceedings and in that way, the conference in Florida mirrored other states' women's conferences, where anti-ERA groups also disputed the conference organizers. The atmosphere at the Orlando conference clearly displayed the tension among women's groups as Florida became a battle ground for passing the ERA. By the time the Women's Conference in Orlando took place, the amendment was approved by thirty-five states and only needed three more states in order to achieve its ratification. In Florida, "the amendment came to a floor vote in one or both houses in 1972, 1973, 1974, 1975, and 1977."[23] The large organization of anti-ERA forces over the course of the 1970s showcased the difficulties that supporters of the ERA were confronted with.

Groomes-McLendon remembers how that tension also influenced her attendance at the 1977 National Women's Conference. As stated previously, due to her sorority's nomination, Groomes-McLendon was able to attend the conference as a Florida delegate, even though she went there to represent Florida's Commission on the Status of Women. Because of her uncertainty about whether she would be able to attend, the excitement of being able to participate in the conference is what Groomes-McLendon remembers most vividly. She was delighted to be meeting women from all over the nation who were committed to push women's rights to the forefront of the nation's consciousness. Not surprisingly, she met AKA sorors from other states who also attended the conference as delegates and attendees, which displays not only the wide network of the

Black sorority, but also puts AKA at the center of the conversation regarding national women's rights. In addition, Groomes-McLendon recognized friends and colleagues, some of whom were fellow delegates and others who were just women interested in attending the conference. She remembers chatting informally about topics that she was concerned with in her position as chairperson of the commission. Since Florida was in the news nationwide with its difficulties of passing the ERA, particularly after its contentious Women's Conference in Orlando, the press in Houston was focused on Groomes-McLendon and were pressing her about what was going on in Florida. The press was quite persistent in trying to find out why the ERA was not being passed in the state and Groomes-McLendon recalls doing her best to respond to their insistent inquiries as the representative of the Commission on the Status of Women.[24] Undoubtedly, it must have been frustrating to her as well, that the commission's and other women's organizations' hard work to try and win the deciding support for the amendment did not bear a quick and desired outcome.

After the National Women's Conference

Groomes-McLendon used her attendance at the 1977 National Women's Conference in Houston as a motivating force for her continued work as an advocate for women and minorities. She saw her attendance at the conference as a reminder to continue to work hard and aggressively on issues pertaining to women's rights in Florida, "in order to make the state in particular, but the United States, in general, a better place" for underrepresented populations.[25] Groomes-McLendon incorporated her motivation from the Houston Conference in her work as a member of Florida's Constitution Revision Commission, to which she was appointed by Governor Askew in the summer of 1977. According to an announcement in the *City News Herald* on July 3, 1977, Groomes-McLendon was only one of two Black members and one out of five women who made up the thirty-seven-member commission. The commission began its meetings in the fall of 1977 and one of its proposals, which Groomes-McLendon strongly supported, was the so-called Little Equal Rights Amendment. On December 8, 1977, the *Daily News* declared that this state-version of the ERA would at least "add a provision barring sexual discrimination to the Florida Constitution."

According to a report in the *Playground Daily News* on May 6, 1978, Groomes-McLendon was determined to prevent members of the Constitutional Revision Commission from turning its "backs on the masses of women in Florida," and fiercely debated the necessity of revising the state Bill of Rights to include the word "sex" in order to give women legal rights and protection under state law. Her own race and gender played a defining factor in her arguments for the revision. Groomes-McLendon made it clear in no uncertain terms that her intersecting position as a Black woman meant that she could not separate her race from her gender.[26] Due to her work as a chairperson on the Commission on the Status of Women as well as her position as executive assistant to the Florida State University's president, overseeing its minority affairs program, Groomes-McLendon knew that race *and* gender needed to be included in the language of Florida's State Constitution in order to guarantee full protection and equal rights for women and minorities.[27] Groomes-McLendon's persistence paid off and the *Sarasota Journal* reported on October 24, 1978, that the proposal was included as Revision 2 on the November ballot in 1978, which would have added the word "sex" to Florida's Bill of Rights, which until then read "no person shall be deprived of any right because of race, religion, or physical handicap." Ultimately, the provision was defeated at the ballot and Florida ended up neither passing this provision, nor the national ERA.

As we continue to bring to the fore African American women's voices, who have been ignored and overlooked, the importance of recording these women's journeys through primary resources and their own firsthand accounts remains crucial to the recovery of Black women's political activism. Groomes-McLendon's achievements and political advocacy for women and minorities show us how Black women, who are not nationally known in the larger narrative of the fight for racial and gender equality in the United States, were an intrinsic part of various organizations and programs that focused on meaningful social change. Groomes-McLendon's member- and leadership in Alpha Kappa Alpha, the Commission on the Status of Women, the Constitutional Revision Commission, as well as her decades-long commitment to increase the number of women and minority students and faculty as the Florida State University president's executive assistant, display the multifaceted ways in which Black women participated in and led major political programs during the decade of the 1977 National Women's Conference.

Notes

1. During the 1970s, Dr. Groomes-McLendon was known by her then-last name Groomes. Newspaper articles cited in this chapter refer to her as Freddie Groomes. However, Dr. Groomes-McLendon has used her hyphenated name for the past sixteen years and prefers her name to be written this way, so I will refer to her as Groomes-McLendon throughout the chapter.

2. Freddie Groomes-McLendon, phone interview with the author, August 24, 2017.

3. Freddie Groomes-McLendon, phone interview with the author, August 24, 2017.

4. Stephanie Y. Evans, "The Vision of Virtuous Women: The Twenty Pearls of Alpha Kappa Alpha Sorority," in *Black Greek-Letter Organizations in the Twenty-First Century*, ed., Gregory S. Parks (Lexington: The University Press of Kentucky, 2008), 41.

5. Deborah Elizabeth Whaley, *Disciplining Women: Alpha Kappa Alpha, Black Counterpublics, and the Cultural Politics of Black Sororities* (Albany: State University of New York Press, 2010), 42.

6. Freddie Groomes-McLendon, phone interview with the author, August 24, 2017.

7. Evans, "The Vision of Virtuous Women," 60.

8. Marybeth Gasman, "Passive Activism: African American Fraternities and Sororities and the Push for Civil Rights," in *Black Greek-Letter Organizations 2.0: New Directions in the Study of African American Fraternities and Sororities*, ed. Matthew W. Hughey et al. (Jackson: University Press of Mississippi, 2011), 36–37.

9. Robert Harris, "Lobbying Congress for Civil Rights: The American Council on Human Rights, 1948–1963," in *African American Fraternities and Sororities: The Legacy and the Vision*, ed. Tamara L. Brown et al. (Lexington: The University Press of Kentucky, 2005), 225.

10. Harris, "Lobbying Congress for Civil Rights," 229.

11. Whaley, *Disciplining Women*, 50.

12. Freddie Groomes-McLendon, phone interview with the author, August 24, 2017.

13. Freddie Groomes-McLendon, phone interview with the author, August 24, 2017.

14. Freddie Groomes-McLendon, phone interview with the author, August 24, 2017.

15. Joan S. Carver, "Women in Florida," *The Journal of Politics* 41, no. 3 (1979): 941.

16. Joan S. Carver, "The Equal Rights Amendment and the Florida Legislature," *The Florida Historical Quarterly* 60, no. 4 (1982): 470.

17. Kimberly Wilmot Voss, "The Florida Fight for Equality: The Equal Rights Amendment, Senator Lori Wilson and Mediated Catfights in the 1970s," *The Florida Historical Quarterly* 88, no. 2 (2009): 181.

18. Freddie Groomes-McLendon, phone interview with the author, August 22, 2018.

19. Freddie Groomes-McLendon, phone interview with the author, August 22, 2018.

20. Doreen J. Mattingly and Jessica L. Nare, "'A Rainbow of Women': Diversity and Unity at the 1977 U.S. International Women's Year Conference," *Journal of Women's History* 26, no. 2 (2014): 92.

21. Freddie Groomes-McLendon, phone interview with the author, August 24, 2017.

22. Freddie Groomes-McLendon, phone interview with the author, August 22, 2018.

23. Carver, "The Equal Rights Amendment," 458.

24. Freddie Groomes-McLendon, phone interview with the author, August 24, 2017.

25. Freddie Groomes-McLendon, phone interview with the author, August 24, 2017.

26. Freddie Groomes-McLendon, phone interview with the author, August 24, 2017.

27. Freddie Groomes-McLendon, phone interview with the author, August 22, 2018.

6

"Each One Teach One"

Dr. Jeffalyn Johnson on the Power of Community, Representation, and Education

LINDSAY AMARAL

Figure 6.1. Dr. Jeffalyn Johnson stands twelfth from the left (*rear*) between Margaret Mealey and Addie Wyatt. Members of the National Commission at the White House, 1978. Diana Mara Henry Papers (PH 51). Special Collections and University Archives, University of Massachusetts Amherst Libraries. https://credo.library.umass.edu/view/full/mupho51-soic-i0027. Copyright © Diana Mara Henry / www.dianamarahenry.com.

IN 1978, PRESIDENT JIMMY CARTER signed *The Spirit of Houston,* a report culminating in the twenty-six planks agreed upon at the National Women's Conference (NWC) in Houston, Texas, the previous year. At the ceremony honoring the leaders of the National Commission on the Observance of International Women's Year, nineteen women gathered at the White House to commemorate their work. The commission's diverse expertise and interests illuminated their efforts in fostering women's equality in the broadest way possible. Honored for their leadership, this group of women understood progress from a kaleidoscope of vantage points. Yet, at this auspicious event, they were photographed under the official presidential portrait of John Tyler, an ardent states' rights advocate and Confederate sympathizer and the irony is inescapable. For Dr. Jeffalyn Johnson, one of nineteen African American NWC commissioners, this moment had been both joyous and trying. "How did I feel about it? That I had to stand in front of it and grin? . . . that's the way it was," she recalled. She drew strength from her mother's teaching, "Bite your tongue and bide your time."[1]

Johnson's enduring commitment to equality for African American women and men was founded in her belief that increasing representation based on gender and race laid a foundation for a more equal society. Activism can be carried out in large or small scales, and Jeffalyn Johnson's life encompassed both. Her work helped create more opportunities at the top levels of business and education for minority people. Through her scholarship and her feminism, she produced tangible change on local, national, and international levels. As a co-founder of the Group of Ten and the Black Women's Agenda at the 1977 National Women's Conference in Houston, Texas, Johnson helped change the way scholars, politicians, and the public embrace human difference and work toward full equality. As an academic, teacher, entrepreneur, artist, and activist, Johnson was a lifelong educator and she lived by the mantra, "each one teach one." She reinforced, in her students, a "sense of responsibility to help teach, develop . . . whoever you came into contact with."[2] She built her career and activism on a sense of community, one that propped up each individual as a deserving member in a more equal society.

Johnson's life was no ordinary one. Her commitment to creating equality in education and employment in the United States stemmed from the legacies left by her parents. Johnson attributed her success to her "phenomenal mother . . . phenomenal parents, really."[3] Her career and lifelong activism were steeped in specific areas of interest including education, ethnic and racial equal representation, policymaking, and community organization. Her parents instilled in her a sense that she carried forth a tradition of African Americans securing their rights through education and demands for legal reform. Theirs was an activism grounded in creating systematic change through institutional channels rather than radical protest.[4]

Jeffalyn Harriette Brown was born on September 7, 1928, in Los Angeles, California. Johnson was the second of three children and her older sister, Betye Saar, became an internationally recognized artist, specifically for her work during the Black Arts Movement of the mid-1960s to the mid-1970s. Their father, Jefferson, and their mother, Beatrice, both attended UCLA in the 1920s and were active in both the YMCA and YWCA. Jefferson died when Jeffalyn was just three years old, and she along with her siblings were raised by their mother. Beatrice's work as a schoolteacher instilled in Jeffalyn a strong interest in education, and her parents' community organizing, mostly centered on politics, nurtured her view that it "all goes to community development and building. You develop a community. You're raised by all of the people around you."[5] Johnson remembered her mother frequently taking all three siblings to "community rallies" and to vote.[6] In addition to community organizing, Johnson believed strongly in the power of education.

In 1950, at the age of twenty-two, Jeffalyn married Alvin Palmer Johnson and the couple had one son named Channing.[7] For her son and for the students she taught, Johnson understood the power of a community because "you don't fail by yourself, you fail because your family, or your friends, or your background didn't provide you with enough support. So, building support was very important."[8] Johnson held a bachelor's degree in political science and economics from the University of California, Los Angeles, in 1949 and a master's degree in political science from California State University, Los Angeles, in 1962. While still taking classes, she began her career as a social caseworker and later taught at the elementary, junior high, high school, and college levels. She also worked as a school counselor and remembered, vividly, the day Martin Luther King Jr. was assassinated as a day she was home sick with the flu but rushed into work to console her shocked, angry, and emotional students.[9] Believing steadfastly in the power of community organization to affect change Johnson stated, "No one has the right to live unto themselves alone. They have a responsibility to build on strength. And strength comes from numbers and strength comes from knowledge and strength comes from cooperation."[10] Johnson realized a need for minority students to gain a sense of identity so that they could reach their full potential. Grounded in this belief, she and other local parents fought to introduce Black and ethnic studies courses into high school curriculum but admitted that they "were constantly at war with the school system."[11] She held the firm conviction that educating all students in a broader and more diverse range of curriculum was the first step toward equality. In addition, Johnson actively worked to create opportunity for Black students. She regularly placed Black students in "white institutions" fostering "a kind of mutualism."[12] Johnson's community activism and cooperative spirit also defined her personal life.

In 1965, responding to the Watts Rebellions and assassination of Malcolm X, artists and intellectuals in Los Angeles came together in a vibrant arts community that was known as the Black Arts Movement (BAM).[13] Johnson was heavily involved in and influenced by this creative political milieu, a swirl of activity that focused on "the necessity of multiple expressions of intellectual activism for social change."[14] The Black Arts Movement was art by Black people for Black people. These artists intended to express their identity, not as an auxiliary portion of the American story, but as integral to its very foundation. In other words, BAM intellectuals and activists reinforced the idea that they were part of America rather than a product or consequence of it and their art shifted themes from avenues of protest to pieces that spoke directly to Black identity.[15] As longtime artists and art activists, Jeffalyn and her sister Betye were involved in the Pasadena art community. Johnson and her husband, Alvin, were avid art collectors, hosting group exhibitions at their home where African American artists "from all over bring their stuff" for viewing.[16]

In 1968, Johnson was hired to teach political science, history, public administration, psychology, and urban community development at Pasadena Community College and in 1972, she earned a doctorate in public administration and political science from the University of Southern California while working and raising her son, Channing.[17] Johnson's enduring curiosity and appetite for knowledge led her to continue her education well past the norm for women at the time, recalling, "most people didn't know I had a PhD and there wasn't many of them."[18]

Interested in the "institutional impact on behavior," Johnson's dissertation, titled "Experiences and Attitudes of Black and White Community College Students Toward Selected Public Institutions," argued for the systematic inclusion of Black studies programs in higher education curriculum for both Black and white students.[19] The dissertation analyzed four institutions: armed forces, law enforcement, politics, and education and studied student protesters involved in the Civil Rights Movement and the Black Panther Party.[20] Johnson "felt that Black students, or anybody, would not be successful without a sense of their history and their identity." She felt "that all people and particularly Black people, people of color I should say, need to know who they are."[21] Johnson's purpose was to expand awareness about the difficulties faced by minority citizens as well as build students' trust in institutions and foster civic engagement.

She crafted her thesis on the framework that "ethnic studies are a legitimate academic pursuit in the university curriculum and can serve to reduce social conflict and foster cultural pluralism."[22] Believing that education was a crucial avenue to promote a multiracial society based on inclusion and equality, Johnson "wanted to inculcate in anybody who touched my life to understand that power came from education, from knowledge, and experience, and cooperative spirit."[23] She argued that "ethnic studies" programs would not only educate white students on the tribulations of Black people but also help Black students form stronger identities and build trust among the institutions that served them. Yet, even as she grounded her research in ideas of inclusivity and trust among institutions, Johnson faced her own hurdles in completing the degree. She remembered the choice to largely omit her research on the gender inequality that she saw in her studies because she attended a "white institution," recalling that as the only African American and female PhD student, "everything you said or did had to be acceptable to the institution."[24]

By 1976, Johnson held a Senior Professor post at the US Civil Service Commission's Federal Executive Institute (FEI) where she authored an article arguing for the importance of representation and equal employment when hiring effective and efficient employees for public jobs in all levels of government bureaucracies.[25] Ideas about acquiring personnel combined with her scholarship on education, trust, and inclusivity were part of the framework that Johnson built her career on and she carried over those ideas in her time as a business owner, activist, and IWY commissioner. While at the FEI, Johnson was recruited as a policy analyst for President Jimmy Carter's 1976 transition team. She was responsible for the "identification, location, development of executives" in his new administration with "special emphasis on locating the most talented African Americans and minorities."[26] Her work in creating paths for African Americans into the top echelons of politics and business primed her for the role.

In 1977, Johnson left politics and embraced entrepreneurship as the president and chief executive officer of her own management consulting firm, Jeffalyn Johnson and Associates, Incorporated. Johnson opened offices in California, Virginia, and Texas. Her company "designed and conducted research, managed project and program evaluations, implemented organization development interventions, conducted training, and provided strategic planning consulting services" for both corporate and government offices.[27] Johnson knew that leaving politics was the right decision. However, her contributions to women's, and specifically Black women's, equality under Carter administration did not end there.

White House aid Midge Costanza recruited Johnson as an IWY commissioner, selecting her for her stature and expertise in management planning. As a commissioner, Johnson was tasked with forming state conferences in Virginia, California, and New Mexico where participants voted on delegations to represent them at the NWC in Houston, "we had to get their energies and activities focused," she recalled.[28] Responsible for the conferences in these three states, Johnson was immersed in different women's community organizing, especially "Chicano affairs."[29] Serving on the commission extended the work Johnson had done in promoting women's fair pay in the government and corporate sectors and provided her an opportunity to apply her research on employment equality for Black women. Representation mattered to Johnson as she fought for both race and gender equality. "One of the most important things was for women to see themselves as valuable," Johnson remembered of the 1977 National Women's Conference in Houston, Texas.[30]

Leading up to the conference, Johnson played a crucial role in developing the Minority Plank, providing scholarship on the discriminatory issues that nonwhite women faced.[31] "Pulling together that Minority Women's Plank was really tough," she recalled, for as a commissioner, "We represented white government."[32] Still, Johnson noted that her "experience and knowledge" in the Black Power Movement "really helped" in the formation of the Minority Plank.[33] Johnson was aware of the many perspectives and goals of the different organizations at the conference and who specifically contributed to the Minority Plank. Often, "these community people would come out of the Black Power Movement" like "labor unions" with varied perspectives "all vying for power" and "trying to be the leader." Ultimately, Johnson helped find cohesion and unity in their ideas and she attributed that success to her lifelong work in "community organizing."[34]

Johnson also contributed to a "Group of Ten," who drafted a "Black Women's Action Plan" before the National Women's Conference convened. They argued that Black women's grievances were unique and they demanded that the conference delegates understand them through a racial and gendered lens."[35] Johnson and her colleagues used statistical data to show that Black women often dealt with inferior educational and employment opportunities that held them in positions of second-class citizenship. Included in *The Spirit of Houston,* the "Black Women's Action Plan" became the intellectual foundation for the Minority Plank.[36] Based on the position paper, these women, led by Dorothy Height of the National Council of Negro Women, formed the Black Women's Agenda, which is still in existence today. The initial goals of the BWA were to implement the demands of the Minority Plank at the National Women's Conference. By 1979, leaders of forty-three Black women's organizations supported the Black Women's Agenda and its goals to work toward "empowering and enriching the lives of Black women and their families."[37]

Looking back at the National Women's Conference, Johnson judged it a success. While she focused her energies on the Minority Plank, she also found it promising that, "all women wanted progress." She felt that "some were more interested in doing it through children and some through labor unions and some through, you know, politics. But, we always found common ground."[38] These issues, she believed, transcended race such as gender-type casting in the workforce.[39] At the NWC, she thought it important to highlight differences on account of race, but also to form an understanding of collective experience as women. The exchanges she had in Houston resonated well after those four days. It was, for her, "a time of awakening. Awakening of self-understanding, self-power, and awareness of community opportunities."[40]

Johnson's activism and career did not end with that momentous 1977 conference. She continued researching and developing plans to help African Americans reach their career goals and gain promotions in executive positions. As a professor, Johnson taught courses on educational policy, public policy, and public administration.[41] Jeffalyn Johnson and Associates, Inc. released studies of both national and international importance. One 1977 report, "African Women in Development: Income Producing Feasibility Study Evaluation Report," evaluated a study designed to organize informal job training to Sahel women to boost their economic equality. Johnson's team of researchers reported on the usefulness and timing of the report and argued for a more efficient strategy to implement the programs.[42]

Over the next several decades, Johnson's work for equality in employment and education for all Black Americans never ceased.[43] She continued her activism through projects like the Angel City Links Achievers Foundation. Founded in California in 1981, Angel City Links aimed to motivate and strengthen young Black men to reach their college and life goals.[44] Johnson's enduring commitment to equality for African American women and men through educational and employment opportunities helped increase awareness and representation of African Americans. From 1991 to 1992, Johnson served as Assistant to President of International Planning and Evaluation and Interim Executive Director for Planning, Evaluation and Budget at the University of North Florida.[45] While at UNF, Johnson authored an opinion to a case study in the *Harvard Business Review* regarding race bias in promoting employees to executive positions."[46] In 1997, Johnson was appointed as a member of the Texaco Equality and Fairness Task Force, where she and her colleagues produced a five-year study where they "monitored and assisted Texaco in the design and implementation of human resources projects."[47] Johnson finished her career as a consultant for large companies like General Electric and General Motors where she "did a lot of work helping corporations to promote women."[48]

Looking back on her career and life's work, Johnson lamented, "I'm so tired of being the first one to do this or the first one to do that. And being accepted when others weren't." She remembered her mother's advice "You're going to have to work for it and you're going to have to work harder . . . once you go in, you're going to have to be smarter, better trained, more experienced."[49] Johnson succeeded in her career and life goals despite the discrimination she faced. Using those lessons as motivation, Johnson spent her career finding ways to increase consciousness and create more opportunities for nonwhite people in educational and business sectors. She visualized a future where being the "first one" would no longer be an indicator of the struggle that minority people faced in gaining equal opportunities in American society. Still active in Los Angeles today, Johnson "had the first Obama headquarters in Los Angeles," during his presidential campaign.[50] She continues to provide strategic consulting to young professionals, believing that workplace advancement is one avenue for African American men and women to cultivate greater rights and visibility. Focusing on education and business, she has devoted her life to making the workplace environment more equitable and women's advancement as leaders of industry more achievable.

Notes

1. Jeffalyn Johnson, phone interview with the author, August 2, 2018.
2. Jeffalyn Johnson, phone interview with the author, August 2, 2018.
3. Jeffalyn Johnson, phone interview with the author, August 2, 2018.
4. Nancy MacLean, *Freedom Is Not Enough: The Opening of the American Workplace* (Cambridge, MA: Harvard University Press, 2006), 118.
5. Jeffalyn Johnson, phone interview with the author, August 2, 2018.
6. Jeffalyn Johnson, phone interview with the author, August 2, 2018.
7. Jeffalyn Johnson, phone interview with the author, August 2, 2018.
8. Jeffalyn Johnson, phone interview with the author, August 2, 2018.
9. Jeffalyn Johnson, phone interview with the author, August 2, 2018.
10. Jeffalyn Johnson, phone interview with the author, August 2, 2018.
11. Jeffalyn Johnson, phone interview with the author, August 2, 2018.
12. Jeffalyn Johnson, phone interview with the author, August 2, 2018.
13. Lisa Gail Collins and Margo Natalie Crawford, eds., *New Thoughts on the Black Arts Movement* (New Brunswick, NJ: Rutgers University Press, 2006), 46.

14. Patricia Hill Collins, *On Intellectual Activism* (Philadelphia: Temple University Press, 2013), x.

15. Mark Godfrey and Zoe Whitley, eds., *Soul of a Nation: Art in the Age of Black Power* (D.A.P./ Distributed Art Publishers Inc., 2017), 7–8.

16. Jeffalyn Johnson, phone interview with the author, August 2, 2018; Kellie Jones, *South of Pico: African American Artists in Los Angeles in the 1960s and 1970s* (Durham, NC: Duke University Press, 2017), Fig. 1.2, 10. Believing in the need to continue the education and expression of Black Americans though art, Jeffalyn and Alvin Johnson later donated their collection to the Museum of Modern Art in New York. *Now Dig This: Art and Black Los Angeles 1960–1980, Museum of Modern Art PS1*, April 15, 2016, https://hammer.ucla.edu/fileadmin/media/Mellon_projects/Now_Dig_This_/Art/Checklists/NDT_Checklist_MoMA_PS1.pdf.

17. Jeffalyn Johnson, phone interview with the author, August 2, 2018; *The HistoryMakers Oral History Video with Jeffalyn Johnson*, Recorded in Los Angeles, California, July 21, 2017, by Harriette Cole.

18. Jeffalyn Johnson, phone interview with the author, August 2, 2018.

19. Jeffalyn Johnson, phone interview with the author, August 2, 2018.

20. Jeffalyn Johnson, "Turning the Public Wheel: Some Issues in Public Personnel Administration," *Ralph Bunche Journal of Public Affairs* 1, no. 1, article 4 (1976): 51–57.

21. Jeffalyn Johnson, phone interview with the author, August 2, 2018.

22. Jeffalyn Harriette Johnson, "Experiences and Attitudes of Black and White Community College Students Toward Selected Public Institutions," dissertation, University of Southern California, 1972.

23. Jeffalyn Johnson, phone interview with the author, August 2, 2018.

24. Jeffalyn Johnson, phone interview with the author, August 2, 2018.

25. Johnson, "Turning the Public Wheel."

26. Jeffalyn Johnson, phone interview with the author, August 2, 2018.

27. Jeffalyn Johnson, phone interview with the author, August 2, 2018.

28. Jeffalyn Johnson, phone interview with the author, August 2, 2018.

29. Jeffalyn Johnson, phone interview with the author, August 2, 2018.

30. Jeffalyn Johnson, phone interview with the author, August 2, 2018.

31. Doreen J. Mattingly and Jessica L. Nare, "'A Rainbow of Women': Diversity and Unity at the 1977 U.S. International Women's Year Conference," *Journal of Women's History* 26, no. 2 (Summer 2014): 88–112.

32. Jeffalyn Johnson, phone interview with the author, August 2, 2018.

33. Jeffalyn Johnson, phone interview with the author, August 2, 2018.

34. Jeffalyn Johnson, phone interview with the author, August 2, 2018.

35. Mattingly and Nare, "'A Rainbow of Women,'" 96.

36. National Commission on the Observance of International Women's Year, *The Spirit of Houston: The First National Women's Conference; An Official Report to the President, the Congress and the People of the United States* (Washington, DC: US Government Printing Office, 1978), 272–77.

37. "History," The Black Women's Agenda, http://www.bwa-inc.org/about.html.

38. Jeffalyn Johnson, phone interview with the author, August 2, 2018.

39. Jeffalyn Johnson, phone interview with the author, August 2, 2018.

40. Jeffalyn Johnson, phone interview with the author, August 2, 2018.

41. Jeffalyn Johnson, PhD CV, Personal Name Files, JAF-KA, University Archives, University of North Florida, Thomas G. Carpenter Library, Special Collections and Archives.

42. Jeffalyn Johnson and Associates, Inc. Management and Organization Specialists, "African Women in Development: Income Producing Feasibility Study Evaluation Report," AID No. 698–0388.8, 1977, i–vii. https://pdf.usaid.gov/pdf_docs/Pdaag650e1.pdf.

43. From 1983 to 1991, Johnson served as an outside consultant for General Motors and worked within affiliated plants in the United States, Canada, and Mexico. Her job consisted of strategic planning, program design and evaluation, and design and delivery of executive development among other duties. Johnson's national and international presence within major corporations was indicative of her successful career in high powered and influential positions.

44. Shirlee Taylor Haizlip, "Links Achievers Pass the Baton: More Than $122,450 Was Awarded in Scholarships at This Year's Event," *Los Angeles Sentinel,* June 19, 2008. https://lasentinel.net/links-achievers-pass-the-baton.html; "138,000 in Scholarships," *Los Angeles Sentinel,* April 23, 2009. https://lasentinel.net/138-000-in-scholarships.html; Achievers: Building Educational Bridges, An Education Linkage Program, The Link Corporation, Link Dene Wallace, Chair. http://www.walinks.org/members/presentations/Program-Education_Acheivers.pdf.

45. Jeffalyn Johnson, CV, 1.

46. Mary C. Gentile, "The Case of the Unequal Opportunity," *Harvard Business Review,* July–August 1991, 9. Personal Name Files, JAF-KA, University Archives, University of North Florida, Thomas G. Carpenter Library, Special Collections and Archives.

47. Jeffalyn Johnson, phone interview with the author, August 2, 2018.

48. Jeffalyn Johnson, phone interview with the author, August 2, 2018.

49. Jeffalyn Johnson, phone interview with the author, August 2, 2018.

50. Jeffalyn Johnson, phone interview with the author, August 2, 2018.

Activist Organizers

NO ONE TRAVELS FAR without crossing a bridge. As Fannie Lou Hamer put it, "Never [. . .] forget where we came from and always praise the bridges that carried us over." Those bridges are not necessarily made of metal and steel. Bridges with melanated skin, crooked backs, tired feet, and hands sore from doing the heavy lifting in the fight for equity. Despite their exhaustion, the "bridges" show up; arguably they never left. They do what they do, not because they were "paid," but because injustice is not an option and can't be conquered without conduits providing direction and compassion.

Activist Organizers are often the "bridge" that get us over. Whether focusing on disability (Georgia McMurray), Lesbian Rights and Revolutionary re-envisionings (Barbara Smith), Welfare Rights (Johnnie Tillmon), Civil Rights and politics (C. Delores Tucker), or everything at once (Florynce Kennedy), the visionaries in this section communicated a way over to a better place.

7

Florynce Kennedy

A Radical Voice

KIRSTEN LENG

Figure 7.1. Florynce Kennedy at the International Women's Year Conference in Mexico City, 1975. Bettye Layne. Courtesy of Duke University Special Collections and Archives.

MEXICO CITY, 1975. The site of the first International Women's Year Conference. Here stands Florynce Kennedy, attorney and political radical, in a photograph taken by Bettye Lane.[1] She is hailing a cab; she is looking the viewer straight in the eye. Kennedy would never back down from a confrontation: as she put it in her own words, she preferred to "kick ass" regularly. Her T-shirt, emblazoned with the laughing mascot of COYOTE (Call Off Your Old Tired Ethics), a pioneering sex workers' rights organization, announces her radical politics. Indeed, while in Mexico City—and later in Houston—Kennedy would promote the decriminalization of prostitution, much to the consternation of her feminist colleagues. Kennedy dressed sharply, here in a white pantsuit and shawl, but certainly in contrast to the staid middle-class norms of feminists her age. Her look certainly rejected the demands of respectability so frequently foisted upon publicly active and prominent Black women, and to which she herself had long adhered. She meant to attract attention—and provoke conversation. Kennedy had long insisted on wearing pants, even in court, in violation of sartorial expectations for female lawyers. In so doing, she distinguished herself also from her professional peers, and even seemed to gesture that the law could be practiced differently. Also visible are her long nails, always painted red, and her false eyelashes. Kennedy's appearance meant to convey a message: she herself conceded, "When I go to do combat, I come dressed for it."[2] A whistle hung around her neck, not just to attract cabs, but ready to lead a crowd in protest or song. Though not at a microphone or in the midst of a political rally, as she so often was, this photo nevertheless captures the reality that Kennedy was often in charge, directing the action around her: as she stands in the midst of traffic, she is utterly unfazed by chaos, seemingly in command of the cars surrounding her.

Florynce Kennedy was born on February 11, 1916, in Kansas City, Missouri. Kennedy attributes her predilection for "kicking ass" and her refusal to bow to authority to her parents, Wiley and Zella. Although her parents were not members of any political organization, Kennedy asserts that they were "political in the sense that [they] never took any shit."[3] Both parents encouraged their children to directly confront racist bullies and defended them against prejudicial authorities, such as school administrators. In interviews and lectures, Kennedy often recounted with great admiration the time her father stood up to members of the Ku Klux Klan who attempted to force the family out of their home in a predominantly white neighborhood using terrorist violence and intimidation.[4]

In the early 1940s, Kennedy moved to New York City with her sister Grayce, where she found employment in the US Treasury Department. In 1944, she enrolled at Columbia University as part of an unprecedented influx of women into the institution during the Second World War.[5] Kennedy's biographer, Sherie Randolph, suggests that Kennedy's experience as part of this flood of women, mostly white, led her to connect the oppression of white women and Black people, and to envision a possible coalition between these groups.[6] While at Columbia, Kennedy took courses with some of the era's leading socialist and communist academics; these classes allowed her to work out intellectual positions on marriage, race relations, and gender relations. She eventually entered Columbia Law School after challenging her rejection on the basis of sex and race and insisting that she would bring forward legal action based on racial discrimination. Only eight women were admitted to Columbia Law School in 1948; she was the only Black woman in her class and went on to become the first Black woman to graduate from Columbia University's law program. Yet Kennedy's entrée into activism predated the 1960s, and even her move to New York City. While still in Kansas City, she helped organize pickets against Coca-Cola to protest their refusal to hire Black truck drivers.[7] She also staged a lunch counter protest against racial discrimination with her sister Grayce at a rest stop in Monroe City, Missouri, in 1942. The latter act of nonviolent civil disobedience had severe consequences for Kennedy's health: the rest stop's angry white patrons broke her spine while violently removing her from her seat, which developed into a painful, lifelong impairment.[8] However, the successful civil suit she filed against the restaurant and bus company precipitated her interest in studying the law.[9]

In her capacity as a lawyer, Kennedy defended the estates of artists such as Billie Holliday, who came under official scrutiny after speaking out against racial violence, and Charlie Parker; in the process, Randolph points out, Kennedy became a campaigner for performing artists' intellectual property rights.[10] Kennedy ultimately developed a keen interest in the media and the sociopolitical power of images and rhetoric. She founded the Media Workshop in 1966 to target racism in the media, and ultimately expanded the organization's remit to consider sexism in the media.[11] In time, Kennedy became disillusioned with the limits of the law to achieve broader change. She ultimately came to focus her energies as a lawyer on social justice causes, above all civil rights and reproductive rights. She provided legal defense for former SNCC chairman H. Rap Brown, *SCUM Manifesto* author Valerie Solanas, and the reputed leader of Black Liberation Army and Black Panther Party, Joanne Chesimard,[12] also known as Assata Shakur.[13] Along with Diane Schulder and other feminist lawyers, she was part of the legal team that prosecuted *Abramowicz v. Lefkowitz* (1970), which challenged New York State's abortion laws. Their efforts are detailed in *Abortion Rap* (1971), which Kennedy and Schulder coedited. She also used her knowledge of the law to pursue social change through large bureaucracies. On behalf of the Feminist Party, a radical multiracial political party that Kennedy cofounded which espoused Black feminist principles and supported Shirley Chisholm's presidential run, Kennedy petitioned the IRS to revoke the Catholic Church's tax-exempt status in light of its vociferous and explicitly political anti-abortion activism.[14]

However, Kennedy never relied exclusively on the law as a vehicle for social change. She was a member of numerous civil society organizations: throughout the 1960s and 1970s, she was involved in a range of civil rights, Black Power, socialist, and antiwar organizations, including Wednesdays in Mississippi (where she was in contact with Dorothy Height and Fannie Lou Hamer), the Freedom and Peace Party, Workers World Party, Youth Against War and Fascism, the Black Power Conferences, and the Black Panther Party.[15] Beginning in the later 1960s and throughout the 1970s, Kennedy became increasingly involved with feminist organizations as well, playing a leading role in founding the New York chapter of the National Organization of Women in 1967, the Feminist Party in 1971, and the National Black Feminist Organization in 1973.[16] Starting in the mid-1960s, she became increasingly focused on the media as a source of power and a vehicle for potential social change. Her creation of the Media Workshop in 1966 acknowledged the power of the media to shape reality, and not only targeted its representations but also its material foundations, urging people to boycott companies that engaged in racist and sexist employment and representational practices. She also became involved with COYOTE, an early sex workers' rights group founded by Margot St. James that advocated the decriminalization of prostitution. By the 1970s, Kennedy's activism also embraced LGBT rights and opposition to the Vietnam War.

While keeping a toehold in legal activism, Kennedy increasingly dedicated her energies to street activism and public speaking. In so doing she was likely inspired by her work within the Media Workshop, which heightened her awareness of the power of the media in drawing attention to a cause. She participated in theatrical, playful protests including the 1968 Miss America protest, and helped organize both the "Flush Palmolive" campaign spearheaded by NOW New York and the Harvard Yard "Pee-In" of 1973 to protest the lack of restroom facilities for female students. Kennedy was insistent that social change could only occur if people were willing to fight anywhere and everywhere power was to be found, whether "in the streets, suites and courtrooms."[17] As the range and tone of her protests suggest, Kennedy routinely deployed humor to great effect. Songs were a key part of her protests, and her witty turns of phrase became oft-cited feminist aphorisms.[18] As Randolph points out, "Kennedy rejected the notion that comedy, especially in the hands of a woman, should be equated with a lack of seriousness. Like Black women radicals Toni Cade Bambara and Queen Mother Moore . . . Kennedy made great use of laughter as a weapon and a shield."[19]

Throughout her years of political activity, Kennedy served as an important and influential mentor to a younger generation of Black and white feminists, including figures such as Margaret Sloan, Ti-Grace Atkinson, and Gloria Steinem. As Randolph notes, she also helped mentor young feminist lawyers such as Diane Schulder and Emily Goodman.[20] Recognizing Kennedy's crucial role as a mentor helps us appreciate the extent of her influence, especially within the women's liberation movement.

Flo Kennedy's commitments to myriad political causes were undergirded by a set of beliefs and analyses that were not only feminist and anti-racist, but also pragmatic and materialist. Kennedy was centrally concerned with power, specifically its operations and its necessity as a means of overcoming oppression and affecting social change. Although Kennedy viewed the control and distribution of capital as critical to the maintenance of power, she viewed the ideological work of the law and especially the media to be critical as well, as they held the power to shape perceptions of reality, obscure social and political priorities, and to distract and diffuse political energy. They were therefore responsible for perpetuating while obscuring the fact that "we have a pathologically, institutionally racist, sexist, classist society."[21] As a result of her comprehensive analysis of power, Kennedy was able to make connections across forms of oppression, and imagine an "alliance of the alienated" that united marginalized groups.[22] However, Kennedy vehemently insisted that marginalized groups ought not revel in their powerlessness, but rather endeavor to seize power for themselves. In her view, "Powerlessness is more corrupting than power"; speaking with regards to women, she hoped to "change [them] and give them a sense of worth so they can fight the establishment and not each other."[23]

Kennedy was not an official delegate to the National Women's Conference. This fact is not surprising: like the feminist theorist Kate Millett, also attending in an unofficial capacity, she was likely far too radical in her orientation and demands for many participants. At this time in Kennedy's career, she was involved with the sex workers' rights group COYOTE, and pushing for the decriminalization of prostitution. Although COYOTE was present at the conference, and even had a booth in the conference's Exhibition Hall, prostitution was not even on the agenda of many state conferences.[24] Yet Kennedy had experience with International Women's Year events. In 1975, she was involved with the unofficial conference associated with the International Women's Year meeting in Mexico City. Referred to as the "Tribune," it was held approximately twenty miles from the official venue. There, Kennedy pressed for prostitutes' rights, contrary to the UN's stated ambition of eradicating sex work globally. She also used the Tribune as an opportunity to conduct talks about other issues, such as the persecution of Assata Shakur.[25] In Kennedy's view, the IWY Conference's remit was too constricted; she was deeply critical of the fact that it was limited to women's issues, narrowly defined and disconnected from larger geopolitical issues.[26]

In addition to her previous IWY involvement, Kennedy was likely drawn to the National Women's Conference because many issues of deep concern to her were present in the official Plan of Action, including media reforms, reproductive rights, and the concerns of "minority women." Kennedy was also a longtime proponent of the Equal Rights Amendment and supported measures to see it passed. Moreover, many of her views regarding intersectional oppression were present in caucus documents such as the "Black Women's Plan of Action" and "It's Our Movement Now." No sources could be found in Kennedy's autobiography, newspaper interviews, archives, or secondary literature that provide direct evidence of Kennedy's thoughts about the official Plan of Action or the caucus documents. However, Kennedy would likely have agreed strongly with the Black Women's Plan of Action's assertions that "The white male power structure has been adept, historically, at shifting arenas of competition, limiting opportunities, and assuming the power of definition in an effort to misrepresent divisions of greatest import in fundamental social change"; and that "as Black women informed by our past we must eschew a view of the women's struggle which takes as its basic assumption opposition to men, as distinguished from organizing around the principle of opposition to the white male power structure's perpetuation of exploitation, subjugation, inequality, and limited opportunities based upon sex and race." She would have especially welcomed the document's insistence that "An ethnocentric women's movement which minimizes, misconstrues, or demonstrates no serious regard for the interests and views of other disadvantaged groups and minorities sows the seeds of its own destruction."[27] Such statements reflect concerns with structural inequality, with imbalances of material, social, and political power, and with redistribution, which Kennedy certainly shared. In their insistence on highlighting the mutually constitutive nature of racism and sexism, as well as the damaging effects of a singular focus on gender within the women's movement, the statements also reflected Kennedy's intersectional perspective. Like the Black Women's Plan of Action, Kennedy stressed the centrality of Black women's perspectives, and indeed argued that Black people's concerns and leadership must constitute the vanguard of contemporary social and political struggle. Kennedy frequently insisted that, based on her experiences in the US and other settler colonies like Canada and Australia, "racism is the crux of the worst problem in the world"; in comparison, sexism is "like a bad case of athlete's foot or a toothache."[28] She also routinely called out white feminists for failing to show up for racial justice, at times going so far as to accuse white women of wanting to use Black women within the movement as "scarecrows to frighten the white men."[29] Yet despite these points of broad agreement, Kennedy likely disagreed with the move to develop an umbrella minority caucus. In her view, unity was not an unequivocally good thing: indeed, in one interview she referred to it as a "mistake," saying, "If I were the Establishment and had the big loaded guns of the various oppressive institutions . . . I would much prefer to see one lion come through the door than 500 mice."[30] At the same time, she did agree that activists from various groups should organize around the things upon which they agree.[31]

Kennedy was dedicated to attending the meeting. In spite of her poor health and physical obstacles, Kennedy rode out the conference's infamous accommodation chaos by sleeping on the floor of the lobby when her room at the Whitehall Hotel was not ready. Her willingness to sleep in the lobby was reported in both mainstream media and official conference documents, offering evidence of her fortitude and determination.[32] Despite not being a delegate, Kennedy was an unmistakable presence. While evidence of her participation in the plenary sessions is scarce, Kennedy played a key role in the "Houston Equal Rights for Women Welcoming Rally" on Friday, November 18 at City Hall. The rally, meant to commemorate suffragist Alice Paul, who coauthored the original Equal Rights Amendment in the 1920s, also featured Dolores Huerta (United Farm Workers Union), Luz Gutierrez (La Raza Unida Party), Lillian Bembow (former president of Delta Sigma Theta), Nikki van Hightower (Houston women's advocate), Billie Carr (Harris County Democrats), Betty Friedan, and the feminist comedy team of Pat Harrison and Robin Tyler.[33] According to the Houston feminist newspaper the *Breakthrough*, approximately 1,500 women attended the rally, which provided "a chance to laugh, cheer, chant and shout." The *Breakthrough* reported that Kennedy (described here as a "humorist") told a "receptive audience" that "We must not let a vocal minority stop us from getting our rights." Reportedly, "her songs set the crowd to clapping and stomping as the 'old pro' of the fundraising hustle passed the hat for the ERA, telling the women to 'get out of the kitchen and back into the streets where you belong!'"[34] A *New York Times* report further described Kennedy, "the doyenne of the disenfranchised," as addressing the audience "in her traditional costume of jeans, beads and boots" and whipping up the audience by declaring, "We've still only spilled menstrual blood. . . . And if you think you can change society without shedding blood you're crazy." She then reportedly led the crowd in a round of a song she often sang in conjunction with COYOTE, "Everybody Needs a Hooker Sometime."[35] The *Breakthrough* further noted that Kennedy "carried the torch of media reform," and called for "women to return to their homes and to immediately begin a campaign to 'ban all commercials (radio-TV) that make women look like imbeciles.'" Kennedy "told the women there are 125 major advertisers who must be made to feel the economic pressure and push of the women's drive for equality."[36] Kennedy clearly worked to push the conference attendees in a more pro-active, radical direction, calling upon them to take action in their own realms and see the interconnections between their local condition and larger forces. Her efforts at the conference also demonstrated her arresting use of humor to communicate blunt, incisive political observations. At the conference, she assumed a few—but certainly not all—of her many activist roles: agitator, advocate, gadfly.

Kennedy was sixty-one years old at the time of the conference. Afterward she continued to perform at speaking gigs, although these became fewer in subsequent decades due to her faltering health. Nonetheless, Kennedy kept up her fight against racism and sexism through new venues, including the media. In 1977, she was named an associate of the Women's Institute for Freedom of the Press, a nonprofit concerned with increasing communication between women and enhancing women's participation within the media. During the 1980s and 1990s she hosted the *Flo Kennedy Show* on Manhattan cable television. In this capacity, she explored a range of radical topics, and interviewed a diverse collection of civil rights and feminist figures, as well as LGBT rights leaders, political radicals, activist lawyers, and New York City, national, and international politicians. She also made a notable quasi-cameo in the feminist cult classic *Born in Flames* (1983). As Zella Wylie,[37] she served as a mentor to one of the film's Black feminist protagonists, Women's Army leader Adelaide Norris, thus reprising a role on film she had often played in life. She further collaborated with William Francis Pepper on a book manuscript entitled *Sex Discrimination in Employment: An Analysis and Guide for Practitioner and Student*, and occasionally took on legal cases, such as Sonia Butler's sex discrimination suit against the National Urban League.[38] She received a number of awards toward the end of her life, including Columbia University's "Owl" Award for outstanding alumni, and City University of New York's Century Award.

Flo Kennedy's life and work challenges narratives about the women's liberation movement in a number of ways. Her activist strategies challenge strict demarcations between liberal and radical wings of feminism. For example, Kennedy was present at the foundation of the New York branch of the National Organization of Women, noted bastion of liberal feminism, in 1967, and was enthusiastic about its goal of challenging sex discrimination—though she repeatedly attempted to move it in a more radical direction by advocating an intersectional approach and antiwar agenda. Moreover, as a trained lawyer, Kennedy realized the power of state institutions, above all the law, to affect meaningful change, especially with regard to reproductive justice. Yet Kennedy was aware of the limits of the law as a tool for meaningful change; as Kennedy pessimistically observed, "law is about power not about justice . . . everything Hitler did was legal."[39]

Kennedy was also a prominent figure who moved across feminist organizations oftentimes defined by race yet maintained an unabashed Black feminist perspective even within white milieus. In the process, she pioneered an intersectional analysis. She worked with primarily white women in organizations such as the National Organization of Women, the Feminist Party, and the National Women's Political Caucus; at the same time, she was also heavily involved in the Black Power Conferences and cofounded the National Black Feminist Organization. Kennedy repudiated what she viewed as a "divide and conquer" strategy that separated oppressed people and prevented them from uniting against ruling groups. She famously coined the term "horizontal hostility" to describe the infighting that could arise among people with common political objectives that further inhibited successful collective action. Yet while willing to work with white women, Kennedy nonetheless prioritized racial oppression, particularly in her later life, as she believed racism was key to understanding oppression writ large. She insisted that Black people should be at the vanguard of political leadership.

Finally, Kennedy's example offers a powerful rebuke to the well-worn claim that feminists are not funny, or that they lacked a sense of humor. As a highly sought orator and expert at street theater, Kennedy deployed humor as a means of bluntly stating a sophisticated political point and keeping her audience's attention. In addition to serving the pedagogic purpose of teaching audiences about injustice and swaying them to adopt a feminist point of view, humor made protest fun: as Kennedy herself noted, "the best way to recruit is to be having fun. . . . [Other] people like to be dreary. I try to be as undreary as I can be."[40] Her humor not only energized her fellow activists but also sustained her feminism. Though playful, it was imbued with serious purpose.

Florynce Kennedy has received scant attention from scholars and historians, yet arguably, to truly understand the plurality of the Second Wave movement, the origins of radical feminism, or the development of a coalitional feminist consciousness, one ought to study her life, work, and ideas. Flo Kennedy illuminates the integral role Black women played in the emergence of Women's Liberation. Kennedy was not only a pivotal figure in some of the key organizations and protests that would define the "second wave," but also a profound influence on other key leaders. She was also instrumental in laying the foundation of an intersectional consciousness and sought to promote the visions and concerns of Black women, both in her speeches and through the creation of groups such as the National Black Feminist Organization. In fact, she repeatedly stressed the interconnections between various forms of oppression as a result of a white male–dominated power structure. Over the course of her life, she adopted radical positions, including decriminalization of sex work, that stood in contrast to many feminists of her generation. Furthermore, she fought power wherever it could be fought—in the courts, through state bureaucracy, on the streets—using a range of tools including the law, policy proposals, boycotts, civil disobedience, and street theater.

Florynce Kennedy never compromised herself or her standpoint, regardless of where or how she conducted politics. Through her words, actions, and example, she demonstrated feminism's full potential as a program for sweeping change: one that embraced not just all women, but all humanity; one that targeted injustice wherever it be found, by any means necessary; and one that could deploy a range of tactics—including humor—in service of transformative social change.

Notes

1. Layne was a colleague of Diana Mara Henry, also renowned for her photographic documentation of the feminist movement.

2. Cited in Sherie Randolph, *Florynce "Flo" Kennedy: The Life of a Black Feminist Radical* (Chapel Hill: University of North Carolina Press, 2015), 154.

3. Kennedy interview with Jacqueline Ceballos, February 18, 1991, Tully-Crenshaw Oral. Cited in Randolph, *Florynce "Flo" Kennedy*, 13.

4. Randolph, *Florynce "Flo" Kennedy*, 12–13.

5. Randolph, *Florynce "Flo" Kennedy*, 37.

6. Sherie Randolph, "Not to Rely Completely on the Courts: Florynce Kennedy and Black Feminist Leadership in the Reproductive Rights Battle," in *Toward an Intellectual History of Black Women*, eds. Mia Bay, Farah J. Griffin, Martha S. Jones, and Barbara D. Savage (Chapel Hill: University of North Carolina Press), 235.

7. See Chris Acemandese Hall and Phyllis Inman, "Tribute to Flo Kennedy: 'When I Get Crazy, People Get Intelligent,'" *New York Beacon*, March 10, 1999, 23; see also Flo Kennedy, "It's Damn Slick Out There," *Social Text* no. 9/10 (Spring–Summer 1984): 347.

8. Randolph, *Florynce "Flo" Kennedy*, 28.

9. Randolph, *Florynce "Flo" Kennedy*, 33.

10. Randolph, *Florynce "Flo" Kennedy*, 77–80. Kennedy increasingly came to view the law as rigged in favor of those with racial, gender, and class privilege. In fact, Kennedy eventually went on to refer to the legal system as a "whorehouse" in a contribution to a 1971 radical law volume edited by Gerald Lefcourt. See Florynce Kennedy, "The Whorehouse Theory of Law," in *Color Me Flo: My Hard Life and Good Times* (Englewood Cliffs, NJ: Prentice-Hall, 1976): 129–137.

11. Randolph, *Florynce "Flo" Kennedy*, 103.

12. "Flo Kennedy talks about 'Yes, We Can,' Feminist Party," *Bay State Banner*, January 24, 1974, 12.

13. Hall and Inman, "Tribute to Flo Kennedy," 23.

14. "Women Take Catholic Church to Court over Abortion," *Feminist Times* (Winter 1972): 4. Kennedy's petition also named Birthright and the Knights of Columbus in violation of IRS rules.

15. Randolph, "Not to Rely Completely on the Courts," 236.

16. See Randolph, "Not to Rely Completely on the Courts," 236; Randolph, *Florynce "Flo" Kennedy*, 188–189, 205–209.

17. Randolph, "Not to Rely Completely on the Courts," 236.

18. See, for example, Gloria Steinem, "The Verbal Karate of Florynce R. Kennedy, Esq." *Ms.* magazine (1973), accessed July 22, 2017, http://www.msmagazine.com/summer2011/verbalkarate.asp.

19. Randolph, *Florynce "Flo" Kennedy*, 155.

20. Randolph, "Not to Rely Completely on the Courts," 234.

21. *Speaking for America: 12 Original Interviews with American Activists Rene Dubos, Ralph Nader, Sissy Farenthold, Julian Bond, Chuck Morgan, Flo Kennedy, and Others*, Princeton, NJ: Visual Education Corporation, 1976, Audiorecording.

22. Randolph, *Florynce "Flo" Kennedy*, 216.

23. Flo Kennedy, "She Who Laughs-Lasts," *Common Ground* (December 1988): 3.

24. Doreen J. Mattingly and Jessica L. Nare, "'A Rainbow of Women': Diversity and Unity at the 1977 U.S. International Women's Year Conference," *Journal of Women's History* 26, no. 2 (Summer 2014): 98.

25. Randolph, *Florynce "Flo" Kennedy*, 217–218.

26. Randolph, *Florynce "Flo" Kennedy*, 218.

27. "Black Women's Plan of Action," in National Commission on the Observance of International Women's Year, *The Spirit of Houston: The First National Women's Conference; An Official Report to the President, the Congress and the People of the United States* (Washington, DC: US Government Printing Office, 1978), 274.

28. Kennedy, *Color Me Flo*, 111; see also "Kennedy Speaks On Black Rights." *New Pittsburgh Courier*, October 18, 1975, 9; Carol Lipton, "Balancing the Scales: Women and Justice," *off our backs* 4, no. 9 (September 30, 1974): 16; Anne Williams, "Power Talk," *off our backs* 4, no. 2 (January 31, 1974): 4; "Flo Kennedy," *Women's Press* (March 1972): 18.

29. Kennedy, *Color Me Flo*, 96.

30. Kennedy, *Color Me Flo*, 113.

31. Kennedy, *Color Me Flo*, 114.

32. Caroline Bird, "Houston Day by Day," in National Commission on the Observance of International Women's Year, *The Spirit of Houston*, 127.

33. "Schedule of Events," *Daily Breakthrough*, November 18, 1977, 17.

34. "Rally Honors Alice Paul," *Daily Breakthrough*, November 19, 1977, 10.

35. Anne Taylor Fleming, "That Week in Houston," *New York Times*, December 25, 1977, 13.

36. "Looking for the Fight: National Media Hits Houston," *Daily Breakthrough*, November 19, 1977, 10.

37. This character's name actually constitutes a combination of Kennedy's parents' names: mother Zella and father Wiley (spelled "Wylie" in the film).

38. See Valerie Burgher, "League said, she said," *The Village Voice*, January 28, 1997, 20, 22.

39. Maria Scipione, "Flo Kennedy. Paying Attention to the Signals," *New Women's Times* (June 1982): 9.

40. Abby Karp, "Flo Kennedy," *Baltimore Sun*, February 14, 1988; cited in Randolph, *Florynce "Flo" Kennedy*, 153.

8

Bringing Depth to the Movement

Race, Gender, and (Dis)Ability in the Life of Georgia McMurray

CRYSTAL LYNN WEBSTER

Figure 8.1. Georgia McMurray (*front, left, in stripes*) and delegates on stage, 1977. Diana Mara Henry Papers (PH 51). Special Collections and University Archives, University of Massachusetts Amherst Libraries. Copyright © Diana Mara Henry / www.dianamarahenry.com.

WHEN COMMISSIONER LIZ CARPENTER gave her opening address at the historic 1977 National Women's Conference and named several significant delegates, she saved Georgia McMurray, the childcare activist and New York delegate, for the finale as a powerful embodiment of the movement. In describing Georgia McMurray as a "longtime leader in movements for civil rights and the disabled," she enthusiastically asserted, "Would you deny this and any of the millions of Black women the right to go as far as their dreams and magnificent talents can take them? Not me!"[1] At this, the audience erupted in applause at Carpenter's portrayal of McMurray and her role in the movement. Diana Mara Henry's photograph of the event captured this moment during Carpenter's speech in which McMurray looked back out at the audience with a modest smile. The photograph shows a seated McMurray gazing at the speaker with an apparent reflective contentment that embodied the characteristics that Liz Carpenter claimed Georgia McMurray brought to the conference: "head and heart."

As academic disciplines including women and gender studies, cultural studies, disability studies, and Black studies increasingly turn toward incorporating intersectionality as a fundamental approach toward fully understanding the nature and range of human experience, Georgia L. McMurray's life and activism demonstrate the critical role of these analytical approaches. As a Black woman who championed for various causes, including daycare, women's rights, and those with disabilities, Georgia L. McMurray's life experiences traverse and transcend across various identities, political endeavors, and activist movements. In this way, her life is emblematic of the diversity and multidimensionality of the twentieth century's women's rights movement.

. . .

Georgia McMurray's life and activism converged around issues concerning minority children, teenagers, and women, as well as health and disability. Although McMurray's importance and influence were reflected in her selection as a delegate from New York and her public recognition from Liz Carpenter, at the same time, McMurray's authority, health, and competence were directly challenged in the city which she represented. This and other key moments in her life were shaped by her experiences as a Black woman with a physical disability. In 1974, she was forced to resign as commissioner of the New York City Agency for Child Development.[2] McMurray defended her life's work and activism in the face of challengers whose claims of her inability to perform her job were embedded in systemic forces of racism, sexism, and ableism. In many ways, the opposition McMurray faced in the years leading up to the conference encapsulated, and complicated, the historic event's stated mission to "evaluate the discrimination that American women face because of their sex."[3]

Early Life and Education

On March 18, 1934, Georgia McMurray was born in Philadelphia, Pennsylvania, to George McMurray and Daisy Gatewood McMurray Fullen. Her mother was from Wadesboro, North Carolina, and her father was born in Tennessee. Both worked, her mother for the garment industry and at a cafeteria, and her father as a barber. The family lived in West Philadelphia on North 41st Street, a traditionally African American neighborhood.[4] McMurray attended Philadelphia's Girls' High School, a historic school established in 1848 under the name, the Girls' Normal School, as the first public school for girls in the area. By the time McMurray attended the school during the second half of the twentieth century, it was known as the Philadelphia High School for Girls, a competitive and academically rigorous institution. McMurray was therefore among a select few with the opportunity to attend such an institution, an even smaller number of which were African American. The school was located across the Schuylkill River, outside of McMurray's childhood neighborhood. However, McMurray undertook the task of traveling the distance to attend Philadelphia High School for Girls, a school that graduated many notable alumni who went on to complete successful, illustrious careers.[5]

As a student at Philadelphia's High School for Girls, McMurray exhibited both academic and musical talent. She performed in the choir Singing City, a progressive group founded in 1948 that traveled the country, including to the South during the Civil Rights Movement.[6] McMurray also sang in the choir at New Bethlehem Baptist Church in Philadelphia. Due to these inclinations, McMurray was awarded the Marian Anderson Scholarship for musical talent by the school. The award was named in honor of Marian Anderson, an African American woman of Philadelphia who became a celebrated classical singer. McMurray's scholarship enabled her to attend Temple University, of which she graduated in 1959 with a degree in Sociology. She went on to study social work at Bryn Mawr College and graduated three years later with her master's degree in 1962.[7]

Project Teen Aid

As a recent graduate of Bryn Mawr College, Georgia McMurray began her career by fiercely advocating for underserved children and youth in New York. Three years after earning her master's, Georgia McMurray received funding from the Office of Economic Opportunity (OEO) for a new initiative called Project Teen Aid. The program was the first of its kind and demonstrated McMurray's commitment to issues affecting young, predominantly Black and Puerto Rican women, in her community. The project launched McMurray's social justice career and garnered her national attention and critical acclaim in the years following its implementation.[8]

Project Teen Aid sought to assist pregnant youth in Brooklyn. At the outset, the project faced opposition from some community members who were concerned with the location of the initiative and its effects toward "contaminating good girls." However, McMurray managed to garner the support of many of those who were initially hesitant by holding meetings with local groups. McMurray described the ways in which those who observed the initiative, including professionals, often had disparaging views of the girls in the program. She claimed, "many still hold traditional, stereotyped views about pregnant unwed teen-agers from minority group families, and are resistant to any departure from old-established customs of practice." These previously established forms of dealing with pregnant teenagers most likely did not include the progressive stances McMurray attempted with her conceptualization of Project Teen Aid, focused on education and activism. The need for the program was apparent and in 1968, the project was funded at the level to provide aid to one hundred pregnant teens.[9]

Project Teen Aid provided assistance for girls between the ages of thirteen and nineteen who were also pregnant or unwed mothers. Many of the teenagers were from the community and of low-income backgrounds, some of whom benefited from welfare programs. The young women entered the program on their own or through referrals from various institutions including local schools, hospitals, welfare centers, and churches.[10] One of the primary aims of the project was to allow teenagers to pursue their education while they were expecting. They continued their academic education while also learning about their pregnancies. McMurray identified the dire need for educational options for pregnant teens, especially African Americans, whose only means of continuing their educations once pregnant were to enter into "maternity centers," like McMurray's that provided financial and childcare assistance and education of which there were "few." The initiative set up classes for the girls to attend led by two teachers once they were no longer able to attend junior and high school. Despite their removal from school, McMurray claimed that the teenagers were "eager" to pursue their schooling. This allowed the girls to continue their pregnancies without it impeding on their education, a factor of both their and their future children's socioeconomic status.[11]

Project Teen Aid also included initiatives that concerned the teenagers' home lives and mental health. Counselors, teachers, and volunteers participated in the project ranging from "resident nonprofessionals" who led homemaking courses, to a licensed beautician. As such, the project relied upon involvement of the local community at various levels, creating avenues of employment and community activism. The program also involved the teenager's families in the outreach activities. Project Teen Aid was met with wide success in the early stages of the program. These successes included the high rate of schooling, as 62 percent of the teenagers returned after giving birth. Twenty-one of the teenagers went on to vocational training or other occupations, and sixteen remained at home.[12]

By founding and implementing Project Teen Aid, Georgia McMurray improved both the lives of minority and low-income young girls and women, and her community's ideas of pregnancy, race, and class. However, McMurray was not satisfied with the work she had accomplished by implementing Project Teen Aid. As she reflected on the success of the program in 1968, she identified an essential issue facing many of the unwed mothers: a lack of childcare resources. This created obstacles for young mothers who attempted to continue their educational or vocational interests after the births of their children. This issue animated McMurray's activism to reach beyond pregnant teens to consider what could be done for the mothers and their children after giving birth.

Work for New York City's Daycare Centers

In 1969, Mayor John Lindsay's administration asked McMurray to serve as director of New York City's Early Childhood Task Force. As director, McMurray helped to establish resources for underserved women, children, and families. In 1971, she was named the first commissioner of the Child Development Agency. Under her leadership, McMurray focused on the creation of new childcare centers, as well as preschool programs. While previously only 5,000 children attended daycares in the city, under McMurray's leadership as commissioner she grew this number to 35,000 children.[13] McMurray led the city in its efforts to provide subsidized, affordable, and quality childcare options for the city's working women, many of whom were working-class women of color.

For many women, access to childcare made a meaningful difference in their livelihood. Many of these daycare centers were publicly funded, allowing working mothers to support their families. A survey conducted by McMurray in 1979 found that an overwhelming majority of the women of working-class backgrounds were working "out of necessity, not choice." However, many did not have access to public daycare. The report emphasized the need for subsidized daycare for families that had been removed from federal programs under the recent cutbacks.[14] As city commissioner, McMurray worked to overcome the odds facing many of these women across various mediums, both by conducting and publishing studies of the issues plaguing the women, and by advocating publicly on their behalf.

Throughout the 1970s, McMurray began to increasingly suffer from symptoms of the degenerative disorder Charcot-Marie-Tooth disease. As a result of the disease, McMurray underwent surgery on both hips and used crutches throughout the early 1970s. Regardless of her physical limitations, McMurray frequented the daycare centers and community meetings regularly and publicly stated, "I've found that in many neighborhoods the first generation immigrants don't understand about day care centers . . . going out and meeting parents is the best part of my job."[15] Despite this clear commitment to her work, in 1974, her position was challenged when Mayor Edward Koch took office. Her physical ability was used as a justification to her inability to properly perform and when all agency administrators participated in the tradition of submitting their letters of resignation under the new administration, McMurray was not surprised to learn that hers was accepted. Andrea Fooner who had worked with her defended her record and claimed, "Georgia's condition may have affected her mobility, but not her ability. She was running the most effective agencies in the cities."[16] Indeed, after she left the position, she remained committed to completing her work throughout the 1970s through 1990s, McMurray's health declined and resulted in her paralysis from the neck down. When McMurray represented New York as a delegate in the 1977 Women's Conference, she attended in a wheelchair.

The 1977 Women's Conference

Georgia McMurray held a significant role at the 1977 Women's Conference as a delegate singled out by Liz Carpenter, and also as a participant. The 1977 Women's Conference recognized the various burdens placed on women and ability with Plank 7: Disabled Women, in which McMurray was involved in drafting. The plank identified specific challenges that disabled women face including equal right to "keep their children" and toward adoption and foster care. The Plank also included recommendations for proper terminology and categorization including that "women" be defined in ways that include those with "disabilities" and "bilingual" include sign language. The Plank referenced intersectional forces of which disabled women faced resulting in "double discrimination" of being neglected in vocational training for their gender and ability.[17] In this way, McMurray would have faced discrimination on three levels, though this expansion of intersectional oppression is not addressed in the Plank. It also encouraged expansion of what is considered to be the challenges women face to those against access to "architectural barriers and communications barriers."[18]

At the 1977 conference, physical issues facing those with disabilities were addressed in arrangements made for the accommodation of participants. These included building additions for accessibility such as ramps, two ASL interpreters, and the usage of braille transcriptions on various signs and of the National Plan of Action.[19] Despite these advanced arrangements, these protections were not legally mandated, and accessibility at the national would not become required until the passage of the Americans with Disabilities Act in 1990.[20] McMurray encountered the very types of "architectural barriers" described in the Plank on disability. The stage upon which she sat during the opening ceremonies did not have a ramp and according to the conference proceeding records, a delegate who participated in the introductory ceremony (likely McMurray), "had to be carried up the stairs to participate."[21] At the conference, Georgia McMurray encountered a space of open and affirmative advocacy for her shared gender, and in some ways (while perhaps marginally) her race. However, she also confronted physical barriers and ableist language in flyers that read "Standing together women shall take their lives in their own keeping."[22]

Months later after leaving Houston, Georgia McMurray published her thoughts on her experience of being Black, a woman, and in a wheelchair, reflecting on her life as "a minority inside a minority" in an opinion piece for the New York Times. In the article, McMurray identified as someone who spoke "on behalf of the nonwhite handicapped." For her, forces of marginalization marked nonwhite handicapped people as "forgotten," and "hidden away even by those who care for them most." McMurray identified the ways in which these experiences are often overlooked by other marginalized groups and observed, "organizations that defend the rights of Blacks and other minorities have overlooked this minority within a minority because it has been silent."[23] McMurray brought this perspective as a handicapped woman of color, as well as her years of public service, to the 1977 Women's Conference.

McMurray continued to speak publicly about her experiences and in 1984 McMurray was the keynote speaker for a conference by the Networking Project for Disabled Women and Girls. Here, she directly also addressed the ways in which her disability impacted her work and described the changes in how she managed this throughout the arc of her career. In her first position after graduating from Bryn Mawr, she struggled to complete the commute and continually fell. Once her supervisor confronted her with this, she concealed her disability. When she was interviewed for the position of commissioner of the Agency for Child Development with Mayor Lindsay and forced to stand at the end of the meeting, she confessed, "Mayor Lindsay, I cannot stand up," to this the Mayor picked her up and continued to do so in their subsequent public appearances.[24]

At the height of McMurray's work and activism while she herself concealed her illness for fear to retribution, activists increased their work toward advocacy and visibility of the issues that people with disabilities faced in their lives and workplaces. In the 1970s and 1980s, activists organized sit-ins and demonstrations of the inaccessibility public transportation. In 1973, activists protested at the Capitol in the face of the Rehabilitation Act of 1973. The act included an expansion of disability rights including barring "employment discrimination because of disability and mandate[ing] the use of affirmative action programs to hire qualified people with disabilities."[25] At the same time of this growing activism in the disability rights community, McMurray focused her work on her community in New York of women, children, and African Americans. She served as deputy general director of the Community Service Society of New York—a nonprofit advocacy group assisting with housing, childcare, healthcare, and more—from 1978 to 1986. Under her leadership, she led initiatives including the 1973 clothing drive that issued coats to more than 2,000 children living on welfare in New York City. She also continually challenged the Koch administration's lack of commitment toward child welfare reform and in 1986 called on the administration to provide families on welfare "a decent place to live."[26] During these years, Georgia McMurray also taught at Fordham University as a Distinguished Professor of Social Policy.

By the time Georgia McMurray was honored in 1992 by Oprah Winfrey and *Essence* magazine for demonstrating the ways in which, "a physical challenge of any kind-whether an early pregnancy or a rare disease-need not be a limitation to excellence," the Americans with Disabilities Act was made into law.[27] At this point in her life and career, McMurray wrote most directly of her disability as she put final words to her physical and emotional struggle with her disability in, "Dreaming, I Can Dance," writing, "My body that wants to fly, that needs to love, lies still. Dreaming, I can dance. So let me sleep, never to wake again. I want to dance once more."[28] That year Georgia McMurray passed away at the age of fifty-eight.

Georgia McMurray's life and legacy illustrates the intersectionality of Black women's lives and activism.[29] Her work and struggles require multidimensional approaches to understanding the feminist movement of the 1970s. For many like McMurray, feminist activism did not align solely with issues that were specifically and particularly felt by all women. Many experienced feminism and activism as a natural extension of their local, community-based work, and that of their own identities and experiences as women, mothers, disabled, and Black. When McMurray attended the 1977 National Women's Conference, she brought with her the personal experience of negotiating these various forces of oppression, an important element of both the conference proceedings on minority experiences and the formation of intersectional approaches to Black feminism.

Notes

1. National Commission on the Observance of International Women's Year, *The Spirit of Houston: The First National Women's Conference; An Official Report to the President, the Congress and the People of the United States* (Washington, DC: US Government Printing Office, 1978), 140. The official record differs slightly from the recording and omits "And so my friends, first ladies, members of the convention and those who are watching." *National Women's Conference. Audiotape Collection of the National Women's Conference, 1977,* Radcliffe Institute for Advanced Study, Harvard University.

2. Jessie Carney Smith, *Notable Black Women: Book II* (Detroit: Gale Research, 1996), 461.

3. National Commission on the Observance of International Women's Year, *The Spirit of Houston,* 10.

4. United States Census, 1940, Philadelphia City, Philadelphia, Ward 24.

5. Smith, *Notable Black Women,* 460. Sarah F. Goldsmith, "The Philadelphia High School for Girls," Historical Society of Pennsylvania: PhilaPlace online resource.

6. http://www.singingcity.org.

7. Smith, *Notable Black Women,* 460.

8. Georgia L. McMurray, "Project Teen Aid: A Community Action Approach to Services for Pregnant Unmarried Teen-Agers," *American Journal of Public Health and the Nation's Health* 58, no. 10 (October 1968): 1848–53, 1849.

9. McMurray, "Project Teen Aid," 1849.

10. McMurray, "Project Teen Aid," 1849.

11. McMurray, "Project Teen Aid," 1849.

12. McMurray, "Project Teen Aid," 1849–51.

13. Wolfgang Saxon, "Georgia L. McMurray, 58, Leader in Services for New York Children," *New York Times,* December 19, 1992.

14. Nadine Brozan, "The Toll of Losing Daycare Is Studied," *New York Times,* June 17, 1982.

15. Smith, *Notable Black Women,* 461.

16. Andrea Fooner, "Against the Odds," *Working Woman* 8 (October 1983): 141–43.

17. National Commission on the Observance of International Women's Year, *The Spirit of Houston,* 33.

18. National Commission on the Observance of International Women's Year, *The Spirit of Houston*, 32.

19. National Commission on the Observance of International Women's Year, *The Spirit of Houston*, 172–73.

20. GovTrack.us. 2017. *S. 933 (101St): Americans With Disabilities Act Of 1990—Senate Vote #173—Sep 7, 1989.* [online] Available at: https://www.govtrack.us/congress/votes/101-1989/s173. Accessed 10 March 2017

21. National Commission on the Observance of International Women's Year, *The Spirit of Houston*, 173.

22. National Commission on the Observance of International Women's Year, *The Spirit of Houston*, 174.

23. Georgia McMurray, "A Minority Inside a Minority," *New York Times*, April 6, 1977.

24. Nadine Brozan, "Disabled Women Meet Role Models," *New York Times*, November 28, 1984.

25. Doris Fleischer and Frieda Zames, *The Disability Rights Movement: From Charity to Confrontation* (Philadelphia: Temple University Press, 2011), 50–51, 88–109.

26. Robert O. Boorstein, "New York Urban League Chapter Honors 5 for Public Service," *New York Times*, January 6, 1986.

27. Smith, *Notable Black Women*, 462.

28. Georgia L. McMurray, "Dreaming, I Can Dance," in *Trials and Tribulations: African American Perspectives on Health, Illness, Aging, and Loss, Vol. 819,* eds. Marian Gray Secundy and Lois LaCivita Nixon (Ann Arbor: University of Michigan Intercultural Press, 1992), 93.

29. Kimberlé Crenshaw, "Demarginalizing the Intersection of Race and Sex: A Black Feminist Critique of Antidiscrimination Doctrine, Feminist Theory and Antiracist Politics," *The University of Chicago Legal Forum* 140 (1989): 139–67.

9

Beyond Combahee

Barbara Smith and Black Radical Feminism

JULIE DE CHANTAL

Figure 9.1. Barbara Smith, class of 1969. Reprinted with permission. The
Mount Holyoke College Archives and Special Collections, South Hadley, MA.

WHEN BARBARA SMITH ATTENDED the 1977 National Women's Conference in Houston as a delegate for the Commonwealth of Massachusetts, she was best known as one of the founders of the Combahee River Collective, a Black radical lesbian feminist group based in Boston. By 1977, the group had worked on "sterilization abuse, abortion rights, battered women, rape and health care."[1] Seldom mentioned in oral histories or in analyses of her career as an activist, Smith's work at the conference remains understudied. Yet, it challenges the ways in which historians reduced the conference to a white middle-class feminist event. Smith's efforts in Houston transcended racial and sexual orientation barriers and spoke to her commitment to build Black feminism through a broader framework, which included gender, race, socioeconomic background, and sexual orientation.

Smith contributed extensively to both the Minority and the Sexual Preference Planks of the Conference Program. However, as both a Black woman and a lesbian, Smith found difficulty in gaining full acceptance into either group. Some lesbian activists within the Sexual Preference Caucus still held racially biased views, while some of the Black delegates of the Minority Caucus were guided by homophobia. Despite, or perhaps because of, these challenges to diversity, Smith managed to build a biracial coalition uniting both Black and lesbian women to secure each of these program planks. She was among the few Black women to tackle what she described as a multi-issue feminism, a feminism which fought against all forms of oppression that women faced. In line with the work that she already performed through the Combahee River Collective and the National Black Feminist Organization, Smith's work at the conference demonstrates the importance of intersectionality as a cornerstone of Black radical feminism in the late 1970s. Ultimately, her success at the conference bolstered her work as an activist and as an editor, setting her on a path to revolutionize the field of feminist studies and to organize women of color all over the world. This chapter brings to light Smith's work, which bridged the civil rights, LGBTQ, and women's rights movements from the 1970s to today.

Born prematurely, a twin, and surviving infancy against all odds, Smith felt that the universe had a plan for her; it was her mission to become an activist fighting not only against injustice, but also to be "outspoken about issues of sexuality as an out Black lesbian."[2] Finding her voice, however, was far from easy. She lived her adolescence and early adulthood "in terror," having "screaming nightmares," because of her sexual orientation.[3] Coming out in the 1960s or 1970s was unthinkable, especially for someone who had received what Smith described as a "very southern and very traditional" upbringing from her female relatives.[4] Her family had moved from a small town near Macon, Georgia, to Cleveland, Ohio, during the first wave of the Great Migration.[5]

In Cleveland, her family grew increasingly politicized, connecting with race leaders through the Church and the early Civil Rights Movement. Smith explained that even at a young age, she knew that she would "commit [her] life to trying to make things better, and to fight injustice."[6] Growing up in segregated Cleveland, her "eyes were pretty quickly opened" as she discovered that she could not use public facilities, drink at white water fountains, or sit at the front of the city bus.[7]

In high school, she joined the Congress of Racial Equality (CORE).[8] Early on, CORE leaders understood the importance of mobilizing the youth, and recruited high school students throughout the Midwest.[9] Through the organization, Smith received mentorship, participated in boycotts, and took part in local civil rights protests. Between her graduation from high school in January 1965 and her enrollment at Mount Holyoke College in September of the same year, she volunteered for CORE, canvassing her neighborhood to discuss housing issues plaguing Cleveland.[10]

Over time, Smith became more politicized. While at Mount Holyoke College, she joined the Civil Actions Group against the US involvement in Vietnam and attended the 1967 March to the United Nations against the war led by Martin Luther King Jr.[11] However, by the early 1970s, her political organizing moved in other directions. When she became a professor at Emerson College in Boston in 1973, she joined the National Black Feminist Organization (NBFO). Contrary to most mainstream organizations, the NBFO was a radical group, which addressed the simultaneous racial and sexual oppressions that Black women encountered on a daily basis.

Like many other Black women, Smith had not been involved in the feminist movement prior to her involvement with the NBFO. She could not "see being and doing political work with predominantly white women or men," though she understood that women's oppression was linked to patriarchy and gender.[12] As the Civil Rights Movement shifted from "integrationist perspectives to a more militant Black nationalist ideology" in the late 1960s, those whom she described as "unprogressive Black nationalists" redefined the role of women's activism in ways that were "a bit too narrow" for her.[13] Stokely Carmichael, one of the leaders of the Black Power Movement, once even joked that the role of women in the SNCC, the Student Nonviolent Coordinating Committee, was "prone."[14] Other groups, less direct in their approach, only gave supporting roles to women, putting men in the spotlight.[15] Yet, like many other Black women, Smith was reluctant to "jeopardize" her "racial credibility" by criticizing what Pauli Murray had described as "Jane Crow," the sexism that Black women experienced at the hands of Black men.[16] Within Black communities, Smith argued, discussing issues of sexism could as likely elicit "attacks and ostracism," as "comprehension and readiness to change."[17] Even Black women had fairly strict and traditional notions of gender.[18] As many scholars point out, heteronormativity often represented the "only privilege" available to Black women and men, as Smith put it, "straightness [was their] last resort."[19] Radical organizations had an even clearer vision sometimes, expecting women to "have babies for the Nation and to walk seven paces behind a man and basically be a maidservant."[20] Smith felt cornered; the NBFO became her "pathway back into activism."[21]

In the NBFO, Smith found women, like Eleanor Holmes Norton, Shirley Chisholm, Faith Ringgold, Flo Kennedy, Alice Walker, and Margaret Sloan, who shared her ideas and concerns.[22] The organization's first conference was held at the Riverside Church in New York City in late 1973, forming ten local chapters of the organization.[23] In late 1974, a *Ms.* magazine article about the NBFO conference in *Ms.* magazine listed Smith's address for the Boston branch. She began receiving letters from women interested in joining the local chapter.[24] Racial tensions had risen in Boston after Judge W. Arthur Garrity rendered his decision in the *Morgan v. Hennigan* desegregation case. Throughout the fall of 1974, violence exploded as white parents from the poverty-stricken neighborhood of South Boston opposed the federal desegregation order.[25] Black women had few places to go to discuss community issues, as women, so the NBFO served as a safe space where they could voice their frustrations.

While the NBFO allowed Smith to fight multiple forms of oppression at once, she still did not feel that the organization was radical enough. Instead of "fixing the system"; she "basically wanted a revolution."[26] She needed to form her own organization, one where she could shape organizational politics and ideological positions.[27] In late 1974, with the participation of several members of the Boston chapter of the NBFO, Smith broke away to form the Combahee River Collective.

Well known for its 1976 manifesto, the Combahee River Collective defined itself as "anti-capitalist, socialist, and revolutionary," focusing on community issues through the lens of sexuality, economic development, and social justice.[28] For example, its members asked city officials why they did not hire people of color to build a new school in the predominantly Black neighborhood of Roxbury. They discussed issues of urban poverty and ghettoization. They supported Willie Saunders, a Black man wrongly accused of raping white women in the predominantly white neighborhood of Brighton; Kenneth Edelin, a Black doctor accused of manslaughter for performing a legal abortion; and Joan Little, a North Carolina inmate accused of stabbing her jailor in self-defense.[29] To the organization, rape, childcare, violence against women, sterilization abuse, quality education, peace, or labor, were neither mutually exclusive causes, nor only of a "Black agenda."[30] The crux of the organization, "identity politics"—the political positions based on group members' multi-faceted identities—was not exclusionary politics. Instead, it was multi-issue politics, directed against oppression at large.

When Smith was elected as a delegate representing the Commonwealth of Massachusetts to the National Women's Conference in Houston in 1977, she brought identity politics to the table. At the time, her friends Lisa Leghorn and Leslie Cagan had heard of a preparatory conference to elect delegates.[31] A number of activists, both on the left and on the right, saw the conference as an opportunity to have their voices heard. Smith, however, knew that right-wing activists, including those whom she nicknamed the "anti-reproductive choice contingent," were planning "to take over the conference," by "stack[ing] that electing convention." To her, it was a life or death situation for the femi-nist movement. Smith, Leghorn, and Cagan, strategized to attend the elec-toral convention themselves and encourage "as many people who were actually committed feminists to go to it." They would also submit their own names as potential delegates, in the hope that a larger number of feminist supporters on the ballot could "counter the rightwing [sic] takeover" of the conference.[32] Her goal was to curb "the right wing's desire to undermine and sabotage the IWY process."[33] Smith and her friends were all quite surprised when they were chosen as official delegates from Massachusetts, but their candidacy was in line with the anti-racist organizing which actively took place in Boston.

Through their nomination, Smith hoped to bring to the conference their "multi-issue, grassroots feminist politics."[34] She understood the need to pro-mote grassroots organizing, since unlike white feminists, Black feminists did not have access to "the big megaphones or microphones." Politically disenfran-chised at home, Black activists seldom had their voices heard in predominantly white settings, like the conference. To help promote their voice at the confer-ence, they put together a newspaper and called themselves the "Lucy Parsons Brigade," to honor the Chicago-based Black Mexican radical anarcho-commu-nist labor organizer, featuring her picture on the newspaper. They printed "tens of thousands" of copies to distribute on site, with Smith describing themselves as looking like newspaper boys, "in those old-fashioned movies," attempting to hand out their stacks of papers in Houston.[35]

Smith's objective at the conference was to protect the Black feminist agenda not only from the right-wing takeover, but also from "bourgeois feminism." She often saw white middle-class feminists reducing the movement to their own agenda, sidelining women of color, lesbians, and poor women. Instead, Smith promoted an intersectional understanding of feminism, and argued that capitalism and imperialism "ruined the lives of virtually everyone on the planet," with the exception of the ruling class.[36] Her newspaper was the voice of the voiceless, of those who could not speak their minds and their needs at the conference. At a time where only a small portion of Black women gravitated toward the feminist movement—a large proportion of these Black women "focus[ed] on elective office and more conventional kinds of political intervention"—Smith felt that she had a particular responsibility to her sisters in the fight.[37] As a result, she participated in the Black Women's Caucus and in the Lesbian Caucus.

Through the Black Caucus, Smith realized her work in Boston was similar to that of other Black women in St. Louis, Chicago, or Jackson, Mississippi. However, she also acknowledged that Black activists lacked the connections or a "central place to know that other people" were organizing in the same way. "But we came," she explained, "we were organizing and trying to get ready as Black women."[38] She continued, "I've been Black [laughs] since at least 1946 and whatever my sisters were doing, I was involved with and interested in that, too."[39] The Black Caucus prioritized sharing information, building networks, and mobilizing.

From this organizing, emerged the Black Women's Plan of Action which encouraged the federal government to rethink education programs for Black women, to address unemployment issues, to establish a placement program specifically designed for Black children facing family difficulties, to take action on housing issues, and described other issues affecting Black communities nationwide.[40] Like Smith's work with the Combahee, the underlying ideas behind the Plank were rooted in a desire for economic development. In order to come to an understanding, members of the Black Caucus adopted strategies that Smith had already used in her work. They built coalitions and used "political quilting," a strategy favoring "supporting, connecting, convening, [and] bringing together."[41] Through Gloria Steinem, who acted as a "shuttle diplomat" between the different groups of the Minority Plank, they found a language common to all women of color, yet acknowledged each group's unique issues.[42] To Smith, the idea of sexual orientation, however, was still missing from the deliberations of the Minority Plank. For that reason, she navigated between the Black Caucus and the Lesbian Caucus.

The Lesbian Caucus produced the most controversial plank of the IWY platform. Less than a decade after the Stonewall Riot, the caucus sought to secure antidiscrimination legislation at the state and federal levels, especially with regard to employment, schools, housing, child custody, and in the banking industry.[43] Due to the controversial nature of the plank, Smith knew that she needed to build a coalition to gain support. None of the groups—left-leaning or right-leaning, white or women of color—pledged their support as a block. Even within the Lesbian Caucus, race, ethnicity, and economic status shaped the priorities and politics of the group. As a Black woman, she hoped that her racial background and her ability to present positions would sway straight Black women in favor of the plank. With the help of the Black Lesbian Caucus, she drafted a petition specifically targeting Black women to ask for their support. "We found some hotel typewriter," Smith recalled, "and we appropriated it." She found a place to photocopy the document and made copies upon copies.[44] Black lesbians then went from delegation to delegation, discussing their plank, and asked for support from Black delegates. Considering her experience with homophobia in the Black community, she rightfully feared that the delegates would reject her ideas. Yet, some signed it, possibly as a quid pro quo, hoping in return to gain support from white lesbians for the Minority Plank.

Even with the Black delegates' vote, other delegates were still divided over the plank. Many delegates in attendance claimed that "they had never met a declared lesbian face to face before they [came] to Houston."[45] Unsurprising at *posteriori*, as many gays and lesbians were not yet open about their sexual orientation, the conference allowed many attendees to humanize and understand lesbians. Some attendees acknowledged that women could have their own private sexual relations. However, they were still homophobic, and couched their argument in the protection of children, "worried about lesbian teachers" who could compromise the innocence of the youth. Some, although seemingly at ease with homosexuality, argued that the conference should focus solely on "areas in which women are discriminated against vis-à-vis-men, or in which [their] services are undervalued, as they are in the home." They failed to acknowledge that the discrimination against lesbians stemmed from the same patriarchal notions of gender roles, as Smith had already pointed out. The fiercest opponents showed their misunderstanding of sexual preference, conflating it with sexual predation and unrestricted libido, as they claimed that they would not "advocate a stoning or a burning at the stake or throwing stones at a homosexual as long as homosexuals keep their sexual preference private, the same as adulterers and adulteresses."[46] Once known for her opposition to what she called "the lavender menace," Betty Friedan came out in "unexpected support" of the plank.

Ultimately, and despite the opposition, delegations from all corners of the nation voted in favor of the plank. Reflecting on the result, Smith understood the importance of coalition building in securing the victory. "We really felt that we had been absolutely instrumental as Black lesbians in getting to Black women to help support the plank," Smith recalled, thinking about the ways that they helped rally seemingly conservative, and possibly homophobic women, to their sisters' fight.[47] Following the conference, Smith returned to Boston where she took on a greater role in community organizing.

Beginning with organizing around what were called "The Roxbury Murders," of twelve African American women killed between January and May of 1979 and the trivialization of these crimes by the media, Smith described her organizing as "the culmination of everything [that she] had done, learned, tried to do until then."[48] Through a critical feminist lens, she highlighted that all of the murders had been committed against women; they were "not just rooted in racial injustice and violence but in widespread hatred and victimization of women."[49] Linking the events in Boston to a national trend, she argued that the murders of Black women were "logically connected," part of a same widespread sexual violence against women.

She wrote a pamphlet which connected sexual violence, race violence, and economic exploitation, and proposed tips for self-protection. According to Smith, "it was the first published, tangible thing that came out about the murders that people could use."[50] More importantly though, it was the first piece which did not blame the victims or shame them for their own death.[51] Combahee River Collective members translated the pamphlet into Spanish to spread the information to the women of the growing Hispanic community in Boston.[52] When discussing the goals of the campaign, Smith explained that she "wanted every woman to feel some kind of solidarity and some kind of protection," notwithstanding their language or their racial background. She explained that the efforts to speak about the murders "embodied the kind of work that [she] felt is most important"; "it was a coalition effort that got at a bottom-line issue—murders—and dealt with a feminist issue, sexual violence."[53] The publication of the pamphlets also confirmed the importance of publishing as a way to shape politics and inform about issues pertaining to women of color.

Smith understood that "writing was crucial to movement building"; publishing was an activist's "lifeline."[54] Women of color, especially, were at the mercy of publishers, as they "did not control the process or the outcomes or the product."[55] Audre Lorde and Smith, who had published with independent presses, knew that publishers, editors, and marketing staff shaped the message that readers received. In 1980, with the help of several other Black activists, they founded a Black women's press.[56] Ultimately, creating a press, directed by women of color for women of color, was the only way to reclaim agency over the publication process.[57]

In 1981, the press announced its name, the Kitchen Table: Women of Color Press, to the public. The name itself diverged from most feminist presses' names. Instead of distancing its name from women's traditional roles by using the movement or Greek Goddesses as their emblem—The Feminist Press, Persephone, Diana Press, for example—the Kitchen Table Press embraced feminine iconography. The idea of the kitchen table reminded them of a shared bond between women, of the ways in which "kitchen is the center of the home, the place where women in particular work and communicate with each other."[58] Furthermore, the name highlighted the fact that the press remained a grassroots-led organization, led by volunteers who did not "rely on inheritances or other benefits of class privilege to do the work," that it did.

The press denoted its autonomy through its slogan, "freedom of press belongs to those who own the press." The need for autonomy mirrored the need of women of color to reclaim agency not only in writing, but in the political and economic spheres in the early 1980s. According to Smith, the press was "a revolutionary tool" as it empowered "the society's most dispossessed, who [had] the greatest potential for making change."[59]

As Smith predicted, the Kitchen Table Press served as a launchpad for grassroots organizing. In the 1970s and 1980s, the United Nations organized several women's conferences around the world.[60] According to Smith, several Black women, who had been reluctant to participate in the feminist movement in the United States "got very excited about an international women's conference in the Motherland," in Nairobi, Kenya.[61] They organized for the conference, even if few of them were able to attend. Smith participated in a "planning preconference" which took place at Morgan State University, in Baltimore.[62] Because of the nature of the conference in Nairobi, Smith wanted to distribute the Combahee River Collective Statement, as it "really lays out Black feminist politics so clearly."[63] She had an epiphany, instead of copying materials that she had published more than a decade earlier, she prepared a new pamphlet specifically for the conference. From this revelation stemmed the *Freedom Organizing Pamphlets* series, a series which was both "affordable and explicitly for organizing." To ensure their display, she copied Nancy Bereano's practice at Firebrand Press of attaching a button, forcing the pamphlets to be displayed face out, while giving the reader a button to state their beliefs.[64]

Through the *Freedom Organizing Pamphlets* series, the press "functioned as a beacon," for women of color and lesbians of color nationally and internationally.[65] Focusing on politics, the press participated in the "Arts Against Apartheid" movement and engaged with the Central American Solidarity Movement.[66]

In the mid-1980s, the Kitchen Table Press struggled financially. In an attempt to save it, Smith relocated the press from New York City to Albany, where she lived at the time.[67] Local friends took over key roles, promising to do "whatever [they] could," to support the endeavor.[68] By 1986, the press could no longer hire paid employees, and it was forced to move to a one-desk space in the Albany's Social Justice Center. Smith continued to work, day in, day out, to fulfill the press's obligations, packing boxes full of books, driving them to nearest United Parcel Service (UPS) shipping locations, and paying bills in order to keep the press open at all cost.[69] She held four jobs—her work at the Kitchen Table Press, a part-time teaching position, "numerous speaking engagements," and teaching a New York State Council on the Arts grant-funded weekend women's writing course at the "Y." During this period, she lived in a motel, and the press required a great deal of uncompensated work.[70]

By the summer of 1987, the Press was doing slightly better financially, and moved to a bigger office located at the Albany's Urban League.[71] In 1995, the Press moved to Brooklyn, and a new staff took over the operation.[72] Smith stepped down as publisher, and was "ecstatic at the prospect of what felt like a whole new life."[73]

In 2005, she ran for Albany Common Council.[74] Following her election, she jokingly wondered "how [she could] stick it to the man, if [she was] the man."[75] Yet, running for office was the "next logical thing to do."[76] Although working as an elected official felt like the opposite of grassroots organizing, she used similar strategies to those for preparing for Houston to represent Arbor Hill, a poor nonwhite neighborhood in the city. Still, she admitted to making concessions especially in terms of her sexuality which she did not mention publicly. She felt like she "betray[ed] [her] roots," and possibly disappointed her colleagues for not speaking overtly about what she had fought for so many years. In 2009, when she ran for her second term, she hoped that she would "have a chance to help to enlighten people more about these issues."[77] As a City Council member, Smith introduced a statewide initiative, which aimed to reduce street violence.[78] She emphasized the importance of education as "violence prevention," working on programs like "Cradle through College through Career." In 2009, she supported the Occupy Movement.

Retiring from political life, Smith continues her work as an activist, fighting against islamophobia, supporting refugees and immigrants, and lecturing about multi-issue activism. Her legacy is undeniable and her work has transformed communities in the United States and abroad. Smith's concept of identity politics redefined Black feminism which prevailed in the 1980s and 1990s and led to the emergence of Third Wave feminism. According to feminist scholars, The Kitchen Table: Women of Color Press "literally transformed the conversation on racism, sexism, and homophobia in the classroom in the last decade."[79] Beyond the use of its texts in the classroom, the Kitchen Table Press gave women of color tools to organize around the world. As Smith said, "until this society completely transforms itself, and justice for all people prevails, there will undoubtedly be a need for Kitchen Table: Women of Color Press."[80]

Notes

1. The Combahee River Collective Statement, 1977.

2. Alethia Jones, Virginia Eubanks, and Barbara Smith, *Ain't Gonna Let Nobody Turn Me Around: Forty Years of Movement Building with Barbara Smith* (Albany, NY: SUNY Press, 2014), 38.

3. Jones, Eubanks, and Smith, *Ain't Gonna Let Nobody Turn Me Around,* 37–38.

4. Barbara Smith interviewed by Loretta J. Ross, May 7–8, 2003, Northampton, MA. *Voices of Feminism Oral History Project.* Sophia Smith Collection, Smith College Northampton, MA (cited hereafter as "Oral History"), 2.

5. "Interview with Virginia Eubanks," in Jones, Eubanks, and Smith, *Ain't Gonna Let Nobody Turn Me Around,* 82.

6. Oral History, 43.

7. Oral History, 40.

8. CORE was founded in 1942 in Chicago, and grew out of the Fellowship of Reconciliation, an organization formed by peace activists during the First World War.

9. August Meier and Elliott M. Rudwick, *CORE: A Study in the Civil Rights Movement, 1942–1968* (Chicago: University of Illinois Press, 1975).

10. Oral History, 45.

11. "Many Draft Cards Burned—Eggs Tossed at Parade," *New York Times,* April 16, 1967.

12. Oral History, 48.

13. Oral History, 46–48.

14. Susan Brownmiller, *In Our Time: Memoir of a Revolution* (New York: The Dial Press, 1999), 14.

15. Jennifer Scanlon. *Until There Is Justice: The Life of Anna Arnold Hedgeman* (New York: Oxford University Press, 2016).

16. Duchess Harris, "From the Kennedy Commission to the Combahee River Collective: Black Feminist Organizing, 1960–1980," in *Sisters in the Struggle,* eds. Bettye Collier-Thomas and V. P. Franklin (New York: New York University Press, 2001), 288.

17. Barbara Smith, ed., *Home Girls: A Black Feminist Anthology* (New Brunswick, NJ: Rutgers University Press, 2000), xiv.

18. Harris, "From the Kennedy Commission to the Combahee River Collective," 286.

19. Barbara Smith. "Toward a Black Feminist Criticism," *The Radical Teacher* 7 (1978): 26.

20. Barbara Smith, interview with Susan Levine Goodwillie, 1994, Boston.

21. Oral History, 48.

22. Eleanor Holmes Norton was the Washington, DC, delegate to the United States Congress and became the first chairwoman of the Equal Employment Opportunity Commission in 1977. Faith Ringgold was an artist and activist who created a series of narrative quilts representing the life and struggles of African Americans in the United States. Alice Walker was a writer and an activist. She is better known for her books *The Color Purple* and *You Can't Keep a Good Woman Down: Stories*.

23. Oral History, 49.

24. Oral History, 50.

25. Judge Garrity's decision ultimately led to the busing crisis in Boston which lasted from 1974 to 1986.

26. Oral History, 56.

27. Oral History, 56.

28. The Combahee River Collective Statement, 1977; Harris, "From the Kennedy Commission to the Combahee River Collective," 292.

29. On the Little Case, see in particular Genna Rae McNeil, "'Joanne Is You and Joanne Is Me': A Consideration of African American Women and the 'Free Joan Little' Movement, 1974–1975," in Collier-Thomas and Franklin, *Sisters in the Struggle*.

30. Oral History, 55.

31. State officials held five regional preparatory meetings, in Boston, Worcester, Springfield, Fall River, and Methuen, regrouping a total of 2,500 attendees. National Commission on the Observance of International Women's Year, *The Spirit of Houston: The First National Women's Conference; An Official Report to the President, the Congress and the People of the United States* (Washington, DC: US Government Printing Office, 1978), 114–15.

32. Oral History, 83.

33. Oral History, 84. Ultimately, Massachusetts regional meetings adopted all of the International Women's Year core recommendations, National Commission on the Observance of International Women's Year *The Spirit of Houston*, 115.

34. Oral History, 84.

35. Oral History, 85.

36. Oral History, 85.

37. Oral History, 86.

38. Oral History, 86.

39. Oral History, 86.

40. National Commission on the Observance of International Women's Year, *The Spirit of Houston*, 70, 272–76. The Black Women's Plan of Action especially focused on the concept of human rights instead of women's rights or civil rights.

41. "Interviews with Matt Richardson, Barbara Ransby, and Kimberly Springer," in Jones, Eubanks, and Smith, *Ain't Gonna Let Nobody Turn Me Around*, 160.

42. Gloria Steinem, *My Life on the Road* (New York: Random House, 2016), 61–66.

43. Oral History, 89–91.

44. Oral History, 87.

45. National Commission on the Observance of International Women's Year, *The Spirit of Houston*, 165.

46. National Commission on the Observance of International Women's Year, *The Spirit of Houston,* 166.

47. Even with the victory, the Minority Report could not be clearer in its opposition to the liberal push toward equality. The conservative writers refused to extend rights to adopt, teach in school, or any other roles which could "promot[e] their way of life," to children. Years before the passage of DOMA, the Defense of Marriage Act passed during Clinton's administration, they also defined the family as a bond uniting a man and a woman, refusing to consider same-sex couples as legitimate. National Commission on the Observance of International Women's Year, *The Spirit of Houston,* 271.

48. Oral History.

49. "Building Black Feminism," in Jones, Eubanks, and Smith, *Ain't Gonna Let Nobody Turn Me Around,* 42.

50. "Building Black Feminism," in Jones, Eubanks, and Smith, *Ain't Gonna Let Nobody Turn Me Around.*

51. Jones, Eubanks, and Smith, *Ain't Gonna Let Nobody Turn Me Around,* 72.

52. The English version of the pamphlet was reprinted in Jones, Eubanks, and Smith, *Ain't Gonna Let Nobody Turn Me Around* in 2014, 66–67.

53. Jones, Eubanks, and Smith, *Ain't Gonna Let Nobody Turn Me Around,* 64.

54. Jones, Eubanks, and Smith, *Ain't Gonna Let Nobody Turn Me Around,* 139, 152.

55. Jones, Eubanks, and Smith, *Ain't Gonna Let Nobody Turn Me Around,* 149.

56. The press was founded under the auspices of Barbara Smith, Audre Lorde, Cherrie Moraga, Hattie Gossett, Myrna Bain, Mariana Roma-Carmona, Rosario Morales, Ana Oliveira, Alma Gomez, Helena Byard, Susan Yung, Rosie Alvarez, and Leota Lone Dog. "Building Kitchen Table Press," in Jones, Eubanks, and Smith, *Ain't Gonna Let Nobody Turn Me Around,* 139.

57. While only Black women attended the first meeting, the Kitchen Table Press aimed to publish works by women of color, notwithstanding their racial or ethnic background.

58. Jones, Eubanks, and Smith, *Ain't Gonna Let Nobody Turn Me Around,* 153.

59. "A Press of Our Own: Kitchen Table: Women of Color Press" (1989), in Jones, Eubanks, and Smith, *Ain't Gonna Let Nobody Turn Me Around,* 155–56.

60. Conferences were held in Mexico City in 1975, in Copenhagen in 1980, in Nairobi in 1985, and in Beijing in 1995. The 1985 conference in Nairobi was titled the "World Conference to review and appraise the achievements of the United Nations Decade for Women: Equality, Development and Peace."

61. "Interview with Matt Richardson, Barbara Ransby, and Kimberly Springer," in Jones, Eubanks, and Smith, *Ain't Gonna Let Nobody Turn Me Around.* 158.

62. Morgan State University is a historically Black university founded in 1867.

63. "Interview with Matt Richardson, Barbara Ransby, and Kimberly Springer," in Jones, Eubanks, and Smith, *Ain't Gonna Let Nobody Turn Me Around,* 158.

64. "Interview with Matt Richardson, Barbara Ransby, and Kimberly Springer," in Jones, Eubanks, and Smith, *Ain't Gonna Let Nobody Turn Me Around,* 159.

65. "Interview with Matt Richardson, Barbara Ransby, and Kimberly Springer," in Jones, Eubanks, and Smith, *Ain't Gonna Let Nobody Turn Me Around.* 161.

66. Some of the archives of the movement are located at Michigan State University, in East Lansing, MI. http://africanactivist.msu.edu/organization.php?name=Art+Against+Apartheid

67. Barbara Smith, "A Rose," in *The Truth That Never Hurts: Writings on Race, Gender, and Freedom* (New Brunswick, NJ: Rutgers University Press, 2000), 197.

68. Smith, "A Rose."

69. Smith, "A Rose," 198–99.

70. Smith, "A Rose," 199.

71. Smith, "A Rose," 201.

72. Jamie M. Grant, "Building Community-Based Coalitions from Academe: The Union Institute and the Kitchen Table: Women of Color Press Transition Coalition," *Feminist Theory and Practice* 21 (1996): 1024–33.

73. Smith, *The Truth That Never Hurts,* 205.

74. She was elected and held office from 2006 to 2013.

75. Barbara Smith, "Black Feminist Activism: My Next Chapter" (2012), in Jones, Eubanks, and Smith, *Ain't Gonna Let Nobody Turn Me Around,* 215.

76. Smith, "Black Feminist Activism."

77. Smith, "Black Feminist Activism," 223.

78. The SNUG initiative, a play on the spelling of "guns" backward, was based on Chicago's CeaseFire model, where former gang members take on grassroots work in the streets.

79. Grant, "Building Community-Based Coalitions from Academe."

80. Barbara Smith, "A Press of Our Own: Kitchen Table: Women of Color Press," in Ramona R Rush and Donna Allen, eds., *Communication at the Crossroads: The Gender Gap Connection* (Norwood, NJ: Ablex Publishing, 1989).

10

Johnnie Tillmon

Welfare as a Women's Issue

LAURA L. LOVETT

Figure 10.1. Welfare activists celebrate, 1977. *Right*, in the front of the group is Johnnie Tillmon; to the left stands Beulah Sanders and then Christine Marsden. Tillmon reaches out to shake the hand of Margaret Prescod. Diana Mara Henry Papers (PH 51). Special Collections and University Archives, University of Massachusetts Amherst Libraries. Copyright © Diana Mara Henry / dianamarahenry.com.

THERE WERE MANY MOMENTS of celebration in Houston as women met to articulate and affirm the principles that they wanted to inform national policies. Diana Mara Henry's photograph, taken after the approval of the plank on Women, Welfare and Poverty captures one. As jubilant as the moment appears, this photograph also allows us to understand the multifaceted nature of the Welfare Rights Movement. On the right, in the front of the group, is Johnnie Tillmon, former president of the National Welfare Rights Organization (NWRO). Next to her stands Beulah Sanders, another nationally renowned leader of the NWRO, with the mink hat she was known for wearing everywhere. To her right stands Christine Marsden, a welfare rights activist from Washington state. Tillmon reaches out to shake the hand of Margaret Prescod, another activist who carries a bag and wears the apron emblematic of the International Black Women for Wages for Housework organization, whose members join in behind. Their signs declare unity under the slogan, "Every mother is a working mother," yet acknowledge different experiences as well, "Black women speak out. Not cuts. Just bucks." For Prescod, Tillmon and Sanders, welfare was the first step toward enumerating the value of unrecognized labor, and for demanding recognition that "WELFARE IS A WAGE," as their signs read.

This image signifies the coalition of welfare activists that came together in Houston. Reflecting on the passing of the Women, Welfare, and Poverty plank, Prescod said, "I don't think the welfare mothers ever dreamed the amount of victory that got in there. . . . [W]elfare women aren't isolated any more. There is some power here." Support for the Women, Welfare and Poverty plank represented an important reaffirmation of welfare as a women's issue, not just within the United States. As a national issue, the welfare movement was under increasing attack by the late 1970s. The centralized National Welfare Rights Organization (NWRO) had dissolved in 1975. Johnnie Tillmon and Beulah Sanders had taken over the struggling organization but could not remedy its financial and organizational challenges. The historiography of Black women's activism around welfare rights work often follows the trajectory of NWRO and marks the late 1970s as a time when there is no national welfare movement and everything becomes local and more isolated.[1] In this context, the passage of a national welfare agenda in 1977 signals that national and international coordination of welfare activism is alive and well, and that poor Women of Color will not compromise. Tillmon, Sanders, Prescod, and others had rejected a conservative proposal and President Carter's proposed welfare reforms in favor of a more radical plank, one that focused on poverty and its causes, insisting that welfare and poverty are major women's issues which must be understood as a result of discriminatory employment practices, social security laws, differential educational access, and lack of adequate childcare.

Johnnie Tillmon's Path to Activism

Johnnie Tillmon played a central role in the rise of a national campaign to recognize the rights of welfare recipients in the United States to receive adequate income, with dignity, justice, and a guarantee of democratic participation. Under her leadership, the welfare rights movement became more inclusive in the early 1970s when they recognized the interconnection of political disenfranchisement, racial discrimination, economic, and educational disempowerment as well as gendered oppression. Despite the significant advances made in the campaign for welfare rights in the 1960s, financial, personal, and political pressures eventually brought the National Welfare Rights Organization to an end in 1975. Nevertheless, Tillmon persisted in her advocacy.

Tillmon's background prepared her for fighting through the long haul. She was born in Scott, Arkansas, in 1926, to parents who were sharecroppers. Her mother died when she was only five. In 1944, she was sent to Little Rock to live with her aunt and attend high school, but she was forced to leave high school to work, first as a domestic, then in a war plant, and, after the expulsion of women war workers to make room for returning GIs, in a laundry.[2] Even as a young woman, her sense of justice and leadership led her to organize her coworkers to demand higher wages at that Little Rock laundry. The push to integrate Central High School in Little Rock, a decade after she was pressured to put the economic needs of her family before her own, meant that her vision of the importance of battling poverty was always multigenerational.[3]

In 1948, Johnnie Percy married James Tillmon. Before their marriage ended in 1952, they had three children together. Tillmon's father died while she was pregnant with her sixth child, and she decided to leave Arkansas for California, where her two brothers lived. In Los Angeles, the former war worker found work again at a laundry, as a shirt-line operator ironing 120 shirts an hour. Unsurprisingly, Tillmon advocated for better working conditions, and was made union shop steward.[4]

In 1962, Tillmon and her family moved to Watts, a predominantly Black neighborhood, where they lived in the Nickerson Gardens housing project. She threw herself into community life, joining the Nickerson Gardens Planning Organization (NGPO) as well as a number of local political campaigns. In January 1963, Tillmon developed a serious case of tonsillitis. A friend in the NGPO suggested that she sign up for Aid to Needy Children (ANC) to help cover the time she was missing at work. The ANC program was California's welfare program for single mothers. At the federal level, the Aid to Dependent Children (ADC) had been created as part of the 1935 Social Security Act and was modified in 1962 to become the Aid to Families with Dependent Children (AFDC) program.[5] Tillmon was reluctant to enroll in the ANC program until she found out that her oldest daughter had been skipping school. It was important to Tillmon that her daughter attend school; as a child, Tillmon did not have an opportunity to finish her education. She believed that her daughter's future depended on her school attendance. With support from the ANC program, Tillmon realized that she could work less and devote more time to parenting.

While the ANC program helped Tillmon and her family, it also exposed them to new forms of discrimination. As a state welfare recipient, her home could be inspected without her permission, her spending was subject to scrutiny, as was her love life—evidence of a man in her house was enough to get her benefits revoked. Not one to stand for unfair treatment, Tillmon began to organize other single mothers in the Nickerson Garden projects and formed ANC Mothers Anonymous. Initially, some women were unwilling to admit that they were on welfare; the promise of anonymity was offered to persuade them to join. As an organization, the ANC Mothers group set up an office in Watts where they offered mutual support, direct assistance, and expertise navigating government bureaucracy.[6]

As word of the ANC Mothers group began to spread, Tillmon was called to help organize and lead wider regional efforts in Los Angeles, and work with the newly formed California Welfare Rights Organization.[7] In 1966, she was invited to speak at the Citizens Crusade Against Poverty (CCAP) meeting in Washington, DC. This was Tillmon's first step onto the national stage, and she was not shy. In her remarks, she directly criticized Sargent Shriver, present at the meeting, calling his efforts as leader of President Lyndon Johnson's War on Poverty almost laughable and noting that the Office of Economic Opportunity had not created "job training and placement programs for poor mothers." As she put it, "When all the money is spent, the rich will get richer and I will still be receiving a welfare check."[8] George Wiley, the national action coordinator for CCAP, was impressed by Tillmon, and he made sure that she was invited to a meeting in Chicago the next year where over 350 welfare activists met to address welfare at the national level.[9] Tillmon was elected to chair that meeting and the resulting National Coordinating Committee which began to lobby the federal government. With George Wiley, Tillmon began planning and organizing the National Welfare Rights Organization.[10] Wiley, an African American chemistry professor who resigned his appointment at Syracuse University to work for the Congress of Racial Equality and anti-poverty groups, became the first executive director of the NWRO.

The NWRO fought for welfare rights at the national level while acting as a communication hub for the many state and local groups around the country. They created a plan to increase the availability of welfare supports, create access to consumer credit for poor women, and to create a "guaranteed annual income" that placed a minimum figure on financial support.[11] To achieve these aims, and many others, the NWRO pursued a strategy that historian Annelise Orleck has called "protest in the streets and negotiation in the suites."[12] The results of protests, sit-ins, and even threats of violence were more successful locally than nationally, but national campaigns sent a powerful message to welfare recipients that affirmed their value and encouraged them to claim their rights.

The welfare rights movement coincided with the women's movement in the 1960s and 1970s. Organizers like Tillmon quickly drew connections between feminism and the welfare movement. In 1972, Tillmon wrote an article for *Ms.* magazine that has become a landmark. "Welfare Is a Women's Issue" placed women's poverty and welfare support at the center of American feminism.[13] In a now famous passage, Tillmon compared welfare to a "super-sexist marriage." In her words, "You trade in a man for the man. But you can't divorce him if he treats you bad. He can divorce you, of course, cut you off anytime he wants. But in that case, he keeps the kids, not you. The man runs everything. . . . The man, the welfare system, controls your money. He tells you what to buy, what not to buy, where to buy it, and how much things cost. . . . He's always right."[14] Drawing on her experience in California, Tillmon gave "the man" a name, Governor Ronald Reagan, who called welfare recipients "lazy parasites," "pigs at the trough," and, when he later ran for president, "welfare queens." For Tillmon, women fighting for welfare rights were the "front-line troops for women's freedom," not because there weren't other women fighting for other issues, but the "right to a living wage for women" was a "right to life itself." Of course, welfare was deeply connected to other major feminist issues such as reproductive freedom and abortion. Stereotyped as hyper-sexual, Black women were portrayed as having children as a way to get higher welfare payments. To this line of thought, Tillmon countered: "People still believe that old lie that AFDC mothers keep on having kids just to get a bigger welfare check. On the average, another baby means $35 a month—barely enough for food and clothing." Historian Premilla Nadasen has argued that Tillmon's feminism challenged cultural ideals of family structure that subordinated women and forced them to be dependent on men. For Tillmon part of the stigma associated with welfare was that attached to single mothers who were castigated for not conforming to a nuclear family ideal. To counter the stereotype of the welfare mother as an African American woman who was unmarried but sexually active, who did not want to work but wanted a government check, Tillmon and the NWRO began a campaign to recognize motherhood and "women's work" as "real work." In other words, they wanted people to reimagine welfare as a living wage paid to women for what had always been the unpaid labor of childrearing and housekeeping.[15]

Given that 99 percent of welfare households were headed by women, it was only a matter of time until growing feminist consciousness of welfare activists led them to question the structure of the NWRO. Although headed by a Black man, George Wiley, the organizing staff in Washington, DC, was primarily made up of middle-class white men. So, even as the NWRO argued against stigmatization of poor, their own organization reified boundaries and power differences based on class, race, and gender. This created resentment among the Black women in the organization who saw themselves as doing what needed to be done, but not getting to make decisions about what needed doing. Tillmon, herself a former welfare recipient, urged greater inclusion of welfare recipients in the organization. While she supported Wiley, she recognized the importance of self-determination for women on welfare. In her words, "It wasn't women organizers against men organizers. Or it wasn't white organizers against Black organizers. . . . Our thing was recipient versus the establishment."[16] Tillmon wanted welfare recipients to be able to determine their own futures. The white middle-class men at the NWRO had a place, but as support staff, not leaders.

In addition to growing tensions among the staff at NRWO, financial problems were beginning to create a strain as the organization fell into debt. As public perception of welfare recipients grew more negative, organizations, such as various Protestant denominations, that had previously offered financial support did not renew their contributions. While Wiley was an accomplished fundraiser, he could not find enough income to cover NWRO's expenses in the early 1970s and resigned in 1972.

Tillmon was named the new executive director and given the incredible task of healing divisions within the NWRO and making it solvent. In the announcement of this transition, Wiley acknowledged the importance of having Tillmon take over, saying, "All along the welfare rights organization has been about proving that welfare recipients, especially women, are capable of leadership. Mrs. Tillmon came up through the ranks and through her achievements represents the many poor, Black women who are moving more and more into responsible roles."[17] Tillmon tried to change the culture of the NWRO but growing national criticism and lack of private funding support meant the organization was doomed.

When the NWRO declared bankruptcy in 1975, Tillmon returned to Los Angeles. Certainly discouraged, Tillmon nevertheless did not give up on the welfare rights movement. The movement, she claimed, "is different but still alive."[18] She attended the 1977 National Women's Conference as the NWRO representative delegate.[19]

A welfare plank had always been part of the National Action Plan, but the original proposal circulated to the state committees was conservative and out of line with the reforms advocated by activists. The initial welfare proposal circulated in the briefing document assumed a policy focus that ignored context entirely.[20] The briefing document sent to state committees included a timeline of important events beginning with Nixon's ad hoc Task Force on Women's Rights and Responsibilities which called attention to the "training needs of impoverished young women." Reflecting an uninterrogated idea about the family found in the Moynihan Report, the timeline claimed that "For many girls living in poor or disorganized families, the inability to find a job means turning to prostitution or other crimes—or having a child to get on welfare. Potential husbands do not earn enough to support an unemployed wife."[21] This kind of equation of morality and sexuality ignored economic (or structural) realities, while at the same time erasing medical realities. When the Report was written, birth control for unmarried individuals was illegal in twenty-six states and abortion was legal in only six states.

This initial welfare proposal called for a federal guarantee of equitable payment in order to account for cost-of-living differences by state, educational, and training support, including childcare, healthcare, and transportation for parents of children over preschool age to allow them to "get off welfare," and special programs to "train AFDC parents for jobs that provide more than subsistence wages." In addition to considering mothers with children at home, the summary background noted that with the median income for women over sixty-five, almost half that of similarly aged men that a minimum guaranteed income "would help millions of elderly women who after lifetimes of caring for their families are left the poorest of the aged."

While these proposals appear in the twenty-fifth plank, they were substantially changed at the conference. The title of the plank itself reflects the radicalness of this shift. The subject is not welfare, the subject is Women, Welfare and Poverty. This reflects the kind of statistics that went out with the briefing report, such as in 1976, twice as many women lived below the poverty line as men and "of the 24.3 million poor people in the US, 19.6 million are women and children." The new plank begins with the call that government should assume a role focusing on welfare and poverty "as major women's issues."

The plank extends the analysis of equity to one that focuses on economic opportunities: "the elimination of poverty must be a priority for all those working for equal rights for women." This jeremiad seems as focused on policy and government priorities just as other participants were on the call for equal rights. What feminist could support an Equal Rights Amendment that ignores the fact poverty acts as a barrier to women who are "subject to the multiple oppression of sexism, racism, and poverty—and they are often old or disabled." What might be called an intersectional analysis makes abundantly clear that the only plank that leads with the word women does so because it is a universal issue for all women. Should this not prove enough of a call for action, the revised plank continues, admonishing that structural issues means that many other women "are just one step away from poverty." Enumerating the way in which issues seemingly covered by calls for equality, especially rooted in middle-class concerns, threaten to come up short: "discriminatory employment practices, social security laws, differential education of men and women and lack of adequate child care."[22]

The resolution cast welfare and poverty as an intersectional issue when it explicitly argued that women in poverty were "subject to the multiple oppression of sexism, racism, and poverty—and they are often old or disabled."[23] In addition, the resolution asked for improvements to social security, childcare, health insurance, and legal support. President Jimmy Carter's proposed welfare reform bill was also called out for its proposed cuts to foods stamps, job training, and day care. He had run on a platform of welfare reform, allowing the message chameleon-like "to help people hear what they were listening for." In the words of Joseph Califano, Carter's Secretary of Health, Education, and Welfare, "Carter never had to say precisely what welfare reform meant to him . . . in one speech stressing simplification; in another, a 'uniform national payment, varying according to cost-of-living differences between communities'; in yet another, eliminating 'waste.'"[24] By the time he proposed reform, Carter's promise to overhaul welfare would be undertaken with no additional funds for reform and with the outcome of cutting valued programs, like CETA, the Comprehensive Employment And Training Act, which trained enrollees in marketable skills.

Some delegates, notably those more concerned with national politics and unfamiliar with the challenges of trying to support a family on AFDC, proposed an amendment eliminating any criticism of the Carter administration's welfare reform. This led to a hard-fought floor battle, one reflected in the jubilance of the celebration of its passage. With signs in the crowd demanding "Wages for Housework" and "Welfare is a Women's Issue," Christine Marsten, Frankie Jeter, and Beulah Sanders read the new resolution. As Caroline Bird remembers the event, "The substitute resolution was adopted by an overwhelming vote after delegates defeated an amendment to eliminate censure of the Carter administration welfare reform bill."[25] The passage of the Women, Poverty, and Welfare plank affirmed the fight for welfare as a women's issue at the national level. This moment on the national stage was significant, and worth celebrating as Diana Mara Henry's photograph portrays.

In Henry's photograph we see the radicalness and optimism of the moment in 1977 when it looked like the country could contemplate considering poverty as a woman's issue. More importantly, we can see the embodiment of a movement that centered Black women's wages as a means to understand the complicated relationship between all labor and wealth. We see something else in the photograph. Johnnie Tillmon stands beside Beulah Sanders, wearing a beautiful pillbox mink hat, even in Houston in November when the daytime temperature averaged seventy degrees. This hat, described by Prescod, as one she wore everywhere meant that she felt she had the right to wear something that made her feel beautiful and decorated with an item associated in the 1970s with luxury. Yet, none of the historical descriptions or books written about Sanders mention this fact about her.

Part of the reason for this may be what came after this moment in time. Just as Marjorie Spruill's work helps us understand that the Houston Conference of 1977 helped to politicize Christian Evangelicals, we need to remember that this era helped usher in a president who used claims about welfare abuse to secure his election. As historian Julilly Kohler-Hausmann notes, publicized efforts, like Reagan's, to shrink welfare rolls, instead of focusing on the broader economic context of the 1970s recession and the recognition of discriminatory practices that had served to exclude whole segments of the population from government support had been called into account by a multiracial movement primarily of women. The reaction to this, in a context of slipping economic resources, led to "the intensity of public vitriol against welfare recipients [that] not only emboldened proponents of tough welfare reforms in the legislature (and chilled their critics) but also steered the campaign in subtle ways, for example toward concern about recipients' access to consumer goods and services."[26] If we look closely at this photograph, we can see the before and after of this moment. Even as Reagan hit on the topic that would define his 1980 campaign, "the Welfare Queen," his 1976 version included abuse that did not document what she looked like. Referring to a story by George Bliss in *The Chicago Tribune*, Reagan described abuse by an unnamed woman who used eighty names, and thirty addresses to collect around $150,000 a year, notably, not only from Welfare and Food Stamps but also from Social Security and in the most explicit discussion "Veteran's benefits from four non-existent deceased veteran husbands."[27] Reagan did not call for limits to Veteran's benefits or to Social Security but by the time he ran again two years later, his discussion of "the Welfare Queen" would feature her "mink coat." Indeed, discussions of Linda Taylor's appearance in court in 1977 for welfare fraud focused almost exclusively on her insistence on wearing a black mink coat, complete with sun-shaped broach. But the coverage before this moment did not focus on women's clothing. It focused on fraud. Rather than linking the abuses to an overtaxed system, with more and more demands and fewer and fewer resources, the 1980 election used the shorthand image of a criminal wearing a mink coat, who extraordinarily defrauded the system, to decry all AFDC recipients. It is no wonder that historians intent on telling the story of the NWRO as progressive did not find anyone who in retrospect spoke of Sanders's mink hat.

Conclusion

After Houston, Tillmon returned to Los Angeles and continued working on behalf of welfare recipients.[28] She passed away at age sixty-nine, just a year before President Bill Clinton replaced AFDC with the Temporary Assistance for Needy Families (TANF) program. While TANF mobilized a new wave of welfare activism, the need had never gone away. Susana Downic's 1987 report on the National Plan of Action ten years after Houston noted that "Poverty in general, but especially among women and children, has deepened and spread in the last decade, while programs such as Food Stamps, low-income housing, supplemental food for pregnant women and infants have been reduced by over $50 billion since 1980. The 'feminization of poverty' has been well documented."[29] Johnnie Tillmon's story embodies the history of the continual feminization of poverty, especially among Black women. But, more importantly, her story embodies resistance to the systems that create poverty and maintain it in communities of color whether through racial stereotype, false ideals of femininity and the family, or legislation that punishes women and children in need.

Notes

1. Premilla Nadasen, *Welfare Warriors: The Welfare Rights Movement in the United States* (New York: Routledge, 2005); Felicia Ann Kornbluh, *The Battle for Welfare Rights: Politics and Poverty in Modern America* (Philadelphia: University of Pennsylvania Press, 2007).

2. Premilla Nadasen, "'We Do Whatever Becomes Necessary': Johnnie Tillmon, Welfare Rights, and Black Power," in *Want to Start a Revolution? Radical Women in the Black Freedom Struggle,* eds. Dayo F. Gore, Jeanne Theoharis, and Komozi Woodard (New York: New York University Press, 2009), 320.

3. Nadasen, *Welfare Warriors.*

4. Nadasen, "'We Do Whatever Becomes Necessary,'" 320–21.

5. Guida West, *The National Welfare Rights Movement: The Social Protest of Poor Women* (New York: Praeger, 1981), 17; Premilla Nadasen, "'Mothers at Work': The Welfare Rights Movement and Welfare Reform in the 1960s," in *The Legal Tender of Gender: Welfare, Law and the Regulation of Women's Poverty,* eds. Shelley Gavin and Dorothy Chunn (Portland, OR: Hart Publishing, 2010), 104.

6. By 1964, ANC Mothers had gained the respect of welfare recipients and case workers as they helped families throughout Watts and argued for expansion of childcare for single mothers. Childcare was a central issue for women on welfare. Without affordable childcare, they could not work. A decade later, in recognition of this important push for basic resources, Mollie Taylor and two other women from ANC Mothers created a childcare center in Watts, naming it after Johnnie Tillmon, who had first organized around this issue. Allison Puglisi, "Identity, Power, and the California Welfare-Rights Struggle, 1963–1975" *Humanities* 6 (2017): 1–12; Annelise Orleck, *Storming Caesar's Palace: How Black Mothers Fought Their Own War on Poverty* (Boston: Beacon Press, 2014), 108.

7. Puglisi, "Identity, Power, and the California Welfare-Rights Struggle;" Nadasen, "'We Do Whatever Becomes Necessary,'" 322.

8. Orleck, *Storming Caesar's Palace,* 115.

9. Kornbluh, *Battle for Welfare Rights,* 59.

10. Kornbluh, *Battle for Welfare Rights,* 59–60.

11. Nadasen, "'We Do Whatever Becomes Necessary,'" 323.

12. Orleck, *Storming Caesar's Palace,* 115.

13. Johnnie Tillmon, "Welfare Is a Women's Issue," *Ms.* magazine, 1972; reprinted in *Ms.* magazine in 1995 and 2002.

14. Tillmon, "Welfare Is a Women's Issue."

15. Nadasen, "'We Do Whatever Becomes Necessary,'" 329.

16. Nadasen, "We Do Whatever Becomes Necessary," 331–32.

17. "Mrs. Tillmon Succeeds Dr. Wiley As NWRO Head," *Cleveland Call and Post,* Jan. 20, 1973.

18. West, *National Welfare Rights Movement,* x.

19. National Commission on the Observance of International Women's Year, *The Spirit of Houston: The First National Women's Conference; An Official Report to the President, the Congress and the People of the United States* (Washington, DC: US Government Printing Office, 1978).

20. Document 146: US National Commission on the Observance of International Wom-

en's Year. *National Women's Conference Official Briefing Book: Houston, Texas, November 18 to 21, 1977* (Washington, DC: National Commission on the Observance of International Women's Year, 1977), 243.

21. Chronology of Women's History, Prepared by Catherine East, Deputy Coordinator of the US Department of State's Secretariat for International Women's Year, for use by the US National Commission on The Observance of International Women's Year, 1975, with grateful acknowledgment to Judy Hole and Ellen Levine. Address of the US National Commission is D/IWY, Room 1004, Department of State, Washington, DC 20520.

22. Of the twenty-six planks, five name women and all might be seen as addressing the issue of poverty: Battered Women, Disabled Women, Minority Women, Older Women, and Rural Women. It's unclear if the organizers for these planks felt the need to reiterate the belonging of women often not depicted in the press as belonging to the feminist community as women, but like the Women, Welfare and Poverty plank, these focused on making abundantly clear that these women could not be removed from the National Women's Conference. These were women, too.

23. "Plank 25: Women, Welfare and Poverty," in National Commission on the Observance of International Women's Year, *The Spirit of Houston,* 93–96.

24. Joseph A. Califano Jr., "Welfare Reform: A Dream That Was Impossible," *Washington Post,* May 22, 1981.

25. Caroline Bird, "Houston Day by Day," in National Commission on the Observance of International Women's Year, *The Spirit of Houston,* 119–70, 167.

26. Julilly Kohler-Hausmann, "Welfare Crises, Penal Solutions, and the Origins of the 'Welfare Queen,'" *Journal of Urban History* 41, no. 5 (2015): 756–771.

27. Kohler-Hausmann, "Welfare Crises."

28. West, *National Welfare Rights Movement.*

29. Susanna Downic, "Welfare and Poverty," in *Decade of Achievement: 1977–1987: A Report on a Survey Based on the National Plan of Action for Women* (Washington, DC: National Women's Conference Committee, 1988), 69–70.

11

Addie Wyatt

Bridging Social Movements

MARCIA WALKER-MCWILLIAMS

Figure 11.1. Addie Wyatt (*left*) stands with fellow National Commission member Ersa Poston (*right*) backstage at the convention. Poston was the first black woman appointed to the Federal Civil Service Commission. Despite different political leanings (Poston was a Republican), both women shared a commitment to improving economic opportunities for women. Diana Mara Henry Papers (PH 51). Special Collections and University Archives, University of Massachusetts Amherst Libraries. Copyright © Diana Mara Henry / dianamarahenry.com.

WHEN BELLA ABZUG, head of the National Commission on the Observance of International Women's Year introduced fellow commissioner Addie Wyatt as chair of the conference's final plenary, women in the audience began to sing the labor tune, "Solidarity Forever." Wyatt, one of the highest ranked African American women in the labor movement, was known to lead the song in labor gatherings. She would ask everyone to join hands while singing the song, literally reinforcing the theme of solidarity. When Wyatt finally took the podium, she chose not to address the convention in her own words, but to open her brief remarks by reciting the lyrics of Carole Etzler's feminist anthem, "Sometimes I Wish My Eyes Hadn't Been Opened." The song explores the awakening of a woman who was once blind to, but eventually comes to see the oppression women face. Etzler likens the slumber to slavery, an unfree state of being that kept women suspended and unable to move forward. She describes the stages of awakening or becoming woke, from the painful realization that one was in fact unfree to longing for ignorance once again. The song eventually transitions to woman understanding her place in a protracted struggle for freedom with others who have awakened to finally resolving to fight for that freedom. The final verse of the song reads:

> Sometimes I wish my eyes hadn't been opened
> But now that they have, I'm determined to see
> That somehow my sisters and I will be one day
> The free people we were created to be.[1]

Etzler's song was a call to consciousness inspired to move women toward collective action against their oppression. Wyatt hoped the lyrics might inspire greater cohesion and solidarity among the women in attendance. Immediately following her recitation of the song, she reminded those in attendance why they were there: "We have arrived here this morning, I hope sincerely for the intent of doing what is necessary to bridge the gap between the promise and the fulfillment of freedom, equality and the fullest opportunities possible for women in America and women in the world."[2] Wyatt, an ordained minister, asked for God's blessings on their efforts and a commitment to rededicate themselves to moving American women forward. For Addie Wyatt, consciousness-raising, organizing, and forming coalitions were all essential steps in building sustainable social movements and positive change. The 1977 National Women's Conference was one such step, intended as a space for consciousness-raising, deliberation, and debate on the pathways to free women from discrimination and improve the experiences and outcomes of their lives.

. . .

That Addie Wyatt presided over the final session of the National Women's Conference is significant. The conference was not a coming out for Wyatt or a moment of crowning achievement on a national stage, but rather a moment not unlike others in Wyatt's decades as an organizer and leader in labor, religious, civil rights, and women's struggles, where finding common ground among disparate perspectives was essential to building movement solidarity and sustainable positive social change. Diana Mara Henry's photograph captures Wyatt backstage at the NWC looking serious and determined, holding a sheaf of papers. Next to her is Ersa Poston, the first Black woman appointed to the Federal Civil Service Commission. Despite different political leanings (Poston was a Republican), both Wyatt and Poston shared a commitment to improving economic opportunities for women.

Wyatt's commitment to movement building began in the 1940s in the labor movement fighting for bread and butter issues like maternity leave, equal pay for equal work, an end to discrimination in job classifications and promotions, and affordable childcare. She also advocated for affirmative action, greater leadership opportunities for women and minorities in the labor movement and for an end to racism, sexism, and ageism in and outside of the workplace. Her involvement with social movements grew even further with her community and faith-based activism in Chicago's Altgeld Gardens Housing Project from the mid-1940s to the mid-1950s, and her support of the Montgomery Bus Boycott, the Fayette County Tent City movement, and the Selma voting rights marches. Her commitment to movement building is also visible through the grassroots and organizational leadership posts she held within the women's movement.

Wyatt and her husband founded the Vernon Park Church of God in Chicago in 1955 and Wyatt became an ordained minister in 1968. She co-pastored the church with her husband and occasionally served as minister of music, hence her strategy of employing song to galvanize gatherings. Wyatt was one of only a few women to seek and gain ordination in the Church of God (Anderson, Indiana), a reformation movement originating in the late nineteenth century that adhered to the principles of spiritual unity with others and a belief in the social gospel. In part inspired by her unshakable Christian faith and informed by her struggles against racism, sexism, and classism, Wyatt developed and adhered to a theology of equality that an enduring and collective struggle for human equality would yield tangible results. Wyatt's faith and theology of equality fell in line with, rather in opposition to social justice movements and the liberation of those burdened by racism, sexism, classism, and other forms of oppression.

Her desire for human dignity beyond difference undergirded her push for labor, gender, and racial equality, often placing her at odds with the Religious Right and those who held more conservative beliefs about the roles of women within the church and society. Though devoted to advocating for labor, civil rights, and women's rights, Wyatt never hesitated to criticize these movements for racism and sexism evident within them. Movement organizing and leadership were so essential for Wyatt because they provided pathways to address her intersectional identity: "I find myself as a Black woman oft times fighting on three fronts—the workers front, the Black front, and the female front—trying to overcome all of these pressures. And I get a three-fold impact of all of these discriminations, 'isms.'"[3] What Black feminist scholars would theorize as intersectionality in the late 1980s, Wyatt had lived and organized around since the 1940s.

Born in Brookhaven, Mississippi, in 1924, Addie Wyatt (née Cameron) migrated with her family to Chicago in 1930, where she would live for the majority of her life. The family worshipped at Langley Avenue Church of God and Addie spent quite a bit of time there as a child singing in the choir and honing her skills as a budding gospel pianist. Her parents, Ambrose and Maggie, struggled to find stable employment during the Great Depression and the family experienced deep poverty. In 1940 at the age of sixteen, Addie married her high school sweetheart, Claude Wyatt Jr., and the couple had two sons, Renaldo and Claude Wyatt III, in 1941 and 1943, respectively.

In need of employment to help provide for her family, Wyatt eventually found work in the meatpacking industry as a canner at Armour & Company in 1942. Race- and sex-based job classifications kept Black women out of the front office as clerical workers and confined to the dirtiest jobs for female workers. It was on the job and through her union, the United Packinghouse Workers of America (UPWA), that Wyatt learned of the dual oppressions of race and sex bearing down on her. Several times she had to utilize the union apparatus to fight unfair demotions. In her first few months working at Armour in one of its interracial, though all-female departments, Wyatt filed her first grievance when a supervisor pulled her off the line and replaced her with a white woman, which overrode Wyatt's seniority and demoted her to a lower pay grade. Wyatt and the union shop steward who represented the grievance, an African American woman named Van Johnson, were successful and Wyatt regained her original post. The UPWA was one of the most progressive unions at the time in terms of its embrace of antidiscrimination and maternity leave, but the union was still dominated by white and male leadership. Black women held shop level influence as stewards, but struggled to get higher leadership positions. In 1955, Addie Wyatt broke through the barrier and became the first African American female president of her local union, UPWA Local 56. She also served on the UPWA's women's affairs, antidiscrimination, and civil rights committees. After one year of leading the local, the head of the UPWA's District One, Charles Hayes, promoted Wyatt to international union representative. In this post, Wyatt traveled throughout the Midwest handling grievances for a largely white membership inhospitable to her presence as a Black woman and unable to see her as an ally in their fight for fair working conditions and wages. Through it all, Wyatt came to see the union as a viable vehicle for collective organizing, recognizing that building solidarity and equality had to start from within the union.[4]

Wyatt's organizational affiliations provide significant insight into the ways in which women's issues simultaneously spanned across a number of groups concerned with labor rights, civil rights, and women's rights. It was precisely Wyatt's activism in the labor movement and experience in mass-based coalitions that led to her appointment on President Kennedy's Commission on the Status of Women (PCSW) in 1961. In exchange for Eleanor Roosevelt's support and endorsement in the 1960 presidential election, Kennedy established the PCSW and placed Roosevelt at the helm. The two-year appointment put Wyatt in contact with a cadre of women from religious, civic, political, and labor organizations from across the country.[5] The goal of the PCSW was to investigate the status of American women and to provide recommendations for addressing prejudice and discrimination against women. Yet from the start, the PCSW navigated tensions between committee members who supported protective labor legislation with some key adjustments, legislation that held separate standards and working conditions for women, and those who supported the Equal Rights Amendment (ERA), a proposed amendment to the United States Constitution which states, "Equality of rights under the law shall not be denied or abridged by the United States or by any State on account of sex." The ERA was first introduced to Congress in the 1920s and proposed annually thereafter.[6] Proponents of the ERA argued that protective labor legislation allowed companies to keep women relegated to "women's work" and less earning power. In the end, the PCSW recommended paid maternity leave, greater access to adult education, state level equal pay for equal work laws, greater access to promotions on the job, but did not endorse the ERA. Wyatt was proud of her appointment to the commission as a member of the Protective Labor Legislation Committee, she voiced her concerns in committee meetings and to her comrades in the UPWA that the committee's report did not have adequate input from women at the local level. Wyatt argued that it was working women who needed to debate the impact of protective labor legislation and the Equal Rights Amendment and have their voices represented in the report.[7]

In October of 1963, just two months after Wyatt attended the March on Washington for Jobs and Freedom as a labor ally, the Commission on the Status of Women submitted their report to President Kennedy. Little was done at the national level to enforce and put into motion the recommendations of the commission—greater involvement of women in political affairs, increased opportunities for higher education, better childcare services, upgrading the status of household employment, equal pay, and maternity benefits for women.[8] One of the outcomes of the commission was the formation of an independent organization, the National Organization for Women (NOW) in 1966 to implement the recommendations made in the 1963 report.[9] NOW founders included a number of women who were members of the PCSW, including civil rights activist, lawyer, and women's rights activist Pauli Murray who helped name and define the mission of NOW, a feminist organization dedicated to improving the lives of women and advocating their political, economic, and social rights to full equality with men. Wyatt attended NOW's first national conference but was not a founder of the organization. Though active in the women's movement in the 1960s, Wyatt placed most of her focus on addressing the plight of working women, specifically labor union women.

Wyatt's involvement in the women's movement did grow throughout the 1960s and 1970s, alongside her commitment to civil rights and organizing within Black communities. She was instrumental in the founding of Operation Breadbasket in Chicago as well as with organizations like the League of Black Women. She was still committed to the labor movement as the best vehicle for enhancing the lives of working women, but she was also critical of ongoing racial and sex discrimination within organized labor. Greater numbers of women and minorities were joining unions but faced significant barriers in job classifications and promotions as well as in union leadership. By 1968, the UPWA merged with the larger less progressive Amalgamated Meat Cutters and Butcher Workmen. Despite this shift, Wyatt became even more outspoken about the need to diversify the labor movement and promote greater access to organization and leadership by workers of color and women workers.

In the early 1970s, Wyatt became a fierce proponent of the Equal Rights Amendment and campaigned nationwide for its ratification after Congress finally passed it in 1972. Nearly a decade after the PCSW, labor women were still divided on the ERA with some opposing the amendment for fear that it would spell an end to protective labor legislation. Others opposed the amendment because they believed it was anti-family and would disrupt traditional gender relations in the home, the workplace, and all areas of life. Wyatt saw the ERA as a legislative tool with the potential to impact not only the progress of the women's movement but working men and women of all races. The ERA fit within her own philosophy of equality as an essential human right and she successfully advocated for her union, the Amalgamated Meat Cutters, to endorse the amendment.

In 1972, alongside longtime friend and ally Charles Hayes, Wyatt helped found the Coalition of Black Trade Unionists (CBTU). The mission of CBTU was to provide a voice for Black trade unionists on political, economic, and social issues in and outside of organized labor and to train future generations of Black labor leaders. In 1974, Wyatt and a small cadre of women labor leaders, including some who had served on the PCSW, formed a similar organization for working women, the Coalition of Labor Union Women (CLUW). According to Wyatt, CLUW addressed the fact that few women in organized labor were visible in the burgeoning feminist movement even though working women had been advocating for equal pay, seniority rights, maternity leave, and respect on the job for at least two decades. Women were also not prevalent in adequate numbers in union leadership: "We did not have women at the table in the labor movement speaking for women on the economic issues. We had to get them there, to train them and to be sure that they were inspired and willing to be a part of the struggle for better jobs and working conditions."[10] Over 3,000 women attended CLUW's founding convention in Chicago, about a quarter of whom were African American.

Wyatt saw the formation of CLUW as a necessary voice for working women in the women's movement and in the labor movement. CLUW sought to bring more women into the fold of feminism and labor by encouraging women to participate in their locals, districts, and at the international level as both members and leaders. It sought to organize unorganized women workers and increase women's awareness of discrimination and help women to lobby for political legislation that would ease the plight of working women.[11]

Not unlike the divisions that would emerge in the 1977 National Women's Conference, CLUW's first convention sparked much debate and tension. Some attendees opposed CLUW's support for the controversial Equal Rights Amendment, while others expressed concerns that CLUW's leadership (all union officers) had an agenda separate and apart from that of rank and file union women and were not radical enough in their demands for equality in the labor movement. Wyatt argued that the leadership of CLUW were women who had in a sense paid their dues by coming up through the ranks organizing and leading unions in the 1950s and 1960s. She also recognized the generational differences among labor women and saw the convention deliberations as a frustrating, though necessary step in creating open communication and solidarity within CLUW. Wyatt served as the organization's first national vice president. She and other Black women leaders in CLUW including Clara Day, Ola Kennedy and Gloria Johnson, mentored younger Black women coming up through the ranks of the labor movement. The formation of CLUW placed Wyatt again on the national stage as a key leader in the women's movement and the labor movement. In 1976, she became International Vice President of her labor union (one of two women on the international board) and head of the union's Department of Women's Affairs, which she had lobbied for. That same year, she was honored as one of *Time* magazine's Women of the Year along with US representative Barbara Jordan, tennis star Billie Jean King, and others.

Addie Wyatt's appointment to the National Commission on the Observance of International Women's Year was not the start of her involvement in the women's movement. Nor was it a break from the women's movement. Rather her involvement with the commission was a continuation of decades of activism on behalf of working women and women of color. In the months leading up to the 1977 National Women's Conference, Wyatt participated in four of the state gatherings sponsored by the commission to raise awareness for the national conference, elect state delegates and debate the issues affecting women. Wyatt recalled her experiences at the state conferences:

> this was to be a time when women in these states would come together to talk about their status and changing roles and to make recommendations to the government on the steps that they felt were needed in order to improve these conditions and to adequately deal with the problems that American women still face. It seems to me that in most of the state conferences that I attended (and I think this true for almost all of them) the women were divided in what was considered pro-ERA and anti-ERA groups. This, I felt was regrettable because it hindered the women in getting together to talk about the real problems they face and it polarized them into at least two diverse groups . . . even though we know all of us might have priorities on our agendas, special interests that meet our particular needs, none of us will really be able to achieve them unless we have some sharing together, whether we agree or disagree.[12]

For Wyatt, years of working in the labor movement as a skilled and successful organizer ingrained in her an appreciation for the importance of establishing bonds of common ground that came only through sharing one's experiences with others. Operating often from a place of difference—be it as a Black woman in the white, male-dominated American labor movement, as a woman in the male-dominated clergy, and as a Black woman in a predominantly white women's movement, Wyatt was accustomed to breaking down or through barriers by finding points of common interest or struggle to win others toward a movement or a vision of equity and justice. From Wyatt's vantage point, the division of women into pro- and anti-ERA contingents, prematurely foreclosed on the opportunity to build common ground. Such a stalemate would not only limit the productivity of the state level conferences but could derail the National Women's Conference and the progress of the women's movement.

Tensions between conservative factions of women and men led by STOP ERA head Phyllis Schlafly, and those in support of the National Commission and the National Plan of Action which embraced the ERA, abortion rights, and sexual preference planks came to a head at the conference in Houston.[13] The inability of some women at the conference to acknowledge and understand the problems of women from different backgrounds frustrated Wyatt: "you had some of them who believed in racism. They were really racist. They did not want to see Black and white women working together. There were some who did not believe in women of all economic classes coming together."[14] Though Wyatt was no stranger to debates and divisive issues in movement building, the inherent tensions between factions at the conference cast a shadow over the proceedings and were captured in the media and memoirs of the conference.

· · ·

It was within this context that Wyatt stepped to the podium on the final day of the 1977 National Women's Conference and recited the lyrics to Carole Etzler's song, likely hoping to invoke a greater solidarity and shared sense of mission for the thousands of women in attendance. Despite significant and contentious debate among conference delegates and attendees, Wyatt and other members of the IWY Commission endorsed a National Plan of Action including a motion to create a committee to oversee a future conference and further action on the plan.[15] The National Plan of Action contained twenty-six planks, ranging from an endorsement of the ERA, full employment and national healthcare coverage, to the rights of welfare mothers and lesbian women, to the calling of legislation to address child abuse, rape, and domestic violence and put an end to the discrimination of women in business, education, and politics. The National Plan of Action also included a plank on minority women, specifically curated by minority women at the conference representing Asian/Pacific American, Hispanic, American Indian, Puerto Rican, and Black women.

When legislation authorizing the IWY Commission expired in 1978, President Carter established the National Advisory Committee for Women (NACW) with Bella Abzug and Carmen Votaw as cochairs. The commission worked hard to get a meeting with President Carter to discuss ways to implement the endorsed National Plan of Action and the level of support they could expect from the Carter administration in the year following the Houston Conference. But Carter, embroiled in the public fallout from the conference, conservative backlash, and other issues, was hesitant to provide much support. On November 22, 1978, a "ceremonial" meeting was scheduled between the committee and Carter, for fifteen minutes, hardly the outcome that the committee wanted and certainly not indicative of the time they felt they deserved with the president. Wyatt was among a contingency of committee members who voted not to attend the meeting, believing that little would be accomplished in a fifteen minute "ceremonial" meeting which they took as a slight and a signal that Carter's support for their mission had waned significantly under conservative pressure.[16] A wider rift grew between the Carter administration and the NACW after the failed meeting and by January of 1979, President Carter fired Abzug as cochair of the committee. Addie Wyatt was one of twenty-three committee members who resigned from the NACW in protest.[17]

After the 1977 National Women's Conference, Wyatt continued to organize for labor, gender, and racial equality. Through yet another union merger, she became head of the Department of Women's Affairs and Civil Rights in the United Food and Commercial Workers (UFCW) in 1979. The position required Wyatt to develop and/or maintain relationships with major civil rights and women's organizations. This was not difficult, given Wyatt's extensive networks in both movements. But Wyatt also had a desire to continue to represent workers and push for greater racial and gender equality in the union. The UFCW had a membership of 1.2 million and Wyatt struggled with the distance between her position as a leader in a more bureaucratic union and rank and file workers. The principles of collective action and solidarity were harder to achieve in her union and in the rapidly changing labor movement.

• • •

Wyatt increased her support for the ERA after the conference. Speaking before the Detroit Chapter of the National Organization for Women (NOW) in 1982, Wyatt extolled the importance of the ERA for Black communities: "Black women and men realize its passage will have a more beneficial effect on our community than on any other, because the Equal Rights is a bread and butter issue. Make no mistake, the amendment is a basic struggle for economic equality. As Black women, we have a special stake in any measure that strengthens our own and our families' well-being."[18] Wyatt argued that Black women had to rally behind the legislation and support it even though it appeared as if the ERA was dying a slow death: "To sentence E.R.A. to death is to sentence our mothers, grandmothers, our men also, to a life of eternal inequality. . . . Why should E.R.A be reduced to a 'women's issue'? It is a human issue, a family issue, a national issue, with implications for the world."[19] Despite support from ERA proponents, opposition to the ERA remained too steep and the amendment was never ratified.

. . .

Not all of Wyatt's movement endeavors ended in vain. A year before she retired from the UFCW in 1984, Wyatt supported the historic campaign of Harold Washington to become the first Black mayor of the city of Chicago. She played a prominent role on the Women's Network for Washington Committee which fundraised, canvassed and promoted Washington's campaigns in 1983 and 1987. The multiracial coalition of women included prominent leaders like Wyatt as well as local everyday women who appreciated Washington's commitment to bringing greater racial, economic, and gender equality in the city of Chicago and city government. Once in office, Washington tapped more women to become heads of city commissions, agencies and departments than any of his predecessors.

. . .

Wyatt's activism waned in the mid to late 1990s, but she left an indelible imprint on the labor movement, women's movement, Civil Rights Movement, and religious movement. While we must acknowledge the need for and achievements of the Black feminism, we must also acknowledge women like Wyatt who played important roles standing at the intersections of the mainstream women's movement and Black feminism.

Notes

1. Carole Etzler, "Sometimes I Wish My Eyes Hadn't Been Opened." Sisters Unlimited.

2. *Sisters of '77: The Struggles and Triumphs in the Battle for Equal Rights,* directed by Allen Mondale (1977; Media Projects, Inc., 2005), DVD.

3. Addie Wyatt, Interview by Elizabeth Balanoff, Oral History Project in Labor History, Roosevelt University, 1977, Chicago, IL.

4. Marcia Walker-McWilliams, *Faith in the Struggle: Reverend Addie Wyatt and the Fight For Labor, Gender and Racial Equality* (Urbana: University of Illinois Press, 2016), 86–88.

5. The commission contained seven separate committees: civil and political rights, education, federal employment, home and community, private employment, protective labor legislation, and social insurance and taxes.

6. Mary Frances Berry, *Why ERA Failed: Politics, Women's Rights, and the Amending Process of the Constitution* (Bloomington: Indiana University Press, 1986), 121.

7. Walker-McWilliams, *Faith in the Struggle,* 108–111.

8. President's Commission on the Status of Women, *American Women,* Reverend Addie Wyatt and Claude Wyatt Papers, Box 117, Folder 8, Vivian G. Harsh Research Collection, Chicago Public Library.

9. Addie Wyatt, interview by Joan McGann Morris, Working Women's History Project, UIC Chicago Labor Education Program, December 14, 2002, Chicago, IL.

10. Addie Wyatt, interview by Joan McGann Morris, Working Women's History Project, UIC Chicago Labor Education Program, December 14, 2002, Chicago, IL.

11. Philip S. Foner, *Women and the American Labor Movement: From the First Trade Unions to the Present* (New York: The Free Press, 1982), 442–46; Silke Roth, *Building Movement Bridges: The Coalition of Labor Union Women* (London: Prager, 2003), 5.

12. Proceedings of State Meetings, President's National Commission on the Observance of International Women's Year, September 1977, Wyatt Papers, Box 140, Folder 6, Harsh.

13. Marjorie J. Spruill, *Divided We Stand: The Battle over Women's Rights and Family Values That Polarized American Politics* (New York: Bloomsbury, 2017), 1–2.

14. *Step by Step: Building a feminist movement,* directed by Joyce Follet (Women Make Movies, 1998), DVD.

15. *Sisters of '77.*

16. Shelah Gilbert Leader and Patricia Rusch Hyatt, *American Women on the Move: The Inside Story of the National Women's Conference, 1977* (Lanham, MD: Lexington Books, 2016), 121.

17. Leader and Hyatt, *American Women on the Move,* 121–22.

18. Addie Wyatt, "E.R.A. and beyond: the future of the women's movement in the black community," NOW Detroit Chapter, April 2, 1982. Wyatt Papers, Box 6, Harsh.

19. Ibid. The original ratification deadline for the ERA brought before congress in 1972 was June 30, 1979. In 1978, that deadline was extended to June 30, 1982. The ERA remains politically controversial and to date has not been ratified as a constitutional amendment. For a lengthier discussion on the trajectory and politics of the ERA, see Mary Frances Berry, *Why ERA Failed;* Donald Critchlow, *Phyllis Schlafly and Grassroots Conservatism: A Woman's Crusade* (Princeton, NJ: Princeton University Press, 2005); and Jane Mansbridge, *Why We Lost the ERA* (Chicago: University of Chicago Press, 1986).

IV

The Politicians

TO BLAZE A TRAIL, one must have vision and innovation and be able to serve as a pioneer and champion for causes, even when hope is hard to come by. To blaze a trial, one must be willing to work, especially when nothing around you is functioning properly. Blazing a trail is something you "do," like politics. While politics govern and organize our daily lives, it is the work of politics that brings politics to center stage. Whether studying the field, drafting legislation, organizing the community, fundraising, marching, or picketing—this is what doing politics look like, and *The Politicians* are no stranger to work.

Barbara Jordan, Shirley Chisholm, C. Delores Tucker, Yvonne Burke, and Maxine Waters were trailblazers. Women who played the game and did the work to improve the conditions of their respective communities. While also encouraging women, especially women of color, to get involved in politics at all levels of scale. The Politicians were visible. They were here to bring the unseen and unheard stories to the fold. They are our voice, when we have been rendered silent.

12

Barbara Jordan

Conveying the Charge and the Challenge

CAMESHA SCRUGGS

Figure 12.1. Barbara Jordan is emphatic at the National Women's Conference. Diana Mara Henry Papers (PH 51). Special Collections and University Archives, University of Massachusetts Amherst Libraries. Copyright © Diana Mara Henry / dianamarahenry.com.

CONSIDER TWO PHOTOGRAPHS of Representative Barbara Jordan at the National Women's Conference in Houston. In the first, Jordan stands before the assembled delegates powerfully delivering the opening keynote address. There is an ease and familiarity in her stance. She is in her hometown. As an elected representative, she is an experienced speaker, debater, and attorney. Her speech articulated a joint sense of purpose for the meeting: as always making the case for equality and the passage of the Equal Rights Amendment. As a Black woman, she understood that this unprecedented national conference could create unstoppable momentum toward legislation. In the second photograph, Jordan smiles broadly as conference attendees throng the stage after her speech seeking to shake her hand and get an autograph. Moments later another photograph captures her sitting at the edge of the stage on a folding chair signing the conference program for her fans and supporters. In the hundreds of photographic images created at this meeting, there is no other of a crowd celebrating a speaker in this way. Jordan was certainly a national figure and a local celebrity, but she made herself available to her supporters. She appreciated the importance of rallying public support in order to create legislative change, especially when it came to racial and gender equality.

Through an examination of selected speeches beginning with the declaration of International Women's Year, leading up to and including the National Women's Conference keynote address, we see Jordan's focus evolve from race-centered to women-inclusive issues. Jordan's actions as an elected representative demonstrated a similar evolution as seen with legislation she drafted, supported, and endorsed as a Texas state senator and house representative. However, civil rights remain at the core of her political life.

Jordan's speeches reflected the acknowledgment of her intersectionality by being a Black woman. This recognition is not new. Prior to her legislative tenure, she recognized the challenge in college and through the legal cases she tried. These challenges served as a catalyst to implore her audiences to continue the efforts of passing legislation and advocating for change. I argue that Jordan's lived experiences directly impacted how she curated her voice, using it to convey the challenge of equal rights; simultaneously, giving the charge to her listeners to participate in the process.

On August 22, 1977, Barbara Jordan received a letter from New York attorney, politician, and women's rights activist Bella Abzug, a key figure in the revival of legislative rights for women on a federal level. The letter was a formal request and invitation for Jordan to "participate in the National Women's Conference as a speaker . . . address the plenary body on the morning of November 19, 1977 at approximately 11:30 a.m."[1] As a result of the efforts of Abzug

Figure 12.2. Barbara Jordan greeting supporters. Diana Mara Henry Papers (PH 51). Special Collections and University Archives, University of Massachusetts Amherst Libraries. Copyright © Diana Mara Henry / dianamarahenry.com.

and others, President Jimmy Carter created a commission devoted to advancing women's rights, known formally as the National Advisory Committee for Women. Abzug wanted Jordan to deliver the keynote at the National Women's Conference meeting in her hometown of Houston, Texas. Jordan, a Congressional representative from Texas, was integral to the Equal Rights Amendment movement in Texas politics. In her letter, Abzug lauded Jordan for the impression she made at the Pennsylvania Women's Conference meeting in Pittsburgh on June 25, 1977.[2] In Jordan's Pittsburgh speech, which she titled "Womankind," she encouraged women to continue fighting for women's rights, specifically for the Equal Rights Amendment (ERA). The ERA was a proposed constitutional amendment designed to ensure that regardless of sex or marital status, all women had rights as citizens. This amendment would protect women from unfair labor practices, and end discrimination regarding divorce and property rights. Jordan explained the ERA as a means to "true equality for all Americans."[3] She charged the audience to educate other women about this issue. She told them, "If we are to succeed in our equal rights campaign our first task remains the winning over of other women to our point of view, [because] many women continue to be ill-informed."[4] Jordan probably had in mind, opposition from women such as Phyllis Schlafly, a lawyer and conservative activist that supported "family values." To answer women like Schlafly, Jordan invoked a familiar tactic in the women's movement, consciousness-raising: "Our strategy—[will be] different women working in different ways to raise the consciousness of all Americans—[including] men and women."[5] In Jordan's words, "all these impediments can be overcome if women accept the challenge to exert their political prowess."[6] Encouraging Black women to make their voices heard in the fight for equality was a constant theme in Jordan's speeches in the years leading up to the conference.

Abzug felt that Jordan would be ideal because of her previous work regarding women's rights in addition to the fact that this meeting was being held in Houston, TX. This was the collaborative efforts of Jordan and Abzug on House Resolution 8093—To Direct the National Commission on the Observance of International Women's Year to Organize and Convene a National Women's Conference and House Resolution 9924—National Women's Conference.[7] Since Jordan had represented the 11th district in the Texas Senate and the 18th district in the US House of Representatives, she had experience and knowledge of her constituents and their legislative concerns. This experience, in addition to interactions with various women across social, economic, and political lines as a student and attorney, qualified her as an ideal speaker who could encourage activism among such a diverse group of attendees. Jordan accepted the invitation on September 9, 1977, and corresponded with Abzug on the specific details.[8] However, long before this invitation to the national stage, Jordan had already been charging audiences to rise to the challenges of civil and women's rights.

While a student on the Texas Southern University debate team, Jordan demonstrated that she was the equal of her male counterparts. This is when Jordan "put aside her feminine wardrobe and haircuts and began to look more androgynous."[9] With this new look and strong debate skills, she built the reputation of the team by winning tournaments against well-known schools.

Jordan's interest in debating and politics led her to Boston University Law School, where she was exposed to postwar discrimination against women in the legal profession. She recalled that her professors rarely called on women in class and said, "We were just tolerated. We weren't considered really top drawer."[10] She persevered and received her law degree from Boston University in 1959. After graduation, she successfully passed the Massachusetts and Texas State Bar exams and went into private practice in Houston with some of her earlier cases including divorce proceedings for female clients.[11] Her early career moves followed trajectories similar to other pioneering Black women in the legal profession such as Pauli Murray, Flo Kennedy, and Edith Sampson.[12] These women examined and practiced legal cases that were foundational within the civil rights and women's rights arenas by demonstrating that collective efforts were necessary in order to progressively move the country toward gender equality.

After returning home, Jordan realized that nothing was actually happening with regard to women's equality and decided that "The only way to move things along was to get into a position where you could implement the laws." Eventually, this became an impetus for going into politics, in addition to her commitment to address issues around race.[13] After two unsuccessful campaigns in 1962 and 1964, she was elected to the Texas Senate in 1966. In addition to being the first Black woman, she was the first Black state senator elected after Reconstruction at the state and federal level. Throughout the political campaigns and career, she was told that her identity was a challenge. She was, a Black woman and "People don't really like that image."[14] Yet, she thought "they were just side issues and that people were going to ignore that."[15] She remembered this initial disparagement and reminded future listeners how little these personal slights mattered in the broader context of women's rights. Through her speeches and actions, Jordan simply went about the task of making changes in Texas and national politics. As she reflected on her time in the Texas Senate, she thought about how important her defiance of any traditional role was. To her mind, defying expectations, not only racial but also gender expectations was key. As her biographer Shelby Hearon put it:

> She made it clear there would be no need to rewrite the rules . . . she didn't look like their dear old mother, and she didn't look like their beauteous young girlfriend, so none of the old patterns needed to operate. Here was someone cut from a different mold, who, being outside their standard frame of reference would not disrupt it.[16]

However, Jordan's views on her legislative career reflected an intersectional understanding of her position, one that insisted on both the gendered and racial aspects of her identity. Specifically, she wrote, "I am a member of two groups long discriminated against . . . but I discovered that the weight of those factors, are a part of what I am."[17]

Jordan became the first congresswoman elected to represent Texas in the US House of Representatives by her own right in 1972. As a congresswoman, she gained equality with fellow colleagues, using similar tactics to the ones honed during her debate team days. With support from President Johnson, she was elected to the House Judiciary Committee. In this position, she garnered national attention during the Nixon impeachment hearings with her important opening statement on July 25, 1974. To the viewing audience, her "honest, forceful voice"[18] presented the case against Nixon and the constitutional grounds for impeachment.[19] After 1974, the nation knew Jordan's voice and appreciated its impact.

That year marked the same year that Jordan began her involvement with the International Women's Year. In a speech marking the beginning of the US efforts in 1974, Jordan laid out what the government hoped to accomplish through the passage of the Equal Rights Amendment.[20] As a legislator and representation of intersectional identities, Jordan was drawn to this work of women's rights and civil rights. Although initially, she felt that she was unqualified to do so. According to an interview with her biographer Mary Beth Rogers, Jordan felt that her "reaction to women's rights was more ambiguous. Not having been married, . . . [I] had not dealt firsthand with such chattel-status matters as credit discrimination or loss of contractual autonomy."[21] However, her experiences in Boston and her law practice in Houston had made her aware of the disenfranchisement of women. As a legislator, Jordan witnessed the reluctance of Congressional bodies to legislate women's rights on a federal level, because she appreciated the significance of legislation for women's rights and how it would advance the rights for all people, commitment to women's rights became a hallmark of Jordan's political career.

Of course, Jordan did not separate race and gender in her understanding of her experience or her legislative agenda. Early in her career, Jordan had focused more on racial equality than on gender equality. While she may not have been a direct participant in the Houston Civil Rights Movement, she was certainly aware of it. Indeed, Jordan's affinity for the law reflected a desire to work for civil rights as a young woman. By the mid-1970s, her speeches began to combine the elements of race and gender. For example, in a speech given at the Black Caucus Dinner on September 29, 1974, she reminded her audience of the significance of the occasion. She praised the honorees Myrlie Evers, Coretta Scott King, Betty Shabazz, and Margaret Young; widows of Medgar Evers, Martin Luther King Jr., Malcolm X, and Whitney M. Young, all considered civil rights pioneers. She spoke of how these women suffered tremendous personal loss in order for the Nation to realize the importance of civil rights. Undeterred by the cost, she encouraged her listeners to take up the same fight and continue to work toward civil rights, including women's rights. This was controversial at the time because many Black women did not collectively see themselves as participants in the struggle for gender equality. Speaking to the Black women in the audience, she challenged them to fight against sexism within their communities and "to open up the consciousness of America, [which] should prepare them in the future to forge a new concept of freedom in America."[22] A year later, Jordan spoke to Black women's experience more directly. In her April 15, 1975, speech to the National Caucus on the Black Aged, Jordan declared that "The Black woman has had a hard time of it. She is conditioned by a lifetime of problems that are degrading and dehumanizing . . . we need to seek out what the needs are, who the recipients are before we can do battle."[23] Jordan acknowledged that the need for equal rights was even more acute for Black women than it was for white women. Her work as a legislator reflected this understanding.

Jordan sponsored legislation recommending a creation of the Commission on the Status of Women. Known as Texas Senate Bill 13, she had begun her legislative work on women's issues in the Texas Senate during the 62nd regular session in 1971. The purpose of this commission had been to "study all subjects relating to the status of women," which included employment, education, medical needs, childcare, and implications of social attitudes.[24] Her work resulted in the passing of the Fair Employment Practices Act in Texas in 1972, leading to the development of the state's Fair Employment Practices Commission and provided for the regulation of discriminatory acts in employment. Enacted as Texas Senate Bill 79, the purpose was to "regularly discriminate acts in employment."[25] Specifically, making it illegal to "discriminate against individual or to limit, segregate, or classify its membership in any way that would tend to deprive the individual of employment opportunities, limit his employment opportunities or otherwise affect adversely his status as an employee or as an applicant for employment, or that would affect adversely his wages, hours, or conditions of employment, on the account of race, color, religion, national origin, sex, or age of the individual."[26] These efforts established Texas as progressive regarding policies on gender and employment, making it an ideal location for the National Women's Conference in 1977 and serving as a foundation for Jordan's later efforts. This was evident through Jordan supporting forty pieces of legislation reflecting the purposes of the commission that she supported as an elected official in Texas. Her efforts extended to the federal level when she served in the House of Representatives from 1973 until 1979.

Jordan continued to advance the cause of women's rights in speeches leading up to the National Women's Conference. In her November 10, 1975, speech at the Women in Public Affairs Symposium meeting in Austin, Texas. She warned the audience "it would be a disastrous moment to rest and contemplate how far we have come along the trail behind us. There must be no let-up now, no slackening of effort. Everything depends on sustaining the momentum of equality for all."[27] Nearly a year earlier, in a speech with the same title, "International Women's Year: The Challenges We Face" she tells the audience that they should "sincerely hope that 1975 will be a year in which American women will develop and exert their full capacities as individuals and as citizens in the search for peace and economic prosperity at home and abroad."[28] As she returned home to Houston, she continued her duties as an elected official through various speaking engagements. On December 14, 1975, she delivered remarks at the Bethune Centennial Recognition Dinner and raised a major question, aligning with the goals of the conference by asking, "Can the discriminated woman be expected to maintain hope for the future?"[29] As a woman of color celebrating the life of Mary McLeod Bethune, Jordan is valid in her inquiry. She pledges to continue doing the work as a legislator and advocate for women's rights. Eventually, she modified her views on women's issues and "intellectually endorsed and voted for the ERA and federal aid for abortion."[30] Jordan's speech at this event is significant because she wanted the audience to realize that the efforts of women like McLeod Bethune set the precedent upon which the audience must continue to build. Just like Mary McLeod Bethune, they were marginalized by race and gender. Yet, that was not a deterrent to advance for equality by any means.

• • •

In 1977, Jordan along with other participants were preparing to come to Houston. In her hometown, she speaks to her constituents in preparation for this event during a congressional break. Explicitly, she speaks to her sorority and charges them to be active in the efforts for Black families and the community at large. In her January 8, 1977, speech at the Delta Sigma Theta Sorority banquet, she reminds them of their founding values:

> The impetus for reform must come from the Black community, [because] congress will never enact meaningful reform unless we demonstrate that those who have the most to gain or lose—the members of the Black community-are willing to address the problem, we can bring to bear on the problem those things that are most intangible yet most important: a feeling of concern that no bureaucrat can convey.[31]

Jordan encourages her sorority sisters to join with other social and political organizations to advance the causes and concerns of the Black family. Using the Moynihan Report in addition to the recent publication and broadcast of Alex Haley's *Roots*, she reminds her sorors that they must help to build a family and do the work. Delta Sigma Theta Sorority, Inc. was represented at the 1977 conference as an organization, with Dorothy Height, civil rights activist and former president of the organization.

On November 19, 1977, Jordan was introduced to the audience by former First Lady, Lady Bird Johnson. Her mother Arlyne and sisters Bennie and Rose Mary were invited guests to the conference.[32] After graciously accepting the accolades and introduction, Jordan proceeds to elucidate the audience on their purpose at this conference. In this speech, Jordan tells the crowd the mission of the conference is to achieve "total recognition and total inclusion."[33] In this speech, she admonishes the women using *Proverbs* 31 as a foundational text. She tells them to go "from virtue to power. What we are about here now will require no small amount of virtue and a great deal of power."[34] Jordan is cognizant of the diversity of women at the conference and tells them it "is inclusive; everybody is here and everyone must be free to define the meaning of total women, for himself. The differences among us at this Conference cannot and should not be ignored."[35] She places emphasis on these words by underlining the words "cannot and should not," in her original draft version of the *Opening Session* speech, preserved in her papers.[36] Using the archetype of Wonder Woman, she reminds the audience that the collective power they possess is a prerequisite necessity in order to achieve the goals of this conference. In her standard manner, using her mother's oratory and grandmother's language and diction influences, she educates the crowd of the legislative measures taken to ensure this conference. She reminds the crowd of the distinguishable characteristics of the United States, particularly, the rights of the individual. Yet she highlights that "The differences among us at this conference cannot and should not be ignored."[37] She focuses on the humanity within these rights which is enveloped in her request that "Intra-women's movement rancor must be displaced by interdependence and mutual respect."[38] She reminds them of the charge that they have been given in addition to the challenge that she places before them. Using biblical principle and extemporaneous flair, she summates it and ends her speech with asking the questions "What will you reap? What will you sow?"[39]

Abzug's selection of Jordan as a keynote speaker for the National Women's Conference was significant for various reasons. According to the invitation letter, Jordan would "set the right tone for the important and challenging work ahead."[40] As a college and law school student, Jordan was aware of the inequity based on gender. As a native Houstonian, Jordan had been fighting for half of her constituents since she began her legislative career. During her time in the Texas Senate, she was instrumental in the passage of fair employment practices. During her tenure in the House of Representatives, Jordan sought equity for women through acts such as the Equal Credit Opportunity Act, providing fairness in business loans given to women, providing them with economic tools for advancement.

Being aware that she is a representation of the intersection of race and gender, she admonishes audiences to advocate for legislation that is beneficial to a larger group. In some speeches, Jordan acknowledges that she is a symbol of intersectionality. In her *Democratic Woman of the Year* acceptance speech in 1975, she spoke of being, "Barbara Jordan, the symbol" which gives the audience an evidentiary sense of progress. She mentions this intersectionality again in her infamous Democratic National Convention speech in 1976 through the acknowledgment that "a Barbara Jordan [was asked] to make a keynote address."[41] Abzug, a New York delegate, is seen during the television broadcast of the address. As the camera pans on her, she is shown to be in awe of the audience's captivity to Jordan's words and listens intently.[42] The impression must have been indelible enough for the request to be submitted a year later in an invitation letter on behalf of the National Commission on the Observance of the International Women's Year and hopes for Jordan to "participate in this historic event in Houston."[43]

Notes

1. August 22, 1977, correspondence from Bella Abzug to Barbara Jordan, Congresswoman Barbara C. Jordan Papers, 1936–1996, 1979BJA001, Special Collections, Texas Southern University (cited hereafter as "Jordan Papers"), box 246, folder 7.

2. August 22, 1977, correspondence from Bella Abzug to Barbara Jordan, Jordan Papers, box 246, folder 7.

3. Barbara Jordan, "Womankind," Pittsburgh, Pennsylvania, text, June 25, 1977 (https://texashistory.unt.edu/ark:/67531/metapth611526/m1/4/: accessed December 30, 2020), University of North Texas Libraries, The Portal to Texas History, https://texashistory.unt.edu; crediting Texas Southern University (cited hereafter as "Texas History").

4. Jordan, "Womankind."

5. Jordan, "Womankind."

6. Jordan, "Womankind."

7. Bills and House Resolutions 1973–1978, Jordan Papers, box 168, folders 13 and 15.

8. September 9, 1977, correspondence from Barbara Jordan to Bella Abzug, Jordan Papers, box 246, folder 7.

9. Barbara Jordan and Shelby Hearon, *Barbara Jordan, A Self-Portrait* (Garden City, NY: Doubleday and Co., 1979), 78.

10. Jordan and Hearon, *Barbara Jordan*, 92.

11. Mary Beth Rogers, *Barbara Jordan: American Hero* (New York: Bantam Books, 1998), 77.

12. For additional information on these women, read Pauli Murrray's autobiography *Song*

in a Weary Throat and Florynce Kennedy's autobiography *Color Me Flo: My Hard Life and Good Times.* At this time, a biography has not been written for Edith Sampson. The Edith Spurlock Sampson Collection is housed in the Schlesinger Library at the Radcliffe Institute for Advanced Study, Harvard University.

13. Jordan and Hearon, *Barbara Jordan*, 105.

14. Jordan and Hearon, *Barbara Jordan*, 115.

15. Jordan and Hearon, *Barbara Jordan*, 116.

16. Jordan and Hearon, *Barbara Jordan*, 113.

17. Jordan and Hearon, *Barbara Jordan*, 148.

18. Jordan and Hearon, *Barbara Jordan*, 197.

19. Rogers, *Barbara Jordan*, 218.

20. Barbara C. Jordan, International Women's Year: The Challenge We Face, text, December 21, 1974 (https://texashistory.unt.edu/ark:/67531/metapth611270/: accessed January 1, 2021), Texas History. However, Jordan is a little unsure and places her hope that women's rights would be resolved by the year 2000 as evidenced in her marginalia of the archived speech draft which displays "year 2000?" inscribed in pencil, suggesting room for change.

21. Rogers, *Barbara Jordan*, 213.

22. Barbara Jordan, 1936–1996. [Remarks of Barbara Jordan, Black Caucus Dinner Speech, September 29, 1974], text, September 28, 1974 (https://texashistory.unt.edu/ark:/67531/metapth595149/: accessed January 14, 2021), Texas History.

23. Barbara Jordan, The Aging Black Woman and Federal Policy, text, April 15, 1975 (https://texashistory.unt.edu/ark:/67531/metapth594988/: accessed January 14, 2021), Texas History.

24. Texas Senate Archives, Austin, TX. Texas Senate Bill 79, 62nd Regular Session. Passed February 25, 1971. https://lrl.texas.gov/legis/billsearch/text.cfm?legSession=62–0&billtypeDetail=SB&billNumberDetail=79&billSuffixDetail= Accessed December 31,2020.

25. Texas Senate Archives, Austin, TX. Texas Senate Bill 79, 62nd Regular Session. Passed February 25, 1971. https://lrl.texas.gov/legis/billsearch/text.cfm?legSession=62–0&billtypeDetail=SB&billNumberDetail=79&billSuffixDetail= Accessed December 31,2020.

26. Jordan and Hearon, *Barbara Jordan*, 149.

27. Barbara C. Jordan, International Women's Year: The Challenge We Face, text, November 10, 1975 (https://texashistory.unt.edu/ark:/67531/metapth611495/: accessed January 14, 2021), Texas History.

28. Barbara C. Jordan, International Women's Year: The Challenge We Face, text, December 21, 1974 (https://texashistory.unt.edu/ark:/67531/metapth611270/: accessed January 14, 2021), Texas History.

29. Barbara Jordan, Speech for Bethune Centennial Recognition Dinner, text, December 14, 1975 (https://texashistory.unt.edu/ark:/67531/metapth595373/: accessed January 1, 2021), Texas History.

30. Jordan and Hearon, *Barbara Jordan*, 214.

31. Barbara Jordan, Saving the Family, text, January 8, 1977 (https://texashistory.unt.edu/ark:/67531/metapth611268/: accessed December 1, 2020), Texas History.

32. September 9, 1977, correspondence from Barbara Jordan to Bella Abzug, Jordan Papers. Box 246, Folder 7.

33. Jordan Keynote Speech National Women's Conference, 1977.

34. Jordan Keynote Speech National Women's Conference, 1977.

35. November 18, 1977, Opening Speech draft, Jordan Papers. Box 246, Folder 7.

36. Jordan Opening Speech Draft National Women's Conference, 1977. Notes and comments from the opening speech draft were converted to the Keynote Speech for the National Women's Conference.

37. Jordan Keynote Speech National Women's Conference, 1977.

38. Jordan Keynote Speech National Women's Conference, 1977.

39. Jordan Keynote Speech National Women's Conference, 1977.

40. August 22, 1977, correspondence from Bella Abzug to Barbara Jordan, Jordan Papers. Box 246, Folder 7.

41. DNC Address July 12, 1976, NYC draft Jordan Papers. Box 266 Folder 2.

42. https://www.youtube.com/watch?v=fo_Lo73FMow Barbara Jordan Democratic National Convention Keynote Speech 1976, Part 3. TSU Jordan Archives. Accessed December 27, 2020.

43. August 22, 1977, correspondence from Bella Abzug to Barbara Jordan, Jordan Papers. Box 246, Folder 7.

13

Beyond the Symbolism

Shirley Chisholm, Black Feminism, and Women's Politics

ZINGA A. FRASER

ON JANUARY 31, 2014, the United States Postal Service unveiled a stamp of Shirley Chisholm, the first Black woman elected to Congress and the first African American and woman to run for president from a major party. The portrait used for the US Postal stamp captures a serious Chisholm with pensive eyes peering from her black spectacles and short black wig. Juxtaposed with the colorful rendering of her orange and blue background is Chisholm's stoic expression and partial frown. No smiles or partial smirk, the artist's bold strokes of her face and eyes solidifies an image of Chisholm that was uncompromising. However, the pictures of Chisholm's early Congressional career reveal a charismatic woman that was not outrageously irate but one who was determined, inviting, and compassionate. Chisholm's jubilant Congressional picture used for her news releases and district newsletters contradicts and corrects print media's depiction of her as angry and emasculating. This framing easily reflected national and local anxieties about Black women in power.

Aware of the media's fascination with her, Chisholm had to confront how her visual presence would play a role in shaping her political life. Chisholm would have to juggle with how certain leadership traits like ambition, boldness, and strength usually associated with male leaders would be seen as incongruous with common characteristics for women in electoral politics. On the one hand, Chisholm and other Black women in electoral and grassroots politics would have to navigate between historical controlling images of Black women that depict them as controlling and emasculating "matriarchs."[1] On the other hand, they would have to contend with the perception that women possess an inherent weakness, subsequently making them ineffective for the rough and tumble world of politics. Black Congressional women like Chisholm, who was an accomplished educator, and Congresswomen Barbara Jordan and Yvonne

Figure 13.1. Shirley Chisholm, 1977. Diana Mara Henry Papers (PH 51). Special Collections and University Archives, University of Massachusetts Amherst Libraries. Copyright © Diana Mara Henry / dianamarahenry.com.

Burke, who were both attorneys, stood in the face of gendered criticisms that Black women were not qualified for public office.

Diana Henry's photograph of Chisholm at the 1977 National Women's Conference captures her determined and compassionate gaze.[2] Chisholm's physical appearance with her coiffed salt-and-pepper wig and flower-embroidered top was consistent with her choice of colorful and bold patterns along with her lush furs that did not conform to the formal Congressional uniform of gray and black suits. Chisholm's style reflected a generational Black women's respectability, associated with tailored suits and dresses. Her incorporation of vibrant textures and colors, along with accessories, represented a non-conventional personal style that easily linked her to radical politics that placed her as an outsider within mainstream politics.

Chisholm's legislative platform revolved around taking a resolute stand against economic, social, and political injustices.[3] Embracing the radical rhetoric and politics of the Black Power Movement she crafted tag lines like, "fighting Chisholm" and the coinage of her mantra "Unbought and Unbossed." Such language served as political markers that she was a political independent who was not beholden to powerful political machines like Brooklyn's Democratic Party. As a Black woman, being "Unbought and Unbossed" was a refutation against a racialized and gendered framing that would otherwise suggest she was subordinate or fearful of direct confrontation. Hence, Chisholm articulated a new political style in women's leadership: one defined by a refusal to be reserved or quiet. As she explained to feminist journalist Susan Brownmiller, "One thing the people in New York and Washington are afraid of is HER MOUTH."[4]

While Chisholm's name is permanently etched in American history due to the honor and burden of being a first, her twenty year political life is largely unfamiliar within American and feminist history. Chisholm's erasure is inextricably linked to the stifling power of symbolism that only sees her symbolic representation instead of her legislative and political accomplishments. The public remembrance of her historic firsts, while essential to ensuring that she is not forgotten, also creates a conflict between her symbolism and legacy. In part, the creation of a heroic Chisholm has minimized her long political life that consisted of significant criticism.

Although Chisholm was an effective politician that was able to mobilize both grassroots and traditional political activists, the framing of Chisholm solely as a passionate activist, robs her from a larger intellectual discourse within American politics. Chisholm operates as what scholar Carol Boyce Davies describes as a "radically transformative intellectual"; her praxis is organized around the production of knowledge that transforms the social contexts in which we live and operate.[5] In the 1970s Chisholm operates as a public intellectual through her speeches, interviews, and articles in accessible publications like the *Black Scholar, Ms.,* and *McCall's.* In her article titled, "I'd Rather Be Black Than a Female" Chisholm discusses the pervasiveness of sexism and how it maintains women's subordinate status in every segment and sphere of society. She argues that "what we need is more women in politics, because we have a very special contribution to make. I hope that the example of my success will convince other women to get into politics—and not just to stuff envelopes, but to run for office."[6] If we look at the totality of Chisholm's politics and intellectual work, we can place her among a number of activist—intellectuals like Fannie Lou Hamer and Florynce Kennedy who sought to transform how America embodies its democratic ideals of equality and justice.[7] What this does is place Chisholm within a larger narrative of the feminist movement that does not isolate the movement but explores the collaborative way in which Black feminist leaders worked within the Black Power and Women's movement.

Shirley Anita St. Hill was born in 1924 to working-class Barbadian parents. Although a native of Brooklyn, Chisholm spent her formative years in Barbados with her maternal grandmother and two sisters, due to the economic hardships faced by her parents in Brooklyn during the Depression. The vulnerability of being poor, Black, and Afro-Caribbean created a heightened sensitivity and understanding of racial and economic oppression. For both African American and Caribbean American families, the attainment of education was seen as the main pathway to alleviate generational poverty. Chisholm excelled academically in Barbados and Brooklyn. As a high school senior at Brooklyn's Girls High she received acceptances from Oberlin and Vassar College. Due to her family's limited means she chose to attend Brooklyn College in the fall of 1942. Brooklyn College was part of the three New York City universities that were tuition free.[8] As an assemblywoman, Chisholm would help pass legislation entitled, Search for Education, Elevation and Knowledge (SEEK) that currently provides aid for New York State low-income students to attend college. Ironically, Chisholm would argue that going to Brooklyn College instead of Vassar freed her from becoming "one of the pseudo white upper-middle class Black professionals or a doctor's wife with furs and airs."[9]

Coming of age in the early 1940s, Chisholm was influenced by her father's admiration of activist Jamaican Marcus Garvey. In this way, her ideological roots were similar to many Black political activists in New York City whose direct or indirect ties to Garvey's Pan-Africanism influenced their desire to pursue their own racial self-interest that took various forms—one being a fight for Black political representation.[10] Chisholm would become a beneficiary of a decade-long community effort by Black activists to create a Black Congressional seat.[11]

By 1960, Chisholm joins Brooklyn's political clubs as a volunteer. As she referenced in her book *Unbought and Unbossed*, the women in Brooklyn's Democratic political clubs were relegated to "envelope stuffers" and excluded from leadership positions.[12] Her move to the Unity Democratic Club that was progressive for the time having a number of women in leadership positions, allowed Chisholm to build a base that would be essential for her to run for political office. No longer satisfied with just supporting Black male candidates and helping Black men enter public office she runs for Brooklyn's 17th Assembly district without major party support. Chisholm's campaign revealed the sexism and the financial disadvantages for women who seek public office. Her victory in both the Democratic primary and general election stemmed from her strategic understanding that gender provided both political advantages and limitations. While the inability of Black male leadership to see Black women in leadership positions was pervasive, Chisholm's experience as a political volunteer also informed her of the invisibility of Black women as a voting constituency. Chisholm's campaign and electoral win helped energize the districts most consistent voting constituency, Black women. Women's organizations like the Brooklyn branch of the Key Women of America, a women's civic organization, served as an integral piece of Chisholm's success.[13] One of the members proclaimed, "We all got in and pitched for her. We went with petitions and everything. We were actually her backbone."[14] Although various racial, ethnic, and gendered constituencies would align themselves with Chisholm and her issues, Black women would serve as her most loyal base.

After her election to the New York State Assembly in 1965, Chisholm benefited from the local and political transitions occurring in New York and Washington. Chisholm crafted a legislative agenda that centered the economic and racial disenfranchisement of minority communities at the center of public discourse as a response to the Civil Rights Act of 1964 and Lyndon B. Johnson's war on poverty.[15] As a former day care administrator, she sponsors Assembly Bill 1250, that would provide single mothers and or families assistance with child day care. Her bill for domestic workers to receive unemployment insurance set the groundwork for what would later become New York State's Domestic Workers' Bill of Rights. The Domestic Workers' Bill of Rights provided unemployment insurance for domestic workers that created a safety net for poor and minority women who operated as the state's domestic worker population. Her legislation around welfare, domestic labor, and education is a clear example of Chisholm's Black feminist politic.

By 1967, two years after Chisholm entered the State Assembly, the creation of Bedford-Stuyvesant's 12th Congressional district created the first opportunity for the predominantly Black community to select Brooklyn's first Black Congressional member. Brooklyn's Black leadership automatically assumed the seat was ordained for a Black man. Chisholm argued, "I almost killed myself because I wanted to show the machine that a little Black woman was going to beat it."[16] Chisholm's continual efforts against the political establishment co-incided with her campaign slogan and political ideology of being "Unbought and Unbossed." As a political ideology, "Unbought and Unbossed" reflected Chisholm's political autonomy from machine politics and her efforts to dismantle status quo politics.[17] Her bold and principled status endeared her to both a local and national constituency. As the underdog and "political outsider," Chisholm's ability to win the Democratic primary solidified that she was not only a strategic politician but also her ability to mobilize a grassroots and multiracial voting constituency.

Chisholm articulated a rebellious Black politics that was irrevocably connected to transforming gender politics. The pervasiveness of a Black masculinist politics within the Black Power era erupts in her campaign against civil rights activist and former national CORE director James Farmer. Despite Farmer's longtime residency in Harlem and his decision to run on the Republican and Liberal ticket in a majority Democratic district, his national exposure and financial backing created a highly competitive race for Chisholm. Farmer's campaign proclaimed him as a "militant Black independent" where his maleness served as the sole criteria for qualifying him as the most viable candidate.[18] Reacting to the campaign's sexist tone, Chisholm utilized what Farmer perceived as a handicap around her gender and re-crafted a strategy that connected her to a broad constituency of marginalized voters in the district, specifically Black women.

After one year in Congress, Chisholm was asked to serve as an honorary president of the National Association for the Repeal of Abortion Laws (NARAL). Having supported abortion reform in the New York State Assembly, she cautiously accepted NARAL's request.[19] Placing abortion on her legislative agenda was a major political decision for any Congressional member but especially for a Black freshman congresswoman. Chisholm's articulation of Black and Puerto Rican women's economic and social reasons around reproductive justice issues in her Congressional special-order speech, the "Abortion Question," highlighted the everyday struggles Black and brown women who had the highest incidences of death from illegal abortions. Beyond the political backlash within Congress, Chisholm's promotion of abortion and birth control placed her in direct opposition to a Black nationalist rhetoric that equated abortions and birth control to a tradition of Black genocide in the United States.[20] Chisholm's Black feminism, simultaneously addressed how reproductive rights were inextricably linked to the fight for women of color to also assert their rights to motherhood and equitable childcare and family planning.

As a congresswoman, Chisholm continued to challenge the exploitation of working-class women and their families by proposing a bill to increase the minimum wage for domestic workers. In an interview with the *Washington Post* she provides this anecdote describing the everyday experiences of domestic workers.

The typical wage earners in this country work 9 to 5 and consider that a full day. A household worker's day begins at 6:30 or 7 a.m. when she feeds her own family, and takes the children to school and takes the baby to the sitter. After a long bus ride, she makes breakfast for her second family, housecleans for the day, makes lunch, dinner . . . and when the last dinner dish is wiped, starts the long ride home again. She has to stretch out her budget with food stamps and clothes from Goodwill.[21]

Chisholm's statement enumerates the plight of Black domestic workers. Lenient tax enforcement allowed from middle- and upper-class white women to manipulate a system that did not require them to pay Social Security benefits for their workers, thereby excluding them from receiving workers' benefits.

Five years prior to the 1977 National Women's Conference, Chisholm's 1972 presidential election attempted to break the ultimate glass ceiling in American politics. Historically the framing of Chisholm's 1972 presidential campaign is seen under the lens of failure, rather than a political experiment for political liberation for marginalized communities. For white feminists, Chisholm's 1972 election would identify the fragility of the feminist movement's attempts to materialize its efforts to increase the number of women in public office. In her presidential announcement speech, she proclaimed,

I am not the candidate of Black America, although I am Black and proud. I am not the candidate of the women's movement of this country, although I am a woman and equally proud of that. I am not the candidate of any political bosses or fat cats or special interests. I stand here now without endorsements from any big politicians or celebrities or any other prop. I am the candidate of the people of America. And my presence before you now symbolizes a new era in American political history.[22]

Chisholm's speech and campaign strategy revolved around her operating as the "people's candidate" where she established broad based alliances and coalitions between students, new voters, poor and working class, minorities and women of all races. Even though her campaign was poorly funded, her efforts to run a grassroots national campaign attracted loyal supporters who sought to transform American politics from the top. Chisholm's progressive stances around the termination of the war in Vietnam, affordable education, reinvestment in programs around poverty, women's rights, environmental reform and expansion of civil rights legislation attracted a broad base of progressive voters and volunteers to her campaign. Organizations like the National Organization for Women, the National Women's Political Caucus (of which Chisholm was a founding member) and the Feminist Party spearheaded by Flo Kennedy who was not only a Chisholm delegate but creator of a coalition of Black and white feminists to support Chisholm's campaign and serve as delegates—had the rare opportunity to elect a woman of their own.[23]

While many white feminists symbolically supported the idea of the first woman president, many could not substantially endorse Chisholm's campaign over the Democratic nominee George McGovern due to the unlikeliness of her win. Similarly, Chisholm would not receive the endorsement of her male Black colleagues from the Congressional Black Caucus (CBC) and other Black male political leaders. Even Black women who were part of coalitions with traditional Black political leadership, like 1977 National Women's Conference attendee Coretta Scott King, did not rally support for Chisholm. They saw her campaign as disruptive to the Black political coalitions that were formed to leverage the Black voter turnout during the 1972 elections. Yvonne Burke and Barbara Jordan, who joined Chisholm as Congressional colleagues in 1973, were also 1977 Women's Conference attendees. Of the two, only Burke campaigned with Chisholm in California. Chisholm's radical rhetoric and political independence alienated a core segment of the Congressional Black Caucus. However, that radicalism also attracted her to number of Black radicals, specifically the leadership of the Black Panther Party who publicly endorsed and campaigned for her.[24] Overwhelmingly, her most consistent and ardent supporters were Black women.

Despite what Chisholm identifies as "luke-warm" support from some of the white women attendees and organizers of the 1977 Women's Conference like Bella Abzug (who was a Democratic delegate in 1972), she continued to support feminist efforts to build lasting coalitions between Black and white feminists. Chisholm's presence in the ever-changing women's movement attempted to help raise white feminists' consciousness about racial and class oppression by rejecting a tokenism that only placed a few Black women in positions of power or addressed issues of race in times of convenience. In an interview, Chisholm recalls a conference for the national political caucus where not one Black or Puerto Rican woman was placed on the agenda. She states, "I have seen too many occasions where they talk sisterhood but when time comes to stand up and really exemplify sisterhood they have got to mean it." Five years after her presidential campaign, part of the 1977 conference's resolution was a commitment to address the pervasive gender inequity for women in elected office. Although there is a paucity of accounts regarding Chisholm's participation at the National Women's Conference of 1977, her attendance and participation reflects her unwavering support for feminist coalitions despite her differences with Black and white women's leadership; she believed that creating networks and systems to support a multiracial coalition was integral to American Democracy.

Beyond the symbolism of Chisholm, part of her legacy was her ability to transform the women's movement by providing an intersectional legislative and political agenda. She contributed to an ideological broadening of women's legislation that sought to engage the lived experiences and struggles of women of color. Most importantly, she provides the freedom dreams for men and women who dare to reimagine their place in American politics.

Notes

1. See Sen. Daniel Patrick Moynihan, *The Negro Family: The Case for National Action* (Washington, DC: Office of Policy Planning and Research, US Department of Labor, March 1965). Moynihan's report helped reinforce controlling images of destructive presence of Black matriarchy. My discussion of controlling images draws from Patricia Hill Collins work on the pervasiveness of these images for Black women. Patricia Hill Collins, *Black Feminist Thought: Knowledge, Consciousness, and the Politics of Empowerment* (Boston: Unwin, Hyman, 1990).

2. PH 51 "Houston Day by Day," in National Commission on the Observance of International Women's Year, *The Spirit of Houston: The First National Women's Conference; An Official Report to the President, the Congress and the People of the United States* (Washington, DC: US Government Printing Office, 1978).

3. Susan Brownmiller, "This Is Fighting Shirley Chisholm," April 13, 1969, *New York Times*, SM32.

4. A copy of the Susan Brownmiller's article was submitted into the Congressional Record. See: *Congressional Record*, Extension of Remarks, May 1, 1969, 1160–1163.

5. Carol Boyce Davies, *Left of Karl Marx: The Political life of Black Communist Claudia Jones* (Durham, NC: Duke University Press, 2007).

6. Shirley Chisholm, "I'd Rather Be Black Than Female," *McCall's*, 1970, 40.

7. See Sherie Randolph's book on Florynce Kennedy, *Florynce "Flo" Kennedy: The Life of a Black Feminist Radical* (Chapel Hill: The University of North Carolina Press); Fannie Lou Hamer, *The Speeches of Fannie Lou Hamer: To Tell It Like It Is*, eds. Maegan Parker Brooks and Davis W. Houck (Jackson: University Press of Mississippi, 2011).

8. Similar to other Black women intellectuals like Audre Lorde and Sonia Sanchez who attended Hunter College these institutions provided the most economical option for Black women in New York City to attend college. See Martha Biondi's work on the student movement in New York City. Martha Biondi, *The Black Revolution on Campus* (Berkeley: University of California Press, 2012).

9. Shirley Chisholm, *Unbought and Unbossed* (Boston: Houghton Mifflin Company, 1970), 23.

10. Robert A. Hill, ed., *The Marcus Garvey and Universal Negro Improvement Association Papers* (Berkeley: University of California Press, 1983); Adam Ewing, *The Age of Garvey: How a Jamaican Activist Created a Mass Movement and Changed Global Black Politics* (Princeton, NJ: Princeton University Press, 2014);

11. Daphne Sheppard, "Hail Supreme Court Reapportionment Decree," *New York Amsterdam News*, Dec. 23, 1967, 25.

12. Chisholm, *Unbought and Unbossed*, 50.

13. As Julie Gallagher indicates in her examination of Chisholm's early political life, she credits the women of the Key Club for "launching her political career." See Julie Gallagher, "Women of Action, In Action: The New Politics of Black Women In New York City, 1944–1972," PhD diss., University of Massachusetts, 2003, 183.

14. "Interview with Shirley Chisholm." Schomburg Center for Research in Black Culture, Moving Sound and Recorded Images, (Sc. Audio c-161 [side 1, nos. 1]), 1968.

15. Barbara Winslow, *Shirley Chisholm: Catalyst for Change* (Boulder, CO: Westview Press, 2014), 51.

16. Chisholm, *Unbought and Unbossed*, 68.

17. See Fraser article for her description and analysis of an "Unbought and Unbossed" political ideology. Zinga Fraser, "The Politics of Trauma: Shirley Chisholm's Political Life," in *In Spite of the Double Drawbacks: African American Women in History and Culture*, eds. Lopez D. Matthews Jr., Kenvi C. Phillips, Ida E. Jones, and Marshanda Smith (Association of Black Women Historians: 2012), 75–87.

18. John Kifner, "Farmer and Woman in Lively Bedford-Stuyvesant Race," *New York Times*, October 26, 1968, 22.

19. Chisholm, *Unbought and Unbossed*, 114.

20. Although abortion was a major political agenda for white middle-class women Chisholm joins other Black feminist efforts to broaden the perspective of abortion as an issue of race, gender and class. See Kimberly Springer, *Living for the Revolution: Black Feminist Organizations 1968–1980*, (Durham, NC: Duke University Press, 2005); and Loretta J. Ross, Lynn Roberts, Erika Derkas, Whitney Peoples, and Pamela Bridgewater, *Radical Reproductive Justice: Foundation, Theory, Practice, Critique* (New York: Feminist Press at the City University of New York, 2017).

21. Marlene Cimons, "Extending the Minimum Wage to Domestic Workers," *Washington Post*, May 14, 1972, K20.

22. Shirley Chisholm, "Announces Her Candidacy for the US Presidency," Jan. 25, 1972.

23. Randolph, *Florynce "Flo" Kennedy*, 186–204.

24. "Huey Newton Backs Race by Mrs. Chisholm." *New York Times*, Apr. 28, 1972, pg. 83.

14

C. Delores Tucker

Delegate-at-Large

SABINA PECK

Figure 14.1. C. Delores Tucker, 1977. Diana Mara Henry Papers (PH 51). Special Collections and University Archives, University of Massachusetts Amherst Libraries. Copyright © Diana Mara Henry / dianamarahenry.com.

CAPTURED APPROACHING THE MICROPHONE at the beginning of the second plenary session of the conference, this photograph shows Cynthia Delores Tucker with a look of earnest determination and concern. Tucker, a delegate-at-large at the conference, is pictured officially objecting to the Mississippi delegation being seated, representing the "indignation of the delegates at the election of a white delegation from a State that was more than a third Black."[1] This concern was not misplaced; other delegates had expressed concern about the all-white group from Mississippi that included men, some of whom were rumored to be part of the Ku Klux Klan.[2] A powerful, charismatic speaker, Tucker drew on the indignation of her fellow delegates to elicit emotion from them, and her words were accompanied by hisses and boos from the rest of the delegation in solidarity with their Black sisters in Mississippi. Cynthia Delores Tucker, or "C" as she was known as to friends, is not often named in accounts of this event. However, her presence as an unnamed, though public, objector to the racist nature of the Mississippi delegation has been acknowledged and considered noteworthy in numerous interpretations of the conference. Her long history of social activism and political participation around racial liberation can help us to understand her outspoken indignation at the National Women's Conference.

Born in Philadelphia in 1927, Tucker was raised by Minister Whitfield and Captilda Nottage in a strict religious home. Her mother, a feminist and entrepreneur, founded an employment agency for Black people who migrated from the South.[3] The legacy of Tucker's conservative upbringing is evident in her approach to political activism and social change. Her emphasis on helping Black people to succeed within existing institutions reflected her mother's work, and her moral outrage and crusade against gangsta rap in the 1990s was shaped by her morals and conservatism. Tucker was first educated at the Philadelphia School for Girls. She later studied public relations at Temple University and real estate appraisal at the University of Pennsylvania.[4] Well educated, motivated, and politically conscious, Tucker became a well-known figure when she became the first Black female Secretary of State to the Commonwealth of Pennsylvania in December 1970. K. Leroy Irvis, a Pennsylvanian legislator, called her "a living symbol of brilliance and effective leadership for all young Black women in the nation."[5] This endorsement and high regard for Tucker was shared by Milton Shapp, the state governor. He called her "brilliant and on the ball," and someone who would be deserving of a governmental post in any administration.[6] By 1972, C. Delores Tucker had been honored as the Black Woman of the Year by various TV and radio announcers in Pennsylvania, and by 1975 she was named as "the woman most qualified to serve as the American

Ambassador to the UN."[7] She was also included in a list of women from all over the USA who could "save America."[8] Her accolades, then, were consistent and far-reaching.

Tucker's plaudits aside, many of her opportunities for political influence arose as a result of the platform Milton Shapp provided for her. He ran as an independent Democratic candidate for governor, winning the primary in May 1970 and subsequently restructuring the State Democratic Party. At that point, he asked C. Delores Tucker to be the vice chairman of the party. Tucker had initially approached Shapp when he was running as an independent candidate, telling him that the key messages of his campaign were not reaching the Black community. She volunteered her own public relations skills and knowledge of the Black community and its needs to enhance his campaign—she believed that she could "motivate the Black community to involve themselves totally in his campaign."[9]

Shapp's subsequent appointment of Tucker as vice-chair of the party was contentious. While garnering Black support was important to Shapp, Tucker explained that the appointment remained a "bold step" as only 7 percent of Pennsylvania's total population was Black—lower than the national average.[10] However, fears about Tucker's blackness and militancy—there were unfounded rumors about her being a Black Panther—were assuaged when she stated that "Yes, I am Black and a militant, but I am Black and a militant that this Democratic Party shall be representative of and responsive to the needs of all the people of Pennsylvania."[11] Rather than attempting to play down her blackness or militancy, C. Delores Tucker used it as a platform from which she could reach out to and include those less privileged. She sought to reach out to women, and particularly women of color, to become more active in politics. Tucker believed that three groups—youths, Black people, and women—were set to be fundamentally important in politics, and jokingly commented that "our state got a bargain . . . it got all three in me!"[12]

In October 1972—five years prior to the National Women's Conference—Tucker addressed a group of women at Dickinson College in Carlisle, Pennsylvania, as part of a panel entitled "Where Do We Go From Here? An Appraisal of the Expanding Role of Women in the 1970s." Her view was that women and racial minorities would become fundamental in decision-making in politics during the 1970s; notably similar to the opinions that prompted the desire to hold the National Women's Conference. Tucker's desire to see more women, particularly Black women, involved in the political structures of the USA, was reflected in the desire for the Houston Conference to highlight to the federal government the issues that women were facing, and to encourage women at the conference itself to become more involved at a political level.

In this address, Tucker seems to have prioritized work around race, and the ways that her experiences had been shaped by race, over work around gender. At her address at Dickinson College, she asserted that the greatest burden she encountered was racism, not sexism.[13] Tucker reiterated her emphasis on race at an Honors Day Convocation at Winston-Salem State University in April 1973. Speaking to an audience of the highest-performing students at the historically Black university, Tucker stated that "Black ain't beautiful when it is dumb," urged the students to "make these the best of times for all and the worst of times for none," and emphasized that "concern for your brother is your greatest honor."[14] Her emphasis on race, and the importance of overcoming obstacles that racism presented, demonstrates her understanding of race and racism as a fundamental stumbling block in working toward political participation—more so than gender. However, this is not to suggest that Tucker was not acutely aware of the specific challenges that were faced by Black women. At a conference on business opportunities for women held in Chicago in 1974, she cited a Harris poll that showed that "the majority of Black women 'still see themselves as powerless spectators in a world where others make the action.'"[15]

Tucker's emphasis on race over gender, and an insistence on racial solidarity of Black people across gender, seems to jar with emerging narratives surrounding Black feminism in the 1970s. The development and rise of Black feminism is frequently understood as inextricably linked to the emergence of an intersectional approach to feminism. Intersectionality as a concept or analysis has been broadly associated with organizing by women of color in the USA since the early nineteenth century—although not necessarily explicitly referred to as such.[16] Kimberly Springer utilizes this intersectional approach to assert her understanding of Black feminism as having operated interstitially—within the cracks between the women's and Black liberation movements.[17] That is, Black feminism is generally accepted to occupy a position that was influenced by Black women's dual experience of sexism *and* racism, rather than prioritizing one over the other. Of course, the approaches to racial and gendered discrimination and solidarity varied depending on particular groups or individuals, and the specific work or organizing that they were doing. C. Delores Tucker publicly and explicitly asserted the prominence of race over gender, demonstrating her commitment to racial liberation movements above the "women's lib" movement. As early as 1971, Tucker communicated her notion that the women's movement was less pertinent in advancing Black women in politics than work around their race. She stated that:

I am not for women's lib as far as the Black woman is concerned because the Black woman has long been liberated in her soul, but I am urging her to become much more involved in political activity at every level. Begin at the bottom—but there's room at the top.[18]

Women's liberation, then, was not the route that Tucker advocated for Black women who wanted to make social change. Instead, she advocated participation of Black people—and specifically Black women—in the existing political system and its institutions.

Much of Tucker's previous social activism reflected her focus on race as a central point of organizing. She was the vice president of the Pennsylvania National Association for the Advancement of Colored People (NAACP) and was a charter member of the Black Democratic society of Pennsylvania. She was also described as having been involved in "everything that is progressive in civil rights," and had attended picket lines, been featured multiple times in *Ebony* magazine, and had joined in the March on Washington.[19] The duration and breadth of her activism around race and gender was so notable that she was honored as early as 1971 by the Women's Auxiliary of the Pittsburgh NAACP Branch, where they lauded her long history of civil rights activism. She had been a delegate to the White House Conference on Civil Rights in 1967, and Tucker herself recognized her "greatest achievement" as participating in the Selma to Montgomery March alongside Martin Luther King Jr. in 1965.[20]

Despite claiming that participating in the Selma March had been her greatest achievement, in 1973 Tucker told members of the Mt. Sinai Baptist Church Credit Union that she'd been able to do more in her two years of political power as Pennsylvania's Secretary of State than she had in all the of the days she'd spent "walking with Dr. King, raising clenched fists and saying I'm Black and I'm proud."[21] Two months later, she told a group of students that emphasizing the importance of handshakes, hair, and dashikis was less important than becoming politically involved. She stated that "you must master the system, learn the rules of the game. There are no examinations in the United States which are given in Swahili."[22] Tucker's priorities, then, had shifted by 1973: grassroots work that centered around racial pride was less useful or productive than political involvement. She encouraged Black people and women to try to make social change by becoming educated and by getting involved in politics.

This emphasis on top-down efforts and organizing reveals a side of activism by women of color which is not frequently discussed in historical literature (save for "public" figures such as Shirley Chisholm). It sets Tucker apart from much of the contemporary social activism by Black women at the time. Historians have broadly agreed that the majority of social organizing by women of color tended to occur at grassroots and community levels, and that access to institutional and political positions of power at the state and national level was limited for many women of color.[23] Tucker, however, was a strong advocate of creating top-down change through participation and involvement with the existing political parties. Examining the life, activities and values of C. Delores Tucker can disrupt the understanding that women of color did not engage in or desire social change via existing social and governmental institutions.

Tucker's approach seems even more pertinent when compared to the covert means that the Mississippi delegation took to flood the Mississippi state meeting and outnumber and outvote the feminist participants there. Marjorie Spruill claims that the Mississippi state meeting was the most notorious, and the most complete, conservative victory. A loose coalition of conservative forces joined together to unexpectedly overrun the meeting at the last minute, thus controlling the outcome of the meeting. Spruill describes male "controllers" as using walkie-talkies to instruct women how to vote.[24] This covert (and arguably underhanded) strategy of gaining a conservative victory in Mississippi throws Tucker's attempts to create change through existing and approved social institutions and channels (like the National Women's Conference) into sharp relief.

Despite the support that Tucker's words against the Mississippi delegation garnered among the attendees of the conference, her challenge failed to pass and the delegation was seated. The International Women's Year Commission condemned the delegation but stated that it could take no action as there had been no irregularities reported during the selection of the Mississippi delegates. It was, they suggested, "merely packed" by the right wing.[25] Tucker's public denigration of the delegation, paired with the commission's condemnation of them and recognition of the dominance of the Right, marks the scene captured in the above photograph as one of the first notable moments at which the National Women's Conference was recognized as a battleground between feminists on the Left and the Right. Tucker's participation at the conference, then, is notable because it is representative of the way that the conference was commonly represented after the fact: as simultaneously a space in which women were able to have their voices heard in a structured environment, and one in which they could and did engage in passionate and intense debate around the legitimacy of both the Left and the Right of feminism.

Each state was supposed to nominate a delegation that fairly represented their diversity. C. Delores Tucker's frustration at the Mississippi delegation's flagrant disregard for these guidelines is not surprising, given her history of work within the political system and her strong sense of fair play. Her means of protest—by objecting officially through the sanctioned channels at the conference—is reflective of her attitudes toward activism more broadly. Rather than promote direct action protest against the Mississippi delegation, as some other delegates did, she sought to undermine their presence by taking the official and institutional route. This is broadly reflective of her attitude toward social change more generally: she believed that creating change from a position of political power was more effective than organizing or agitating at the grassroots.

It is not clear the extent to which C. Delores Tucker's life was directly changed by the National Women's Conference of 1977. It is clear that her desire to increase the participation of Black women in politics continued throughout her political life. In 1984, she cofounded the National Political Congress of Black Women (now the NCBW) alongside Shirley Chisholm. They established the NCBW because they felt that Black women were not being adequately represented in the political process, and wanted to encourage women to "participate in the development of political parties' policies, platforms and strategies beneficial to the needs and aspirations of the African-American community."[26] Tucker's emphasis on political participation for Black women clearly did not wane after she left the position of Secretary of State for Pennsylvania.

Indeed, Tucker's work around Black women continued into the 1990s when she became deeply involved in a campaign against gangsta rap and hip-hop music. She believed that gangsta rap lyrics demeaned and undermined Black women in the USA, and she and the NCBW feared the damage that the music would do to the future political prospects of African American women.[27] Departing from her usual top-down style of protest, Tucker took to the streets and picketed outside notable record stores. She handed out leaflets and encouraged passers-by to read gangsta rap lyrics aloud in an effort to raise awareness of the misogyny they contained.[28] In addition to her direct action techniques, Tucker organized congressional hearings to discuss the production and dissemination of controversial rap music—though these failed to create significant change within the music industry and record companies.[29] Her actions gained her a level of notoriety within the industry to the extent that her name was used critically by a number of rappers in their music. Most notably, Tupac Shakur rapped that "C. Delores Tucker you's a motherfucker/Instead of trying to help a nigga you destroy a brother." Aside from the obvious criticism of Tucker, the suggestion that her actions against rap were actively damaging the Black male community seem to contradict Tucker's past history of advocating for improving positions in society for African Americans. Shortly after Tupac's death, Tucker filed a lawsuit against Tupac's estate and significant record companies producing rap music. She stated that:

> I feel that those who produce, and promote this recording all over the world are equally guilty of defamation. Not only have I been defamed, I feel thousands of young women have been defamed by this greed driven, race driven and drug driven music. This sexist lyrical filth [. . .] particularly defames Black women.[30]

This last stage of Tucker's political career sees a move away from her previous approach of prioritizing race over gender. Her actions in her crusade against gangsta rap are clearly based in an effort to protect Black women, and came under fire from many Black men, both publicly and privately.

It is clear that C. Delores Tucker was concerned with tackling racial and gendered oppression throughout her political career, and it is possible to identify a shift from a focus on the former to the latter throughout her life. A notable woman in many ways, she elicited high praise from individuals and institutions both locally in Philadelphia and from national figures. Her main contribution to the National Women's Conference—publicly denouncing the Mississippi delegation—marks a perfect example of Tucker's dedication to fighting racism through existing and approved institutional structures and frameworks. Her husband, William Tucker, described her as "one of the most fearless individuals I have ever known. She will take on anyone, anything, if that is what she thinks is right."[31] Similarly, Tucker herself said that "prejudice can rear its ugly head in any party or public office—and when it does, I hope to have the courage to stand and fight it."[32] Truly, this tenacity, courage, and dedication were evident throughout her political and activist life.

Notes

1. Though most delegates at the National Women's Conference were nominated and elected from the state conferences that preceded it, some (like Tucker) were chosen by the National Commission on the International Women's Year to be delegates-at-large. These delegates were chosen to balance out demographic inequities within the delegation as a whole, and were usually notable or well-known women. Though she spoke out about the Mississippi delegation at the National Women's Conference, Tucker was born in and lived in Philadelphia, PA. Her frustration at the racism and inequality within the Mississippi delegation highlights the extent to which racism within the women's movement, and particularly within Mississippi, was perceived as a national issue to be tackled and not just a regional or local problem. Caroline Bird, "Houston Day by Day," in National Commission on the Observance

of International Women's Year, *The Spirit of Houston: The First National Women's Conference; An Official Report to the President, the Congress and the People of the United States* (Washington, DC: US Government Printing Office, 1978), 142.

2. Megan Rosenfeld, "Mrs. Carter Vows Support To Women," *Boston Globe*, November 1977.

3. Jordan A. Conway, "Living in a Gangsta's Paradise: Dr. C. Delores Tucker's Crusade Against Gangsta Rap Music in the 1990s," MA thesis, Virginia Commonwealth University, 2015, 13.

4. "Mrs. Tucker Gets Another Appointment," *New Pittsburgh Courier*, August 1971.

5. Toki Shalk Johnson, "Shapp Names Black Woman Commonwealth Secretary," *New Pittsburgh Courier*, December 1970.

6. Johnson, "Shapp Names Black Woman Commonwealth Secretary."

7. "Nixon Is Blamed For Decrease Of Blacks in Public Television," *Tri-State Defender*, September 1972; Lewis J. Ulen, "Harrisburg Windmill," *New Pittsburgh Courier*, April 1975.

8. Ulen, "Harrisburg Windmill."

9. Sheryl M. Butler, "Meet Mrs. C. Delores Tucker, 1st Black Woman Secretary," *Chicago Daily Defender*, May 1971.

10. Butler, "Meet Mrs. C. Delores Tucker."

11. Butler, "Meet Mrs. C. Delores Tucker."

12. Butler, "Meet Mrs. C. Delores Tucker."

13. "Tucker Gives Warning to Women," *Pittsburgh Courier*, October 1972.

14. "If 'Black Dumb' It Is Not Beautiful," *New Journal and Guide,* April 1973.

15. "Black Women Powerless?," *Chicago Defender*, March 1974.

16. See, for example, Kimberlé Crenshaw, "Mapping the Margins: Intersectionality, Identity Politics, and Violence against Women of Color," *Stanford Law Review* 43, no. 6 (1991). Crenshaw's article is one of the foundational texts to consider intersectionality and provides an analysis of how race and gender intersect in considerations of violence against women of color; Anna Carastathis, *Intersectionality: Origins, Contestations, Horizons* (Lincoln: University of Nebraska Press, 2016) for a broader overview of intersectionality as a concept, as well as a good historiographical overview of its origins in Black feminist organizing; Kathryn T. Gines, "Race Women, Race Men and Early Expressions of Proto-Intersectionality, 1830s–1930s," in *Why Race and Gender Still Matter: An Intersectional Approach,* eds. Namita Goswami, Maeve M. O'Donovan, and Lisa Yount (Brookfield: Pickering and Chatto, 2014), for an exploration of "early" or "proto" intersectional analyses among women of color's organizing; Kimberly Springer, "The Interstitial Politics of Black Feminist Organizations," *Meridians: Feminism, Race, Transnationalism* 1, no. 2 (Spring 2001), for an assessment of how intersectional identities inform the locations of Black feminism; and Patricia Hill Collins, "Gender, Black Feminism and Black Political Economy," *Annals of the American Academy of Political and Social Sciences* 568 (March 2000): 41–53, for an analysis of varying sociological approaches to Black feminism, including that of intersectionality. This list is neither complete nor exhaustive.

17. Springer, "The Interstitial Politics of Black Feminist Organizations," 156.

18. "First Black Woman in Pa. Cabinet Tells Cheyney Students of Goals," *Afro-American*, January 1971.

19. Johnson, "Shapp Names Black Woman Commonwealth Secretary"; "Pittsburgh's

NAACP Women's Auxiliary Meets to Honor State Secretary C. DeLores Tucker," *New Pittsburgh Courier*, January 1971.

20. "Pittsburgh's NAACP Women's Auxiliary Meets."

21. James Lawrence, "Blacks Must Learn to Segregate Money: Pennsylvania Secretary of State Says," *Call and Post*, February 1973.

22. "If 'Black Dumb' It Is Not Beautiful."

23. See, for example, Premilla Nadasen, "Expanding the Boundaries of the Women's Movement: Black Feminism and the Struggle for Welfare Rights," *Feminist Studies* 28, no. 2 (Summer 2002), 270–301, for an analysis of Black women's work at the grassroots around welfare rights; Winifred Breines, *The Trouble Between Us: An Uneasy History of White and Black Women in the Feminist Movement* (Oxford: Oxford University Press, 2006)—especially chapter four—for an analysis of radical separatist Black feminist activism at the grassroots in the Combahee River Collective; Kimberly Springer, *Living for the Revolution* (Durham, NC: Duke University Press, 2005); and Sherna Berger Gluck, "Whose Feminism, Whose History? Reflections on Excavating the History of (the) US Woman's Movement(s)," in *Community Activism and Feminist Politics: Organizing across Race, Class and Gender,* ed. Nancy A. Naples (New York: Routledge, 1998), for an analysis of the chronology and locations of differently raced "feminisms," which asserts that black activism at community levels emerged at the same or similar times to white feminism, despite previous historiographical suggestions.

24. Marjorie J. Spruill, *Divided We Stand: The Battle over Women's Rights and Family Values That Polarized American Politics* (New York: Bloomsbury Press, 2017), 186–87.

25. Leslie Cagan, "Houston in Retrospect: Equality Within the System," *WIN*, January 1978.

26. National Women's History Museum Website, "The National Congress of Black Women, Inc.," *A History of the NWHM*, 2007, https://www.nwhm.org/online-exhibits/coalition/15.htm [Last Accessed 18/4/17]; Conway, "Living in a Gangsta's Paradise," 14.

27. Conway, "Living in a Gangsta's Paradise," 16.

28. Yvonna Shinhoster Lamb, "C. Delores Tucker Dies at 78; Rights and Anti-Rap Activist," *Washington Post*, October 2005.

29. Conway, "Living in a Gangsta's Paradise," 27–35.

30. "Dr. C. Delores Tucker Files Multi-Million Suit Against Record Producers of Gansta Rap 'Filth,'" *Hyde Park Citizen* 8, issue 38 (August 1997): 2.

31. Lamb, "C. Delores Tucker Dies."

32. "Pennsylvania's Secretary Asks Black Nations to Have Nixon Clarify Policy," *New Pittsburgh Courier*, September 1971, 2.

15

"I Was Me"

Yvonne Burke and the Politics of Representation

SARAH B. ROWLEY

Figure 15.1. Yvonne Burke, 1972. Diana Mara Henry Papers (PH 51). Special Collections and University Archives, University of Massachusetts Amherst Libraries. Copyright © Diana Mara Henry / dianamarahenry.com.

LEADING UP TO THE 1977 National Women's Conference, ten press briefings were held around the country to raise awareness and support for the gathering. In Los Angeles, California, the two people tasked to be the public faces of the IWY Conference were the actress Jean Stapleton and Yvonne Brathwaite Burke, a member of Congress representing L.A.'s 28th District.[1] Stapleton, selected as an IWY commissioner, was most famous to audiences around the country for her role as Edith Bunker on the hit sitcom *All in the Family*. But Burke brought her own star power. As one of the first Black women to be elected to Congress, and as the first representative to give birth while serving, Burke garnered significant national attention in the 1970s. When she was introduced on stage in Houston in November by Chair Mary Anne Krupsak, many people in the audience would have been familiar with the California Democrat.

Throughout her time in Congress, Burke used the novelty of her very presence as a Black woman politician to garner public attention for issues related to gender and racial equality. Her commitments to women's rights and Blacks' rights were inextricable—less two overlapping concerns than one unified agenda against interlocking discrimination, rooted in her embodied experiences as both Black and female.[2] A high-profile professional mother, Burke did not shy away from serving as a public symbol of a new era for women. Where others often noted her many historic "firsts," in her frequent speeches and writings, Burke reframed her own successes by contextualizing them within a longer history, demanding her audiences make progress toward equality. Explicitly locating herself along a genealogy of feminist and antiracist activism, connected both to forbearers in the past and potential successors in the future, Burke embraced her role as a trailblazing "symbol of the new wave in politics."[3]

The New Democratic Politics

Born in Los Angeles in 1932 to a mother who was a real estate agent and a father who, as a janitor at MGM Studios, led the service employees union there, Burke grew up with a professional, working mother and a commitment to collective politics as norms in her household.[4] She attended mostly white schools, including the University of California at Los Angeles and the University of Southern California Law School, where she was one of the first Black women to be admitted as a student. Faced with discrimination in the legal job market upon graduation, Burke pursued private practice and took on public service positions including an appointment as a staff attorney to the 1965 Mc-

Cone Commission, which investigated the Watts riots of that summer.[5] The following year she became the first African American woman elected to the California State Assembly. She won reelection in her Los Angeles district in 1968 and 1972.

Burke's national debut came during the 1972 Democratic National Convention in Miami Beach, Florida, when she was a candidate for the US Congress. To foreclose another violent public spectacle like the bloody riots at the 1968 convention in Chicago, party leaders convened a commission to reform the processes of selecting a presidential nominee. The reforms disempowered conservatives and machine politicians while favoring the party's left wing and ensuring the equitable participation of female, young, and minority delegates. Accordingly, the meeting in Miami Beach was "the fairest and most open political conclave ever in American history."[6] As Burke noted in her acceptance speech when elected vice-chairperson (a position created by the commission's reforms to ensure a top-level spot for a woman), the convention was "symbolic of the new politics" within the party—and Burke was a chief symbol herself.[7]

Wielding the gavel as she presided over much of the contentious convention with "a spirit of frankness,"[8] Burke's very presence as "madam chairman" and her "calm" wrangling with delegates over parliamentary procedure illustrated an irrefutable shift in the complexion of Democratic party politics.[9] In Burke's retelling, the chair, Larry O'Brien, ceded control of the convention to her because he "decided it was too much, and the people were too much trouble."[10] Burke stayed up all night to preside over the approval of the platform in a record-setting session that finally adjourned at 6:20 a.m. Though Burke came as a supporter of George McGovern's candidacy rather than Shirley Chisholm's, her prominent role in the convention represented the same new landscape of Democratic politics for Black women that Chisholm's presidential run seemed to offer. Black women could be the leaders, the standard bearers, the rule keepers of the party, which seemed to be undergoing a reinvention within that noisy convention hall in Miami.

Yet these new roles for Black women in the party raised complicated issues of representation. Both Blacks and women advocating for reform wanted to claim the visibility of the vice-chair position. The National Women's Political Caucus (NWPC) chose Hawaii representative (and Asian American) Patsy Mink as their first choice, but Burke was the compromise between the NWPC and the Congressional Black Caucus (CBC).[11] Burke knew that as a Black woman, she could serve both groups' representational goals, but she had no intention of serving merely as "window dressing."[12] Aware of the risk of having her symbolism move out of her own control, Burke insisted that if she were to have such a high-profile role in the party, she would be a strong advocate for the entire Black population and would not be used as "part of a cop out that keeps the black man where he has been for 200 years—totally eliminated from moving up."[13]

Once in Washington, she made clear that she intended to achieve more than the mere fact of her presence among the much-heralded "triumvirate of Negro Congresswomen" elected in 1972.[14] Throughout her tenure in the House, Burke worked with other women members not only to push for women's rights legislation, but also to enable access to amenities and power on Capitol Hill itself. For example, she reluctantly agreed to chair the Select Committee on the House Beauty Shop (extant from 1967 through 1977) after the former chair, Rep. Martha Griffiths, retired from Congress. The committee provided oversight to and reformed the management of a business that had, for decades, been mismanaged and overlooked by the overwhelmingly male members of Congress. Burke later described the position as a thankless but nevertheless important job to insist on the equal rights and dignity of women workers and customers, the latter of which included not just congresswomen but also congressional employees, wives of male representatives, and the public.[15] Legislation she introduced regularized House administration of the beauty shop and brought its staff under the umbrella of federal employment protections, which entitled them for the first time to pay and benefits equal to the rest of the Capitol Hill support staff—including employees of the barber shops that serviced congressmen.[16] Burke's push for the beauty shop employees coincided with other demands by women for access to multiple spaces on Capitol Hill—from fitness facilities to restrooms and offices—from which they had been historically excluded.[17] Burke socialized and strategized with other women in the House on these issues, and she became the inaugural treasurer of the new bipartisan, feminist Congresswomen's Caucus in 1976.[18] Burke considered herself as much a representative of the House Beauty Shop employees and women of Congress as the residents of her Los Angeles district. In all cases, she fought the "unfair acceptance of the status quo" and pushed for equity.[19]

Burke proved that institutional reforms exceeded mere symbolism when she won a seat on the Appropriations Committee as a first-term representative—a highly sought-after assignment given the power of the purse. With Barbara Jordan on the House Judiciary Committee investigating the Watergate scandal, and Burke on Appropriations, Black women occupied new, influential ground in Washington. When Burke was elected to lead the CBC in 1974, she became the first woman to do so and used the press attention already on her to amplify CBC's agenda to a nationwide audience.[20] In that role, Burke appeared on television programs, held press conferences, gave interviews, and wrote articles for newspapers around the country. She used her public profile to defend busing as a method of school desegregation, call for investigations into incidences of racially motivated miscarriages of justice, and rail against court efforts to undermine affirmative action, insisting that "'reverse discrimination' is a fraud."[21]

For Burke, the concerns of women and Blacks were never separate. Shirley Chisholm had famously written in her 1970 memoir that gender had presented more obstacles than race in her life.[22] Burke later responded that race had been the bigger cause of discrimination in her experience, but she also expressed some discomfort at the framing of race versus gender.[23] Through pursuing policies such as affirmative action in government contracts, reproductive freedom, full employment, and expanded access to the welfare state, Burke forwarded a liberal Democratic politics that enshrined women's and Blacks' rights without separating the two into distinct categories. She hoped that increased representation of minorities and women in government would not only increase opportunities for individuals but would provide a "new consciousness" in policymaking and would lead to real, tangible advancements.[24]

A New Mother in Congress

Eleven months into Burke's first term in the House, she added to her long list of historic "firsts" by becoming the first sitting member of Congress to give birth when she had her daughter Autumn. Burke had already drawn attention for continuing to carry out the business of the House while visibly pregnant as well as for becoming pregnant at the relatively late age of forty. She responded by incorporating a modern, feminist, and race-conscious maternalism into her larger agenda and public persona.

On the March 1974 cover of *Ebony*, Burke smiled warmly and held her infant daughter, who was nestled into her mother's chest and looking up sleepily. In the corresponding cover article, "The Kind of World I Want for My Child," Burke assessed the challenging social conditions faced by Blacks and laid out the hopes she held for Autumn's generation. Here and elsewhere, Burke explicitly politicized her motherhood and used it as an opportunity to advocate Black women's advancement. She acknowledged the power of representation and her own role as a public symbol of progress and achievement:

Aside from what I may be able to contribute to a better world as a legislator, there are those responsibilities I have as a result of the attention being drawn to me as a mother by virtue of my position. Perhaps one of them is to help other women feel that they can do things. If, at my age, I can have a child and maintain a demanding career, others will try it. Many have told me so. And young girls, who have always felt they must choose between a family and a career can see that it is possible to combine the two.[25]

Burke was participating in a larger cultural and political trend of debating the meanings and boundaries of motherhood. Some radical women's liberationists saw the hegemonic feminine, maternal, domestic ideal as the root of women's oppression, while a growing number of feminists in the 1970s hoped that refocusing on motherhood as natural and powerful could provide a universal bond among women amid movement divisions.[26] Feminists of color in liberation movements such as the Black Panthers and Young Lords vigorously debated with men over the role of women and the meaning of childbearing within the context of racial pride and power.[27] The conservative response to the entire spectrum of feminist and radical interpretations of reproduction and mothering further elevated the issues into national political consciousness throughout the decade, especially given demographic changes that saw increasing numbers of American women working outside the home.[28]

Burke's endorsement of blending work and motherhood was of particular note for the press and ordinary observers. Reporters often noted the unusual arrangement between Yvonne and her new husband Bill, given her prominent public career. The *Chicago Tribune's* Louise Hutchinson remarked that despite being one of only four husbands of congresswomen in Washington, Bill Burke's ego "remain[ed] marvelously intact."[29] Though journalists focused on the novelty, Yvonne and Bill framed their public statements to normalize a working mother in a two-career marriage: "my husband and I agree that it takes two to do the job of rearing a child."[30]

It is crucial to recognize that this was no race-neutral feminist expression. Daniel Patrick Moynihan's 1965 study *The Negro Family*, which identified a "tangle of pathology" and unnatural matriarchal rule in Black families, loomed large in 1970s debates about gender, family, race, and liberal politics.[31] For example, Burke's *Ebony* article followed another in the same issue that intended to delegitimize the report's depiction of Black family life "as a sort of defective variant of a dominant white model."[32] Championing monogamy, marriage, and moral values, Burke articulated a uniquely Black feminist vision of motherhood that both insisted on an egalitarian marriage but also demonstrated that her Black family was anything but deviant or dysfunctional. She did so amid a larger cultural conversation about the dignity and health of Black family life.

Readers of the magazine responded to her article in ways that make clear they understood the stakes of Burke's personal story as extending beyond one individual's parenting choice. One woman praised Burke as a working mother amid "this era of childless marriages, abortions and swinging singles." Her comment demonstrates that for at least some Black women readers, the salience of combining motherhood and career differed from the white norm; the meaning of "traditional" families and mothers within them always filtered through a racial lens. Though Burke supported policies to enlarge abortion access and unmarried women's economic security, to this reader the famous working mother holding her infant on the cover personified moral, conventional femininity. However, the majority of letters to the editor responded negatively. Several proponents of population control resented Burke's "baby sell" and one writer perceived hypocrisy from the pro-choice congresswoman who he interpreted as participating in the genocide of Black babies.[33] Notably, these critics not only attacked Burke on reproductive policy grounds but also as skeptics of combining career and motherhood. As one woman wrote, "the two cannot be combined effectively. . . . This is not being responsible—either as a parent or as a career person." In her highly public role as a working mother, Burke represented Black womanhood more broadly at a moment of social upheaval around (racialized) gender roles.

Burke's often-reported-upon beauty may have served, along with her maternal status, as evidence of traditional femininity despite her unusual public position and feminist politics. Journalists frequently lavished complimentary adjectives to describe the former model's looks. Betty Wisham, writing for *Essence* in 1974, opened her feature on Burke—which ran just five months after her *Ebony* cover issue—by highlighting the congresswoman's appearance, which seemed to illuminate her character:

> That splash of sunshine smile hits you, and dissolves doubts. The lady vibrates. Not only has the press succumbed to her radiance, charm, and intelligence—the nation has also fallen under her spell. Yvonne Brathwaite Burke is 41 this year, but she doesn't look a day over 28. Slender, graceful and very much in touch with Yvonne, she is a natural beauty—no excess makeup, no jewelry, no frills. The glow comes from within, capturing you when she speaks.[34]

A writer for *Harper's Bazaar* described her as "one of the most attractive women in politics."[35] Democratic leader Liz Carpenter thought she looked more like an actress or "a cover girl" than a typical politician.[36] It is hard not to read this glowing coverage against descriptions of the other Black women in Congress, since they were often linked in the press. One syndicated story that ran right before the 1972 election identified Burke as "a charming beauty described by one colleague as 'the woman who will make the world forget Shirley Chisholm.'"[37]

If reporters often insisted on foregrounding Burke's beauty in a way that might have discounted her intellectual heft, professional record, and political convictions, she responded by adopting what the feminist scholar Brittney Cooper has called an "embodied discourse": using the physical fact of her Black female body—particularly her reproductive capability—to assert the right to craft her own narrative about her role in the political arena.[38] Insistent upon being more than just a series of pioneering "firsts," Burke ensured that if she were to be a symbol, she would be in control. She inserted her maternal body into her 1974 *Ebony* article as a way to highlight the particular vulnerability of Black people, describing how she was sure to get proper nutrition and avoided anesthesia during birth "because I felt that a Black child coming into this world needs all its faculties, every advantage it can have."[39] Similarly, on Dinah Shore's television show the same year, she announced that she was breastfeeding her infant daughter.[40] She also foregrounded the realities of the vulnerabilities of other female and/or Black bodies in her speeches and articles. She spoke out about "the countless ways in which a woman's life is shaped by the persistent threat of rape,"[41] the persistent injustices perpetrated against Blacks in the judicial system (including Joan Little, who was sexually assaulted by her white male jailer),[42] and the seriousness of domestic violence.[43] Though she was often depicted as glamorous, Burke repeatedly used her position to call attention to the corporeal realities of discrimination suffered by those she represented.

As the first woman to receive maternity leave from Congress, Burke embodied the policy needs of working women but also pushed for homemakers' rights.[44] She supported a variety of changes to expand married women's access to husbands' Social Security benefits, job training programs, counseling services, and even unemployment insurance. For Burke, these policies were natural extensions that would render the existing welfare state fairer and more responsive to poor women's needs. In 1975 testimony to a House subcommittee considering her Displaced Homemakers Act, Burke highlighted the "triple bind" in which older minority women found themselves. Pointing out the negative economic impact of these intersecting oppressions based on gender, age, and race, she highlighted the feminization of poverty and the plight of "displaced homemakers" who had "fulfilled society's traditional definition of a woman's role" only to be left vulnerable upon a husband's death or divorce.[45]

A supporter of abortion rights, sex education, and birth control, Burke used her own motherhood to her advantage, to demonstrate that she supported the full range of reproductive choices for women.[46] She spoke out against unfair penalties aimed at mothers on welfare, which especially affected southern Black women.[47] In response to congressional debate over the passage of the Hyde Amendment, she assailed the imminent return of "back-alley and self-induced abortions" among poor women.[48] In a hearing the previous year, she had argued for family planning funds using an explicitly feminist justification: "I believe that if women are to fully explore their potential as human beings, they must be given the opportunity to plan their families and their futures."[49]

Burke was modeling a type of modern, feminist motherhood that did not exclusively define nor was separate from her wider political agenda. Her identity as a mother entwined with her identity as an African American, a woman, a liberal, and a Californian. The combination of these provided her with a particular standpoint from which she argued passionately for policies she saw as just and equitable—though this did not always go without criticism. *Essence* magazine reported that certain "militant" women's groups worried during and after Burke's pregnancy that she was letting the press use her to shore up a traditional stereotype of woman as wife and mother. Yet in representing the compatibility of a public, legislative career with motherhood—and in particular in representing functional, loving, equitable *Black* motherhood, Burke was not simply reifying traditional stereotypes but was challenging their boundaries.

National Women's Conference

In addition to cosponsoring the legislation to fund IWY with other women in Congress, Burke lent her public persona to the cause.[50] In her home state of California, Burke participated in the state meeting, "a political arena for many polarized groups," which required maneuvering through tense racial politics.[51] In the lead up to the June 1977 meeting, set to take place in Los Angeles, several Black women raised concerns about racial representation among the leaders of the organizing committee. The controversy quickly escalated into a "fiasco" that implicated Burke. She held a meeting at her Inglewood office for various constituencies to discuss their concerns in an attempt to "resolve the thornier issues," but rumors flew about her potentially divided loyalties.[52] Though Burke feared the optics of having to cross a potential picket line, in the end she accepted the invitation to deliver the keynote address.[53] In the speech, Burke referenced the herculean and probably impossible task of attaining perfectly balanced representation of all women in the state, and she acknowledged "squabbling and backbiting," but called for attendees to overcome differences in the pursuit of common goals.[54] She was elected as one of the diverse slate of California delegates to the national conference in Houston later that year.[55] As Burke remembers, this brouhaha was mainly political jockeying among groups and individuals for influence.[56] The conflict also seems to have stemmed in part from fears that conservative women perhaps with the help of the state IWY cochair (and Ronald Reagan appointee) Anita Miller, would overrun the California meeting as they had in other states.[57] Yet the controversy still pointed to the racial tensions surrounding both IWY specifically and feminism more broadly.

When it came to the national conference, though she used her public stature to promote IWY, Burke was not a central player. She was nearly four thousand miles away when attendees began streaming into Houston. When the ERAmerica fundraiser to support ratification of the Equal Rights Amendment kicked off at 5:30 p.m. at the Hyatt Regency Hotel, Yvonne Burke's name was printed on the programs as a patron, yet she was not in attendance.[58] Instead, Burke was addressing the YWCA of Oahu on the topic of women's political involvement. "In order to increase women's participation in the public world," Burke told the audience, "we must effect change in patterns of social conditioning as well as in social institutions. We must move at once and in several directions to broaden the aspirations of American women and to widen the routes of access to our political institutions."[59] Burke considered it part of her duty as a Black woman public official to accept speaking invitations around the country. She saw herself as representing three distinct constituencies: 1) residents of her Los Angeles district, 2) all African Americans, and 3) all American women.[60] Accordingly, Burke saw traveling around the country to give speeches to various organizations—especially women's and Black groups—as crucial to her responsibilities.

Burke did manage to attend and participate in the IWY Conference, though. On Sunday morning in Houston, Burke co-led an ad hoc hearing on disarmament and peace issues with Colorado Rep. Patricia Schroeder. Also participating were the famous anthropologist Margaret Mead and activists from a variety of organizations who were working for disarmament. Organizers hoped that the panel "would not only contribute substantively to public discussion of arms control, but would demonstrate that women can and do master the technical aspects of strategic and other security questions."[61] Also underlying the hearing was the long tradition of women's maternalist antiwar activism. Mead spoke to it directly: "It has been women's task throughout history to go on believing in life when there was almost no hope. If we are united, we may be able to produce a world in which our children and other people's children will be safe."[62] With two young children, Schroeder's public persona, like Burke's, was shaped by the fact that she was a professional working mother. Their maternal identities resonated, along with participants from groups such as Women Strike for Peace, with a long tradition of women engaging in politics *as mothers*. Yet both updated the tradition for the feminist era. Both women had opposed the Vietnam War, and both carried that opposition forward into their congressional service.[63]

Forty years later, Burke did not remember the 1977 Houston Conference; despite other participants' recollection of the National Women's Conference as a galvanizing moment, it made no lasting impression on Burke.[64] Yet the Plan of Action approved at the conference significantly overlaps with Burke's political agenda. From full employment to benefits for displaced homemakers to abortion rights and affirmative action, these had been the issues at the heart of Burke's public speeches and writings during her congressional terms.[65]

Going Forward

Despite a robust public presence in the 1970s, Yvonne Burke has not received much scholarly attention. Even some of the women who traveled down the trail she helped blaze have misunderstood her significance. In the 1990s, Democratic Representative Marcy Kaptur's book lumped Burke into a group of women representatives who gave birth while in office and subsequently decided not to run for reelection because of the difficulty of blending motherhood and career.[66] Yet although it is true that Burke did leave Congress after having her daughter, she did so in 1978, after winning another two elections[67] Moreover, while family concerns (particularly the bicoastal commute) may have influenced Burke's decision to resign her seat, she did so primarily to run for the California state attorney general, which if successful would have made her the first woman from any state to hold such a position. Gender was a primary issue for Burke in that election, as she faced hostility toward the notion that a woman could be tough enough to be the "top cop" in the state.[68] But she did not sacrifice her career in the interests of motherhood, because she never saw the two as being incompatible.

After her loss of the state attorney general race, Governor Brown appointed Burke to the Los Angeles County Board of Supervisors, where she was the first female and first racial minority member.[69] Burke continued to be a voice in national politics for women's and family issues from a liberal perspective, even as the conservative Right was claiming "family values" rhetoric for its own purposes. In 1979 the Board of Supervisors named her to lead a blue-ribbon committee for Jimmy Carter's White House Conference on Families.[70] After a year and a half on the board, she remained active in the Los Angeles political scene while pursuing a private legal career throughout the 1980s. For example, Burke was instrumental in bringing the 1984 Olympic Games to Los Angeles. In 1992 she resumed her service as a Los Angeles County Supervisor, this time after a successful campaign, which made her the first African American elected to the board.[71] Burke served in that role until her retirement in 2008. Her pioneering career successfully provided a model for at least one young Black woman to follow: her daughter Autumn, who was elected to the member of the California Assembly in 2014.

In a 1974 speech, Burke said, "It is not enough to have more black women in politics. Changing the color and sex of politicians will not necessarily change the character of government. Black women must bring a new vision and awareness to the political process that will answer the people's demand for integrity and honesty in government."[72] A recurring theme in her public speeches, especially on topics of race and gender equity, was the importance of role models who inspired others to break down barriers. Not a "bra burner," "firebrand," or "screamer," Burke nonetheless identified as an active member of a less radical, yet crucial, segment of the women's movement that worked for liberal policies and economic equity for women.[73] For Burke, as for so many other Black women predecessors and contemporaries, issues of racial and gender-based discrimination were interconnected, not to mention deeply personal and relevant to her own history. She was never siloed into supporting just "Black issues" or "women's issues," as if they could be separated, and she was active in a wide range of issues central to the politics of the day. She later reflected on her congressional career that she tried to bring the two challenges together in a way that was authentic for her. Looking back she said, "I was direct. I was me."[74] Studying the history of liberal lawmakers like Burke can add to our understanding of the ways that Black women in the 1970s used their public positions to represent underserved populations within partisan politics, reframe and challenge limiting stereotypes of Black womanhood, and enact the policy goals of Black feminism.

Notes

1. Lynne Gallagher, "Unity in Houston: They Said It Couldn't Be Done," *American Association of University Women Journal* (January 1978): 2.

2. I am borrowing the term "interlocking" from the 1977 Combahee River Collective, "The Combahee River Collective Statement," in *Home Girls: A Black Feminist Anthology,* ed. Barbara Smith (New Brunswick, NJ: Rutgers University Press, 2000; orig. 1983), 264.

3. Lacey Fosburgh, "Women's Status a Key Factor in Race by Rep. Burke," *New York Times,* May 13, 1978, 10.

4. Yvonne Brathwaite Burke, interview with the author, July 21, 2017, transcript, in author's possession, 1.

5. Pamela Lee Gray, "Yvonne Brathwaite Burke: The Congressional Career of California's First Black Congresswoman, 1972–1978," PhD diss., University of Southern California, 1987, 22–25; "The Honorable Yvonne Brathwaite Burke Oral History Interview," Office of the Historian, US House of Representatives, July 22, 2015, i, http://history.house.gov/Oral-History/Women/Representative-Burke/, accessed August 19, 2017; Governor's Commission on the Los Angeles Riots, *Violence in the City—An End or a Beginning?* (1965), 89.

6. Sheila Hixson and Ruth Rose, eds., *The Official Proceedings of the Democratic National Convention* (Washington, DC: Democratic National Committee, 1972), 488.

7. Hixson and Rose, *Official Proceedings,* 232.

8. Hixson and Rose, *Official Proceedings,* 426.

9. "2 Black Women Head for House," *New York Times,* October 7, 1972, 18; Hixson and Rose, *Official Proceedings,* 298.

10. "The Honorable Yvonne Brathwaite Burke Oral History Interview," 7.

11. Gray, "Yvonne Brathwaite Burke," 32.

12. Gay Pauley, "Yvonne Proud of New Duties," *Desert Sun,* July 14, 1972, A3.

13. "2 Black Women Head for House," 18.

14. "Black Women Make New Look for 93rd Congress," *Wichita Times,* April 19, 1973, 4.

15. "The Honorable Yvonne Brathwaite Burke Oral History Interview," 27; *Report by the Comptroller General of the United States: Audit of the House of Representatives Beauty Shop, Calendar Year 1977* (Washington, DC: United States General Accounting Office, 1978).

16. *Congressional Record,* vol. 123, 95th Cong. 1st. Sess., 36298–36303.

17. For discussion of access to the gym and pool, see Leonor Sullivan to all women members of Congress, January 31, 1975, box 111, folder 22, Yvonne Brathwaite Burke Papers: California State Assembly, US Congress, Los Angeles County Board of Supervisors, and California Attorney General Campaign 0218.1, University of Southern California Special Collections.

18. Yvonne Brathwaite Burke to women members of Congress, June 24, 1975, box 111, folder 22, Burke Papers; "The Honorable Yvonne Brathwaite Burke Oral History Interview," 15–18; Associated Press, "Women Form Caucus in House," *Baltimore Sun,* April 6, 1977, clipping, box 22, folder 17, Burke Papers.

19. *Congressional Record,* vol. 123, 95th Cong. 1st. Sess., 36299.

20. "The Honorable Yvonne Brathwaite Burke Oral History Interview," 20.

21. Yvonne Brathwaite Burke, speech to East Chicago NAACP, April 26, 1975, box 21, folder 7, Burke Papers; *African American News Service,* "Perjury Charged in Kitty Hawk

Case," *Chicago Metro News,* March 10, 1973, 20; Yvonne Brathwaite Burke, "'Reverse Discrimination' Is a Fraud," *Westside Gazette,* October 20, 1977, 4.

22. Shirley Chisholm, *Unbought and Unbossed* (Boston: Houghton Mifflin, 1970), xii.

23. Burke, interview with author, 16–17; "The Honorable Yvonne Brathwaite Burke Oral History Interview," 19–20.

24. Yvonne Brathwaite Burke, "Black Women in Politics, Today," *Contact* 5 (Fall 1974): 64.

25. Yvonne Brathwaite Burke, "The Kind of World I Want for My Child," *Ebony,* March 1974, 147.

26. Lauri Umanski, *Motherhood Reconceived: Feminism and the Legacies of the Sixties* (New York: New York University Press, 1996).

27. Jennifer Nelson, *Women of Color and the Reproductive Rights Movement* (New York: New York University Press, 2003).

28. Natasha Zaretsky, *No Direction Home: The American Family and the Fear of National Decline, 1968–1980* (Chapel Hill: University of North Carolina Press, 2007); Robert O. Self, *All in the Family: The Realignment of American Democracy since the 1960s* (New York: Hill and Wang, 2012).

29. Louise Hutchinson, "Bill Burke: Connubial Commuter," *Chicago Tribune,* March 31, 1973.

30. Burke, "The Kind of World I Want for My Child," 153.

31. Daniel Patrick Moynihan, *The Negro Family: The Case for National Action* (Washington, DC: Office of Policy Planning and Research, U.S. Department of Labor, 1965), 29.

32. Hamilton Bims, "The Black Family: A Proud Reappraisal" *Ebony,* March 1974, 120.

33. Kathy Hawkins, letter to the editor, *Ebony,* June 1974, 17; S. Brown, letter to the editor, *Ebony,* June 1974, 20.

34. Betty Wisham, "Yvonne Brathwaite Burke: Day by Day" *Essence,* November 1974, 72.

35. "You and Your Job: The Complete Fashion and Beauty Guide for America's Thinking Working Woman," *Harper's Bazaar,* August 1974, clipping, box 396, folder 81, Burke Papers.

36. Yvonne Brathwaite Burke, "Why I Am Optimistic about America" *Redbook,* May 1976, 79.

37. United Press International, "State Sure to Choose Black Congresswoman," *Desert Sun,* Nov. 3, 1972, A3.

38. Brittney C. Cooper, *Beyond Respectability: The Intellectual Thought of Race Women* (Champaign: University of Illinois Press, 2017), 3.

39. Burke, "The Kind of World I Want for My Child," 147.

40. Wisham, "Yvonne Brathwaite Burke," 88.

41. Yvonne Brathwaite Burke, address before the International Platform Association Convention, August 1, 1974, box 21, folder 12, Burke Papers.

42. Yvonne Brathwaite Burke, speech to East Chicago NAACP, April 26, 1975, box 21, folder 7, Burke Papers.

43. Yvonne Brathwaite Burke, "Battered Women: A Time for Action," May 14, 1977, box 162, folder 28, Burke Papers.

44. "Historic First," *New York Times,* November 11, 1973; Yvonne Brathwaite Burke to Patricia Neighbors, October 3, 1977, box 428, folder 14, Burke Papers; Marlene Cimons, "Dusting Off the Homemaker's Image," *Los Angeles Times,* June 8, 1976, OC_B15A; Nan Robertson, "The Martha Movement: Growing Advocate for Homemakers," *New York Times,* October 29, 1977, 40.

45. *Hearings Before the Subcommittee on Retirement Income and the Employment of the Select Committee on Aging on Minority and Low Income Older Women and the Displaced Homemakers Act,* 95th Cong. (1975) (testimony of the Honorable Yvonne Brathwaite Burke, member of Congress), box 21, folder 41, Burke Papers.

46. Burke, interview with author, 14; Study of Adolescent Pregnancies questionnaire, [September 28, 1977], box 428, folder 33, Burke Papers; Statement by the Honorable Yvonne Brathwaite Burke for the Baltimore Sun—Morning Editorial, September 7, 1977, box 22, folder 5, Burke Papers.

47. Burke, interview with author, 8.

48. Yvonne Brathwaite Burke, "Again, 'Back-Alley and Self-Induced Abortions,'" *New York Times,* August 22, 1977, 23.

49. Statement of the Honorable Yvonne Brathwaite Burke before the Labor-HEW Subcommittee, House Committee on Appropriations, April 7, 1976, on Funding for Family Services, box 150, folder 20, Burke Papers.

50. John Mack Carter to Burke, October 13, 1977, box 22, folder 1, Burke Papers; "Women of Congress Speak Out," *Good Housekeeping,* November 1977, 26–27; Carter to Burke, October 13, 1977, box 22, folder 1, Burke Papers.

51. National Commission on the Observance of International Women's Year, *The Spirit of Houston: The First National Women's Conference; An Official Report to the President, the Congress, and the People of the United States* (Washington, DC, 1978), 108.

52. Burke to Anita Miller, June 7, 1977, box 425, folder 48, Burke Papers; Marguerite Archie to Burke, memorandum, June 13, 1977, ibid.; James H. Cleaver, "Women Charge Bias," *Los Angeles Sentinel,* June 16, 1977, A1; Caffie Green to Dorothy Tucker, May 2, 1977, box 425, folder 48, Burke Papers.

53. Burke to Sally Martinez, June 7, 1977, box 425, folder 48, Burke Papers; Draft mailgram from Burke to Bella Abzug, May 27, 1977, ibid. Program, California State Meeting on the Observance of International Women's Year, [1977], box 425, folder 48, Burke Papers; Yvonne Brathwaite Burke, speech to International Women's Year, California state meeting, transcript, June 17 [1977], ibid.; "Schedule for the IWY Meeting," *Los Angeles Times,* June 16, 1977, F5; Burke, interview with author, 10.

54. Burke, "Women in Politics," 3, box 425, folder 48, Burke Papers.

55. List of California delegates to IWY, n.d., box 428, folder 24, Burke Papers.

56. Burke, interview with author, 9.

57. Barbara Johnson, Jackie Martin, and Geraldine Rickman to Burke, telegram, June 13, 1977, box 425, folder 48, Burke Papers; handwritten phone message from Caffie Green to Marguerite Archie, May 27, 1977, ibid.; "Stop Phyllis Schlafly" leaflet, n.d., ibid.; Handwritten meeting notes, n.d., ibid.

58. ERA fundraiser invitation, November 18, 1977, box 1, folder 14, Linda May Papers, University of Houston Libraries; Burke to Liz Carpenter, October 7, 1977, box 24, folder 5, Burke Papers.

59. Yvonne Brathwaite Burke, "Emerging Women" (speech to YWCA of Oahu, Hawaii, November 18, 1977), box 227, folder 14, Burke Papers.

60. "The Honorable Yvonne Brathwaite Burke Oral History Interview," 34–35.

61. Maxine Hitchcock to Beverly King, September 23, 1977, box 227, folder 13, Burke Papers.

62. National Commission on the Observance of International Women's Year, *The Spirit of Houston*, 153.

63. Burke, interview with author, 11.

64. Burke, interview with author, 9–11.

65. National Commission on the Observance of International Women's Year, *The Spirit of Houston*, 13–97.

66. Marcy Kaptur, *Women of Congress: A Twentieth-Century Odyssey* (Washington, DC: Congressional Quarterly, 1996), 145.

67. Kaptur, *Women of Congress*.

68. Fosburgh, "Women's Status a Key Factor in Race by Rep. Burke," 10.

69. Gray, "Yvonne Brathwaite Burke," 193.

70. "Burke Heads U.S. Family Committee," *Los Angeles Sentinel*, Nov. 8, 1979. On this controversial conference, see J. Brooks Flippen, *Jimmy Carter, the Politics of Family, and the Rise of the Religious Right* (Athens: University of Georgia Press, 2011).

71. Associated Press, "Ex-lawmaker Seems Victor in Los Angeles," *New York Times*, November 22, 1992.

72. Burke, "Black Women in Politics," 64.

73. Burke, interview with author, 6; "The Honorable Yvonne Brathwaite Burke Oral History Interview," 9.

74. Burke, interview with author, 18; "The Honorable Yvonne Brathwaite Burke Oral History Interview," 9.

16

Maxine Waters

"I stood with Coretta Scott King"

CARLYN FERRARI

Figure 16.1. Reading the Minority Plank, 1977. *From left to right*: Rita Elway, Carmela Lacayo, Gloria Scott, Ethel Allen, Mariko Tse, Coretta Scott King, Angela Cabrera, and Maxine Waters. Courtesy of Getty Images.

"FLASHBACK: IN 1977, I stood with Coretta Scott King at the 1st National Women's Conference #InternationalWomensDay."[1] Congresswoman Maxine Waters tweeted this message along with the above photograph on March 8, 2017. Dressed sharply in a dark-colored suit paired with a patterned blouse, Waters is standing to the left of King. At first glance, one might not easily spot Waters. Her gaze is fixed intently, noticeably downward, and she stands out among her colleagues who are looking forward as King addresses the audience. Perhaps Waters is looking down at the microphone pointed in front of her, or perhaps she is pensive and contemplating the magnitude of this moment.

For Waters, the 1977 conference was a career-defining moment because she demonstrated her prowess as a politician, organizer, and community-builder. In some ways, the 1977 conference was the beginning of her formal—and very public—career in politics, but it was also the culmination of the grassroots-level politics and organizing that was a part of her life. Noting the structure and organization of the conference, Waters recalls how it differed vastly from traditional political conventions:

> The Women's Conference at Houston was unique in politics, and un-like any other convention I've ever seen. At a national political convention, there are different centers of power, and people come ready to keep somebody else from doing something. At Houston, the challenge was to learn the rules so you could get something done that was being over-looked. You didn't have to fight somebody who was really against you.[2]

The organizational uniqueness Waters names is important because it reveals that her relational awareness informs how she navigates the political realm. Those four days in Houston allowed—and invited—Waters to bridge her formal, political training and personal, community experiences. She was able to establish herself as a solidarity-builder, and it was something she was proud of at the conference because she saw herself as "bridging the gap, and offering explanations to both sides."[3] The "both sides" Waters was referring to are Black and white women, who in 1977 were divided on issues of race and were not in agreement on what constituted "women's issues" or "feminism."[4]

As a bridge-builder, Waters believed "through unity we will open the doors for everyone," and it was this ethos that served as a guiding principle for both her time at the conference and her career.[5] She specifically credits the support of women and people of color for encouraging her to pursue a career in public office. In a 2017 interview with television producer and screenwriter Shonda Rhimes, Waters explains how the support and mentorship of women played a pivotal role in her career:

I mean, all of those women just let me in. And I just followed them and worked with them and they became some of my biggest supporters, you know? So when I ran for office, I knew the community very well but also something else had happened to me: I was focused on the women's movement. I was beginning to know the women in the National Organization for Women and the National Women's Political Caucus. I began paying attention to women like Gloria Steinem and Bella Abzug and eventually ended up working very closely with them. So in a way, I was kind of at the early opportunities that were opening up for women to run for office because of the feminist movement. And the Black women were not considered feminists but they really were.[6]

What is important to note here is that Waters names Steinem and Abzug, two women with whom she worked closely at the 1977 conference who also served as her mentors. For Waters, part of the "Spirit of Houston" came from the convergence of women who were diverse both racially and in terms of political experience. The opportunity to work with, be mentored by, and learn from this group of women that included career politicians and grassroots activists was a powerful learning experience for Waters, one that taught her the importance of being both tolerant and patient.[7]

A "Special Black Perspective"

At the conference, Waters was a part of a coalition of Black, Native American, Asian American, Alaskan Native, and Hispanic women—the United Minority Caucus—who had just presented what would become known as the "Minority Plank," a series of carefully crafted resolutions that addressed the nuanced, "double-jeopardy" race-and-gender-based discrimination minority women faced. Waters played a pivotal role in getting this resolution passed. She presented a substitute motion on behalf of the United Minority Caucus that contained the group's requested revisions. For Waters, it was important that the minority perspective was not additive but instead rooted in the everyday lived experiences of Black people:

There is a Black perspective in all the feminist issues in the National Plan. Battered women, for example. There's a special Black perspective because of the frustration of men in the Black community. Black women have been able to get jobs when Black men could not, and are often hired under affirmative action plans because they meet two criteria: 1) as women, and 2) as Blacks. The frustration of the men in seeking employment added to other sexist socialization, often leads to wife-beating. When I was growing up, I often saw women beaten in the streets. We see less of that now as people rise out of poverty, but it still goes on behind closed doors.[8]

This "special Black perspective" Waters references is due to the "Black Women's Action Plan" that Audrey Rowe Colom and Jeffalyn Johnson helped to orchestrate. This Action Plan led to the drafting of "The Black Women's Agenda."[9] In addition to advocating for an intersectional approach to Black women's issues, this document served "as a basis for discussion and the creation of the language in the final plank."[10] What is crucial to note here is that Waters was considering the Black community as a whole—and specifically naming men—because she understood how the plights of Black men and women were interconnected and inextricably linked. In other words, she knew that she could not address Black women's issues without also naming and addressing Black men's issues as well. For Waters, this intracultural specificity mattered. She carefully and explicitly names Black women's vulnerability and the misogynoir they experience, and she does so using a personal anecdote, a situation that is most familiar to her. Therefore, the "special Black perspective" she names is special, in part, because she was drawing from personal experience, and, in doing so, she signals a kind of grassroots politics that demonstrates her internal knowledge of and commitment to the everyday Black family and their concerns. Waters was not speaking of a general, hypothetical Black community. She makes it clear that she is speaking about *her* Black community as well.

The women implicitly engaged the Combahee River Collective's emancipatory proclamation, "If Black women were free, it would mean that everyone else would have to be free" and drew heavily upon identity politics to build their coalition and craft an inclusive plan.[11] As historians and Doreen J. Mattingly and Jessica L. Nare explain, this Minority Women Resolution was noteworthy not just because of its interracial composition but also because of its multi-issue, comprehensive scope:

> The longest and most detailed in the Plan of Action, the revised plan was over six pages. It addressed issues shared by all women of color and those specific to each group. The common problems discussed included: forced sterilizations, monolingual education, culturally biased testing, high infant mortality rate, confinement to low-paying jobs and poor housing, failure to enforce affirmative action and special admission programs, and bias in health insurance.[12]

The resolution passed and received a chorus of "thunderous applause."[13] Recalling this moment, Waters notes, "Everyone joined in singing 'We Shall Overcome' and women were crying and hugging each other. It was an especially big moment for me because I led off the reading of the resolution we had spent three days and nights drafting."[14]

By linking the unemployment of Black men to "sexual socialization" and "wife-beating," Waters evokes the 1965 report on African American families entitled *The Negro Family: The Case for National Action,* more commonly known as the "Moynihan Report" after its author, Assistant Secretary of Labor Daniel Patrick Moynihan. In this controversial report, Moynihan pathologized the Black family and argued that if Black women would allow Black men to "strut," the purported "tangle of pathology" that plagued the Black family could be alleviated. For Moynihan, the Black family was "inextricably knotted by a matriarchal head of the household" because Black men suffered more than Black women: "It was the Negro Male who was the most humiliated. . . . Segregation and the submissiveness it exacts, is surely more destructive to the male than the female personality."[15] By naming Black men's and Black women's issues in tandem—as opposed to ranking them—Waters and the "Black Women's Action Plan" document that she helped craft, did the work that the Moynihan Report failed to do. In doing so, she provided both a powerful critique and an urgent reframing of the pervasive myths and stereotypes about the Black community. Namely, she did not blame Black people for the issues in their communities; instead, she drew upon her knowledge of experience with the Black community to craft a solution. This "special Black perspective" was more than a personal anecdote; it was the framework for action.

A Head Start in Politics

Of all women in this volume whose contributions have been overlooked and rendered invisible in both popular memory and historical accounts, Waters's erasure is among the most curious—and surprising—because the National Women's Conference of 1977 arguably cemented her political career, a career in which she has been anything but invisible. Waters stood out as a rising star at the conference, and, as historian Marjorie J. Spruill explains, for some of the women, like Waters, the 1977 conference helped launch their careers: "For many feminists who attended, particularly new to the movement, the National Women's Conference was a defining, life-changing moment. The 'Spirit of Houston' would continue to thrill and inspire them for a long time to come. Houston broadened their horizons as they encountered people and ideas with which they might never have come into contact and made them feel empowered."[16] This was certainly true for Waters, who was one of forty women appointed as a member of the National Advisory Committee on Women under President Carter's administration in 1978. Waters' formal career in politics began in 1973 when she began working as chief deputy to City Councilman David S. Cunningham Jr. However, at the time of the 1977 conference, Waters was still relatively new to the political realm and was an unknown delegate from California. She had recently been elected to the California State Assembly in 1976, a position she would hold until 1991 before being elected to the US House of Representatives where she currently serves representing the 43rd congressional district of California.

As a child, Waters dreamed of being a social worker or a dancer and was particularly fond of Katherine Dunham.[17] While politics may not have been her ultimate career objective, her life experiences positioned her to be an advocate and public servant. Raised by a single mother in inner-city St. Louis, Missouri, Waters was one of thirteen children and worked in a whites-only restaurant during her early teenage years. Citing her mother's involvement in politics "at the precinct, the grass-roots level," Waters makes clear that the world of politics was not entirely unfamiliar to her.[18] She married shortly after graduating from high school and relocated to Los Angeles, California, where the 1965 race riots inspired her to become parent-involvement and volunteer-service supervisor for a Head Start program in Watts in 1966. In this role, she became increasingly concerned with parents' rights, and she empowered parents to demand budget increases to meet the community's needs. As she explains, "It was my job to bring parents into the decision-making process."[19]

Founded in 1965 as a part of Lyndon B. Johnson's larger "War on Poverty" initiative, Head Start was created to stop the cycle of poverty by being a "comprehensive child development program that would help communities meet the needs of disadvantaged preschool children."[20] The program fell under the auspices of the newly organized Office of Economic Opportunity (OEO), an office created after the Economic Opportunity Act (EOA) of 1964 was passed.[21] At the core of the Head Start program was a "culturally responsive," multi-tiered plan that sought to address the specific needs of low-income, disadvantaged families. This comprehensive program sought to meet the "emotional, social, health, nutritional and psychological needs" of these families, who were disproportionately families of color.[22] One of the hallmark features of the program was its emphasis on community empowerment and engagement. In a program that was akin to grassroots activism training, the OEO promised to train teachers to serve their community, which some officials hoped would generate tangible community reform. This community service focus was evident in the early years of the program, as the majority of the volunteer teaching staff were women and parents of the Head Start children.[23]

Though the OEO ultimately fell short of its goal, this emphasis on training and empowering individuals to serve within their own communities arguably helped Waters think about how she wanted to define her own career around advocacy and amplifying the voices of the most vulnerable. And perhaps this is why she encouraged Head Start parents to advocate for themselves and make budget demands when their needs were not being met. Childcare was a major agenda item at the 1977 conference, especially for minority women, who wanted affordable, easily accessible, quality care for their children. As a Head Start teacher, Waters was able to see firsthand the lack of resources available to low-income families of color. What is evident from Waters' above comments about how what she witnessed in her own community informed the "special Black perspective" in the Minority Plank, is that she is comfortable drawing from—and learning from—her community members. So her experience with Head Start only sharpened her lens and provided her with a more intimate understanding of low-income families' needs. This experience also taught her how to navigate the political terrain, which not only enabled her to be a better parent advocate but also how to navigate as a politician. Reflecting on her time at Head Start, Waters is careful to note how Head Start equipped her with the necessary, on-the-ground training that helped her transition into a career in politics:

> I learned to interact with politicians, and to lobby for what we needed. I began to work for specific candidates, and learned that there was a need for technicians, for people who could run campaigns. I managed campaigns for other people, and then ran myself for a seat in the California State Assembly. I'd spent ten years building a political base, years of community involvement, and I knew what had to be done—how to organize, how to raise money.[24]

She Won't Change

In recent years, Waters has garnered a multigenerational, celebrity-like fanbase earning her the affectionate nickname "Auntie Maxine." In 2017, she became a viral sensation after using the phrase "reclaiming my time," a phrase she uttered repeatedly while she was questioning Secretary of Finance Steven Mnuchin during a House Financial Services Committee meeting. As one of the few prominent Black women in politics, Waters has endured her share of racist, sexist criticisms about her physical appearance and been labeled as an "angry Black woman." However, Waters has remained audaciously unfazed and resolute. In 1990 just before winning her first race for Congress, she vehemently rejected the notion that she needed to change and adopt a more "congressional" demeanor saying, "I didn't create an image for myself. . . . I'm just me and I won't change."[25] And she has not changed.

The opening photograph is both a visual testimony of the relentless solidarity of the women of color who were present at the conference of 1977 and a blueprint foreshadowing the trajectory of Maxine Waters' nearly five decadeslong career of public service and her unwavering commitment to "standing with" and advocating for communities of color, women, children, and the poor. Forty years after this historic conference took place and on International Women's Day, Waters succinctly articulates what the conference meant to her. From this tweet, it is clear that the National Women's Conference still figures prominently—and fondly—in her thinking. Waters notes that she "stood with" King. These two words signal the unity that took place on that stage and among women of color in the United Minority Caucus. Waters' word choice and her nod to International Women's Day are also emblematic of an ethos of solidarity that provided the architecture and inspiration for her career, a career in which she has envisioned herself as an advocate and an agent of change: "My life has to be about optimism. I can never believe that nothing can be done. I can never believe that there can't be change. I have to believe that not only can we change things, but that I can contribute to that."[26]

Notes

1. Maxine Waters (@RepMaxineWaters), "Flashback: In 1977, I stood with Coretta Scott King at the 1st National Women's Conference #InternationalWomensDay," Twitter, March, 8, 2017. https://twitter.com/RepMaxineWaters/status/839464430165495808?ref_src=twsrc%5Etfw%7Ctwcamp%5Etweetembed%7Ctwterm%5E839464430165495808%7Ctwgr%5E%7Ctwcon%5Es1_&ref_url=https%3A%2F%2Fwww.vibe.com%2F2017%2F03%2Fmaxine-waters-throwback-photo-with-coretta-scott-king.

2. Caroline Bird, *What Women Want: From the Official Report to the President, the Congress, and the People of the United States* (New York: Simon and Schuster, 1979), 24–25.

3. Bird, *What Women Want*, 25.

4. As an author, I choose to capitalize "Black," and I draw on historian Martha Biondi's explanation for the capitalization of "Black": "'Black' is capitalized because it is used much as 'Negro' or 'African American' is used. As a proper noun, it reflects the self-naming and self-identification of a people whose national or ethnic origins have been obscured by a history of capture and enslavement. Similarly, 'white' is not capitalized because historically it has been

deployed as a signifier of social denomination and privilege, rather than as an indicator of ethnic or national origin." Martha Biondi, *To Stand and Fight: The Struggle for Civil Rights in Postwar New York City* (Cambridge, MA: Harvard University Press, 2003). The direct quotes in which "Black" is not capitalized may reflect the decisions of each author as well as the stylistic and societal norms during the original publication date.

5. Biondi, *To Stand and Fight*, 24.

6. Shonda Rhimes, "Rep. Maxine Waters Spills the Tea," *Shondaland*, October 11, 2017, https://www.shondaland.com/inspire/by-shonda/a12246001/rep-maxine-waters-shonda-rhimes-interview/

7. Bird, *What Women Want*, 24–25.

8. Bird, *What Women Want*.

9. See chapter 13 for a discussion of Jeffalyn Johnson's involvement in the 1977 Women's Convention.

10. Doreen J. Mattingly and Jessa L. Nare, "'A Rainbow of Women': Diversity and Unity at the 1977 U.S. International Women's Year Conference" *Journal of Women's History* 26, no. 2 (2014): 97. DOI: 10.1353/jowh.2014.0036.

11. Combahee River Collective, "A Black Feminist Statement," *Monthly Review (New York. 1949)* 70, no. 8 (2019): 33–34. DOI: https://doi.org/10.14452/MR-070-08-2019-01_3.

12. Mattingly and Nare, "'A Rainbow of Women.'"

13. Mattingly and Nare, "'A Rainbow of Women.'"

14. Bird, *What Women Want*, 24.

15. Paula Giddings, *When and Where I Enter: The Impact of Black Women on Race and Sex in America* (New York: William Morrow, 1984), 326.

16. Marjorie Julian Spruill, *Divided We Stand: The Battle over Women's Rights and Family Values That Polarized American Politics* (New York: Bloomsbury, 2017), 189.

17. Rhimes, "Rep. Maxine Waters Spills the Tea."

18. Bird, *What Women Want*, 24.

19. Bird, *What Women Want*.

20. "About the Office of Head Start," The Administration for Children and Families, accessed January 24, 2021, https://www.acf.hhs.gov/ohs/about.

21. Maris A. Vinovskis, *The Birth of Head Start* (Chicago: University of Chicago Press, 2005), 60.

22. "About the Office of Head Start."

23. Vinovskis, *The Birth of Head Start*, 95.

24. Bird, *What Women Want*, 24.

25. Mark Gladstone, "Local Elections: Congress Maxine Waters Already Is Staking Out Her Claim: [Home Edition]." *Los Angeles Times (Pre-1997 Fulltext)*, Oct 01, 1990. http://login.proxy.seattleu.edu/login?url=https://www-proquest-com.proxy.seattleu.edu/newspapers/local-elections-congress-maxine-waters-already-is/docview/281186379/se-2?accountid=28598.

26. Douglas P. Shuit, "Waters Focuses Her Rage at System Politics: She Says Inner-City Woes Have Been Simmering and Need Action: [Home Edition]." *Los Angeles Times (Pre-1997 Full text)*, May 10, 1992. http://login.proxy.seattleu.edu/login?url=https://www-pro-quest-com.proxy.seattleu.edu/newspapers/waters-focuses-her-rage-at-system-politics-she/docview/281679416/se-2?accountid=28598.

V

Communicating Change

EVERYONE HAS A STORY. But everyone's story isn't covered, isn't told. Some stories are deemed unworthy simply due to their cast. Language, voice, and image have the ability to shatter systems of oppression. To disrupt narratives that counter humanity, justice, and liberation. To promote love. To change the world. Yet, you can't speak the language, hear the voice, see the image, nor share the story without a conduit.

You need someone who isn't afraid to take risks. Someone who values lived experiences and understands the need to engage with them. You need someone who is willing to capture the complexity, nuance, and contradictions of everyday life. Someone who's relatable, who knows the people and speaks their tongue.

You need Clara McLaughlin, Melba Tolliver, and Diana Mara Henry. Professional women invested in and committed to communicating change whether that be by making the news as a television journalist or a photojournalist or by owning the media itself. These women worked diligently and deliberately to not just do their job and share a story. They sought to share language, voice, and image, while building community and communicating the change we seek.

17

Clara McLaughlin

"I don't want ON, I want O-W-N."

DESTINEY LINKER

Figure 17.1. Clara McLaughlin and her daughter Rinetta, 1977. Diana Mara Henry Papers (PH 51). Special Collections and University Archives, University of Massachusetts Amherst Libraries. Copyright © Diana Mara Henry / dianamarahenry.com.

CLARA MCLAUGHLIN, a future media mogul, entered the 1977 Women's Conference with her daughter Rinetta and a sense of purpose. McLaughlin attended the conference with Rinetta in order to introduce her daughter to the women's movement and women's leadership. McLaughlin was no stranger to either, and at the time, was best known as the author of the *Black Parent's Handbook*. Published the year before the conference, the *Handbook* was Clara McLaughlin's effort to convey the importance of emotional warmth, creative and intellectual stimulation, and safe, clean living environments for raising Black children. In doing so, she subverted cultural narratives that denied Black children their childhoods. Raising a child of her own "helped make th[is] need visible," as the *Handbook*'s dedication to Rinetta and "all Black children" clarified.[1]

In 1977, McLaughlin was on the way to becoming a media pioneer. She served as a board member for the YWCA, one of the key nongovernmental organizations involved in making the conference possible. McLaughlin was involved in organizing for the conference. When the board members decided they wanted to open the conference with a patriotic song, McLaughlin brainstormed and offered her daughter for the singing spot. No doubt convinced of her daughter's exceptional talents, McLaughlin volunteered Rinetta to sing "My Country 'Tis of Thee" at the opening of the conference. The conference attendees were gracious and kind to the young singer. The moment was one that Rinetta would remember for the rest of her life and identify as a source of confidence. McLaughlin also marveled that, after Rinetta sang in front of the conference attendees, she was able to sit through the rest of the conference proceedings, "[r]eady to be a feminist!"[2]

In Diana Mara Henry's photograph, Clara and Rinetta sit at the front of the conference hall, Rinetta beaming for the camera and wearing support for the Equal Rights Amendment (ERA) pinned to her chest. In other photos, Rinetta used the conference program as a coloring book while her mother approvingly looked over her shoulder.[3] McLaughlin intended to bring her daughter to the NWC to impress upon her the urgent need for women's leadership. Allowing her child to perform in front of others and gain confidence also aligned with McLaughlin's mission to educate Black parents on cultivating "bountiful" environments for their children. McLaughlin understood that the importance of a conference devoted partly to opening opportunities for women's national leadership and economic opportunities could provide space for her daughter to find encouragement and empowerment. McLaughlin insisted through her career and activism that control of media narratives about their own communities was necessary for realizing Black Power, for fostering future generations, and for creating space for Black girls and women to excel.

McLaughlin's determination to model ambition and success for her daughter drew also from the examples of Black women in her family. Born on November 22, 1939, in Brunswick, Georgia, McLaughlin grew up in Gainesville, Florida, where her mother's, grandmother's, and great-grandmother's example shaped her ideas of leadership. For McLaughlin, a leader was a woman who "did things."[4] Leadership for the McLaughlin women developed organically through the daily grind to secure their family's future. In her formative years, Clara McLaughlin witnessed the business acumen and thriftiness of her great-grandmother, who "would be at the courthouse to buy property every month."[5] From her grandmother's life as a preacher and her mother's career as director of a day care center, she cultivated an entrepreneurial spirit and assumed their work ethic.

From toiling in a crab-canning factory to playing piano and singing in a church on the weekends, McLaughlin's resourcefulness and forward ambition manifested early.[6] She took an early interest in journalism as the writer, editor, and distributor for her high school's student newsletter—which she founded. This was the first in many circumstances in which McLaughlin found herself working to fulfill a community's media needs. Because of her sole initiative, her small Gainesville, Florida, high school enjoyed a student newsletter.

After serving two and a half years in the Navy to help pay for college, McLaughlin enrolled at Howard University in 1965. She began her studies while working part-time in Howard's public relations office. McLaughlin discovered that Howard did not offer a major in journalism. This would not do. After a series of conversations about her demands, Howard opened the School of Communications in 1971 with some classes designed and faculty recruited by the persistent McLaughlin. In the process, McLaughlin demonstrated that she had a talent for identifying resources where there appeared to be none and was, as a result, emboldened to take control of her own education. She blended her interest in journalism with her activism by backing the creation of Black and Chicano/a studies at Howard. At a pivotal time when marches for Civil Rights turned into rallies calling for Black Power, McLaughlin knew that the medium was as important as the message. She remembers thinking that "Blacks . . . needed to really get out there and use the media. My thing was, how can [we] have Black Power . . . [if] we don't know what to do with the media?"[7]

McLaughlin's passion for Black Power politics also was apparent in her work for *The Bison*, Howard University's yearbook. She served as co-editor-in-chief for the 1971 issue of the yearbook, and as editor for the 1972 edition. Black

Power politics suffused these two editions of *The Bison*. *The Bison* staff, helmed in part by McLaughlin, chose an image of a Black man with a raised fist to grace the cover of the 1971 edition of the yearbook. The 1972 edition was particularly political. The issue's page for *The Bison* staff theorized, "How do we go about building a Black Nation? The first step is to develop a sense of unity. This year, the Bison Yearbook is designed to emphasize the humanistic part of Howard University . . . that is, YOU, one of 11,000 students, a faculty member, an administrator, or a staff member. It is our way of doing our share in building Black Unity, the only road to a Black Nation."[8]

McLaughlin's politics as embodied in her work on *The Bison* corresponded to wider struggles over social justice and education, and her determined crusade to win a major in journalism spoke to Black Power demands for greater response to student needs and the question of what powers should govern and determine curriculum. During the Black Power era, just as during the Civil Rights Movement, the campus was a significant site of contestation. The campus served many purposes as it represented a place to broadcast and debate ideas, but also an institution that perpetuated racism. As Martha Biondi has demonstrated, Black Power activists on US campuses insisted that public institutions like universities should serve public interests and reflect the diversity of the students that filled their rosters—that they should "Serve the People." Their demands included greater transparency in admissions decisions, making college education more affordable, and, specifically at HBCUs, a greater emphasis on Black self-reliance rather than integration into white institutions.[9] Whereas the protests of the Civil Rights Movement "featured courteous young men and women in dresses and suits and ties," their Black Power era counterparts "hurled defiant vocabulary, wore African-inspired or countercultural clothing, and otherwise pushed the line between Black bourgeois ideals and revolutionary aesthetics."[10] Arguably the most prominent HBCU in the nation, Howard University was a locus of the Black freedom struggle on campus. Notably, it was one of the few federally funded colleges in the nation, and, thus, a challenge issued to Howard's mission and curriculum by its students could be translated into contestations over public institutions in general.

In 1974, McLaughlin, her husband, and their young child Rinetta moved to Houston. When Rinetta was born, McLaughlin believed that she was brilliant, but her grandmother told her that Rinetta was a typical child. McLaughlin's work as an editorial assistant for the *Journal of the National Medical Association* with Dr. W. Montague Cobb at Howard prepared her to evaluate the social, economic, political, cultural, and historical conditions that shaped the experiences of Black children. McLaughlin rejected any insinuation that Black children were biologically or culturally inferior to white children. However, citing surveys conducted by herself and contributors to the *Handbook*, McLaughlin insisted that there were differences and disparities in Black and white child development.[11] Popular parenting guides like Benjamin Spock's *Baby and Child Care* did not reflect the needs or development trends unique to her daughter and other Black children.[12] McLaughlin decided to write a child development guide herself. In doing so, she addressed a need among African American parents, especially Black mothers. Her efforts anticipated similar organizations that would later address the health of Black communities and especially Black women, such as the National Black Women's Health Project, founded in 1984 in Atlanta.

To this day, *The Black Parents' Handbook: A Guide to Healthy Pregnancy, Birth, and Child Care* remains a vital resource for Black parents. The book begins with conception and extends to five years. McLaughlin offered the book as a means for cultivating Black pride: "Many Blacks hate themselves for being Black. The hate stems from the teachings of this society and is reinforced by economic deprivation, political subjugation, and cultural degradation. . . . This book is designed to guide Black parents in rearing their children to develop self-esteem and reach their full potential."[13] McLaughlin addressed a variety of issues specific to African American parents that she saw neglected in other parenting handbooks, from environmental health challenges to "Black folk medicine practices" to sex education.[14] The *Handbook* encouraged Black parents to interrogate their own internalized racism, especially a "widespread syndrome" McLaughlin called "if it's white it's right."[15] Even though Black doctors better understood how to treat Black patients, many Black women deferred to the opinion of the white medical profession, McLaughlin argued. This was not because those doctors were less competent, but because centuries of scientific racism had prejudiced many African Americans against accepting the competency of doctors who looked like them.[16]

Given her work, for McLaughlin, one of the greatest lessons of the Black Power era was the need for positive representation for African Americans, especially Black women. The written word and the broadcasted image became a way to offer her communities information, connections, and power. For McLaughlin, Black Power was at the center of her politics and her career goals. She viewed it as a vehicle for Black Americans to demand more respect. In some ways, McLaughlin's politics advocated both Black Nationalism and Black capitalism, the economic advancement of African Americans as a bastion against racism. She argued:

[Y]ou can't have any power unless you have some media ability. And, working for a company is not it. I mean you are working for the company. I watch the reporters, and they read their scripts. They don't wander from it. But, if you're [the] owner, you can let them know what you can allow. You want to do what is right for your community. And, that's still my goal.[17]

When she first relocated to Houston in 1974, she was by her own admission, "not a TV watcher." As she began to watch though, she realized that the depictions of women and African Americans were overwhelmingly negative and stereotyping. McLaughlin understood that white-owned and operated news media would do little to ameliorate these negative representations of African Americans. She petitioned the FCC to open a station in Longview, since it was the closest area to Houston that had an allocation not being used. It took her ten years to get her own station.

In the interim, McLaughlin's work with the YWCA brought her to the National Women's Conference. For McLaughlin, the NWC was exactly the exposure to positive examples of women's leadership, especially Black women's leadership, that she wanted for her daughter and for all children. The NWC's agenda mirrored and fortified her own views regarding women's empowerment. The major achievement of the conference, the National Plan of Action issued twenty-six planks with recommendations and demands for the nation to improve the lives of all women in the United States. Much of the National Action Plan was organized around the issues of specific groups of women based on identity—disabled women and "minority" women, for example. The "Media" plank tasked the nation's media to take affirmative steps to increase representation and realistic portrayals of all women. It also encouraged all sectors of the communications industry to invest in hiring and training of women into its ranks.[18] The demands of the "Media" plank aligned with Clara McLaughlin's mission to transform cultural narratives and representation of Black women. The relative invisibility of the diversity of Black women's experiences framed McLaughlin's experiences with a communications industry dominated by (white) men.

Clara McLaughlin's and her daughter's presence at the NWC highlighted her support for national efforts to reform laws and cultural narratives about Black women, but her career and activism leading up to 1977 revealed McLaughlin was not content to wait on these changes. Her study and application of Black Power politics fostered her belief that Black people had to construct their own institutions in order to protect and affirm the wholeness and complexity of Black life from conception to adulthood.

Thus, in the years following the conference, McLaughlin redoubled her efforts to found and operate her own television station, becoming the first African American woman to do so. During this time, representatives of the cable news network CNN offered McLaughlin a spot on one of their news shows. Her response was: "I don't want ON, I want O-W-N."[19] As Crystal M. Moten notes, in the 1970s, "Black nationalists developed grassroots organizations and community development corporations to bring economic justice to Black communities across the country."[20] McLaughlin got her first opportunity to "O-W-N" in 1984 when she opened a CBS-affiliated television station KLMG-TV in Longview, Texas.[21] She designed the station from the bottom up. The programming at KLMG-TV included basic CBS broadcasts, along with special comedic and progressive programs offered by Norman Lear. McLaughlin had to compete with neighboring stations that were more established and had greater funds to purchase programming to keep it out of her station's hands.

Money was not McLaughlin's only obstacle. Institutionalized racism and sexism affected her loan negotiations. In an interview, McLaughlin recalled: "There was a banker in New York. I had never seen him, but he knew I was a female, knew that I was Black. I was calling him, and he said, 'I really want you to have the money,' he said, 'but I have difficulty with certain things.' He said, 'I want to speak to the man in charge.' [I said], 'I am the man in charge!'"[22] McLaughlin's tongue-in-cheek, yet daring retort reflected her determination to challenge predominantly white male arenas and issued a challenge to the speaker to deny a Black woman's ability to lead as effectively as any man. During another business meeting, one man said to McLaughlin's lawyer, "Clara doesn't understand. We're not used to women telling us what to do here in East Texas." Her lawyer replied, "That's Clara McLaughlin. Get used to it." Clara McLaughlin refused to soften her ambitions to placate white men's expectations of who she should be or how she should act.

In 1987, *Ebony* magazine profiled McLaughlin and her achievements. Describing McLaughlin as "a woman who has always loved a challenge." The profiler Marilyn Marshall, understood that "obtaining the station was a lofty goal. The competitive and lucrative world of TV broadcasting has long been the domain of White men, and few Black men and no Black woman had ever owned a station."[23] For McLaughlin, the difficulties of running her own television station were compounded by the fact that she was both Black and a woman. This "double discrimination" had not yet been labeled intersectionality by Kimberlé Crenshaw, but McLaughlin like many of the Black women at the NWC knew it all too well.[24] McLaughlin also emphasized her belief in media as a means of empowerment and education: "I've always felt that if we wanted to have any real power, we would have to be involved with the media," she said. "It is so important to our survival and our ability to make it, because it helps develop our minds."[25] McLaughlin had conquered the challenges of being the first Black woman to own and operate her own television station.

McLaughlin wielded her television station to shape how African Americans were represented. Plans for a Ku Klux Klan demonstration organized by a gubernatorial candidate in Longview quickly attracted her attention and intervention. Though KLMG-TV initially intended to televise the KKK march, McLaughlin "vetoed coverage 'because airing the story would be promoting [the KKK-affiliated gubernatorial candidate] and giving him free publicity.'"[26] In addition to denying a platform to white supremacists, the station helped raise funds for three United Negro College Fund area colleges and aired shows that might interest Black citizens in Longview.

As the new millennium neared, McLaughlin relocated to Jacksonville, Florida. The change of location also signaled a shift in McLaughlin's media focus. The Longview station would continue to operate, but McLaughlin shifted to print media. In 2002, she purchased *The Florida Star*, a Jacksonville-based African American newspaper printed since 1951. In January 2007, the newspaper expanded to include a Georgia edition, *The Georgia Star*. She purchased the newspaper from the family of its original founder, Eric O. Simpson, and assumed the production of the newspaper with the help of the existing staff. McLaughlin noticed when she bought the paper that it was heavy on crime. Continuing her lifelong mission of shaping media representation of African Americans, McLaughlin took efforts to turn the paper in a more positive direction.

When you ask McLaughlin today about her legacy, she will smile demurely and reply with some variation of the following: "I do things because [they] need to be done."[27] In nearly all of her endeavors, she identified a need, located necessary resources, and then worked determinedly to meet that need. Though she may have benefited financially from opening a television station and owning a newspaper, McLaughlin sought collective power, self-determination, and transformational education for African Americans as she became more successful herself. Following the example of Black women before her and setting an example for her daughter to follow, McLaughlin wasted no time asking for things to be done when she could do it herself. She carried this spirit into the 1977 NWC when she decided to show daughter the full spectrum of women's experiences and leadership. Clara McLaughlin claimed space for Black girls and women. The future belonged to them, if they could see it and build it.

Notes

1. Clara McLaughlin, *The Black Parents' Handbook: A Guide to Healthy Pregnancy, Birth, and Child Care* (New York: Harcourt Brace Jovanovich, 1976), dedication page.

2. Clara McLaughlin, interview with Destiney Linker and Crystal Webster, September 26, 2016, transcript, 1.

3. Kathleen Hendrix, "Shelters, Colleges Start to Address the Needs of Women," *Austin American-Statesman* (Austin, TX), December 4, 1987, 85.

4. McLaughlin, interview with Linker and Webster, 9.

5. McLaughlin, interview with Linker and Webster, 9.

6. Marilyn Marshall, "Texas TV Pioneer," *Ebony*, March 1987, 84.

7. McLaughlin, interview with Linker and Webster, 3–4.

8. Howard University, *The Bison* (Marceline, MO: Walsworth Publishing Company, 1972), digital, http://hustorage.wrlc.org/disk1/1972bison/#4 (accessed July 7, 2017), 42.

9. Martha Biondi, *The Black Revolution on Campus* (Berkeley: University of California Press, 2012), 7–9, 113.

10. Biondi, *Black Revolution on Campus*, 17.

11. McLaughlin, *Black Parents' Handbook*, xi. One reviewer questioned the sources for and validity of McLaughlin's claims of different rates of child development based on race. McLaughlin was demonstrably influenced by Dr. W. Montague Cobb, whose studies in the 1930s and 1940s at Howard had rejected racial hierarchy while still maintaining belief in the biological reality of race. Judith S. Andrews, book review, "*The Black Parents' Handbook: A Guide to Healthy Pregnancy, Birth, and Child Care*," *New Directions* 3, no. 4, article 10 (1976); Rachel J. Watkins, "Knowledge from the Margins: W. Montague Cobb's Pioneering Research in Biocultural Anthropology," *American Anthropologist* 109, no. 1 (Mar. 2007), 190–91.

12. McLaughlin, interview with Linker and Webster, 19.

13. McLaughlin, *Black Parents' Handbook*, xii.

14. McLaughlin, *Black Parents' Handbook*, xii.

15. McLaughlin, *Black Parents' Handbook*, 27; Marilyn Marshall, "Help for Black Parent: Instilling Self-Respect Top Priority," *The Austin American-Statesman*, 1 Mar. 1977, B3, *Newspapers.com* (accessed 21 Dec. 2020).

16. McLaughlin, *Black Parents' Handbook*, 27–28.

17. McLaughlin, interview with Linker and Webster, 4.

18. *National Plan of Action Adopted at National Women's Conference, November 18–21, 1977, Houston, Texas* (Washington, DC: National Commission on the Observance of International Women's Year), 19.

19. McLaughlin, interview with Linker and Webster, 4.

20. Crystal M. Moten, "'Fighting Their Own Economic Battles': Saint Charles Lockett, Ethnic Enterprises, and the Challenges of Black Capitalism in 1970s Milwaukee," *Souls* 18, no. 1 (2016): 106–25, 108.

21. "Five Kool Achievers Named for 1987 Awards" *PR Newswire*, Aug. 24, 1987, p. NYFNS5. *General OneFile*, go.galegroup.com.silk.library.umass.edu/ps/i.do?p=ITOF&sw=w&u=9211h aea&v=2.1&it=r&id=GALE%7CA5124400&sid=ebsco&asid=373cf6198c316dbfe0398391d106 a37b. Accessed Aug. 9, 2017.

22. McLaughlin, interview with Linker and Webster, 8.

23. Marshall, "Texas TV Pioneer," 78.

24. Kimberlé Crenshaw, "Demarginalizing the Intersection of Race and Sex: A Black Feminist Critique of Antidiscrimination Doctrine, Feminist Theory and Antiracist Politics," *University of Chicago Legal Forum* (1989): 139–68.

25. Marshall, "Texas TV Pioneer" 78.

26. Marshall, "Texas TV Pioneer," 84.

27. McLaughlin, interview with Linker and Webster, 14.

18

An Everyday Anchorwoman

MELBA TOLLIVER

Figure 18.1. Melba Tolliver in the press room at the New York State Women's Meeting. Diana Mara Henry. Diana Mara Henry Papers (PH 51) Special Collections and University Archives, University of Massachusetts Amherst. Copyright © Diana Mara Henry / dianamarahenry.com.

I WAS NOT A DELEGATE, an activist, or a politician pushing an agenda at the 1977 National Women's Conference in Houston. I was there as a reporter for WNBC TV *News Center 4*, the New York City local affiliate and flagship station of NBC.

The work was exciting and exhausting. And sometimes looked and felt like creative chaos. Through all of it I reminded myself—and still do today—of the filters which shape my reporting practice:

> I am unique and so is everyone else.
> I want to give the folks I call "everyday people" their due in my reporting.
> I want to question labels, the ones we give each other and the ones we accept for ourselves, and stay aware of useful distinctions.
> I want to stay alert to the fact that words matter.
> I want to keep watch not to be surprised by events—and when I am surprised, ask "why?"

Why did Norman Fein, my news director, and his producers choose to cover a conference happening more than sixteen hundred miles away and taking a hefty hit to the news budget to do so? I believe it had to do with the temper of the times, the demands of the so-called women's lib movement, and the ongoing ratings war between local news operations to claim the biggest share of 17 million viewers living in our market of New York, New Jersey, and Connecticut. What better way to give our station a leg up than having a presence at what was potentially an important gathering of women, and giving precious airtime to, among others, recognizable New Yorkers like Bella Abzug, chair of the event, Gloria Steinem, and Betty Friedan? And why did they tap *me* for the Houston assignment? No one in charge would have admitted that my being female and Black was a consideration. But they and I knew that I was a "two-fer," slang for one who could be counted and checked off in two boxes when complying with and reporting to federal regulators and others charged with keeping data on the employment of women and "minorities." Rather, my bosses would have said the assignment was made strictly on the merits, that I was a capable, seasoned journalist.

I was born in Rome, Georgia, and brought to Cleveland, Ohio, when my parents moved north, part of the Great Migration.[1] I was two. My father got a job as a chauffeur. My mother joined an older sister as "help" in the homes of well-to-do white families. It was a start. I had a baby sister by the time my parents moved to Akron. And when my mother divorced my father, her role changed, no longer a wife but a single mother and head of household. Extended family also had a hand in raising my sister and me. Neither my mother nor adult family and friends ever used the word homeschooling back then and the word would have had a different meaning if they had. Even so, home is where my mother—my first and only Black teacher—schooled my sister and me in how to be in the world. She educated my sister and me in the domestic arts of cleaning, cooking, sewing, ironing the creases and wrinkles out of "rough dry" freshly washed laundry, setting the table, making a house home. She showed us how to make things, paper dolls and cornbread, and in the process how to make sense of our experiences and make up our minds when confronted with choices and conflicting thoughts. From her we learned to unlock the big front door, ride a bike, engage in serious play with dolls and jacks and "You're IT!" She gave us instructions on how to take the bus downtown and pay the telephone and electric bills. We learned from her how to dress up and to sit down when she told us to. She showed us how clothes bought at the Goodwill were often good as new. And, as one of the few perks of her employment, those previously worn clothes were cleaned and pressed—and altered if need be—in one of the various, environmentally toxic dry cleaners where she spent five and a half days of her week working.

Later in life, as a journalist and writer, I would realize that my mother had, from early on, always been teaching me by example that words matter. In retrospect, as I became a grownup, I understood that she exercised her agency over language. By instinct or intuition, she chose to ignore or outright reject vocabulary that portrayed people like us as inferior, incompetent, or incapable. She shielded us as best she could from, language intended to exploit and manipulate, language that when all else failed, sought to make people like us invisible. She never told us we were "poor" or "poverty-stricken" though she sometimes said she was "broke;" that she had run out of money or close to it before her next pay day. I grew up never hearing the phrase, "broken home." Ours was whole and holy. Lods Street and Kossuth Court where we lived in Akron were not "hoods" or "ghettoes." They were neighborhoods, places next door to folks where the wife worked, the families mostly went to church on Sundays, the kids played in the streets and knew to be home before dark.

We knew that when we or someone else used the word Negroes, it meant people like us. But talking about ourselves we were "colored people," period. Minorities, people of color, diverse, marginalized populations were unheard of, words and phrases yet to be invented. Use of the word "nigger" was more complex; sometimes it was said as an insult, other times spoken as a tease, a put-down by and among insiders who knew the difference. "Niggras" was spoken by certain kinds of white folks, none that we knew personally. And none of my people called ourselves "African-Americans" or "afro-Americans." Hyphenated Americans were unknown to people raising me in the 1940s and '50s. And being American was nothing to dwell on, examine, or discuss. I grew up pledging allegiance to the flag at the start of the school days and singing the national anthem before the first pitch at a Cleveland Indians baseball game.

My mother even taught my sister and me a few French words: *parlez vous, bonjour,* and *tout suite* . . . remnant reminders of the high school education that she, a younger sister, and two of their brothers completed at a segregated Presbyterian boarding school in Anniston, Alabama, miles away from home. Their tuition paid by the family's eldest daughter who sent money home from New York where she had become a registered nurse. A consistent admonition underlying all of my homeschooling: to be successful in the larger world dominated by white people, we must be twice as smart, work twice as hard. This was not said in malice, but as cold hard fact based on the lived experience of the people who raised me.

Thanks to Susan Tolliver and other like-minded folks, my sister Constance and I were well schooled before setting a foot in our neighborhood public schools where most of the students were Black and all the teachers white and mostly women. Three of those women made lasting impressions on me: in 5th grade, my response to a class reading prompted the teacher, Mrs. Lewis, to say, "Melba, you have a good mind (pause) when you use it." On another occasion, thinking she might like to know more about me, I made a halfhearted and unsuccessful attempt to educate her about "nappy" hair. In tenth grade, when the names of the new cheerleaders were announced, and mine was one of them— the first Black girl in South High School's history—my French teacher, Miss Van Dis looked at me, her eyes lit up and her face broke into a broad, crooked grin that said she was proud of my accomplishment. In my senior year, Miss Wolfe encouraged my interest in history and personally steered me to be active with the debate team. I never felt inferior in the eyes of these white women. Just the opposite, all these decades later I remember them, their names, who was tall and skinny, who had a wooden leg, who wore glasses and her hair in a bun, and most of all when I have thought about them over the years, I believe they recognized something in me that they nurtured in their own way. They simply complimented the teachings of my mother and others.

As a working woman and sole breadwinner, before day care was invented, my mother did as other women before and after her have done. She paid a relative to keep her kids during the week. That taught my sister and me at an early age some of the choices and sacrifices some women must make. In her case, it meant living in a rented room and uniting with her kids on weekends. Saving up enough money from her low paid labor, for which she was enormously over-qualified, and borrowing the rest for the down payment on a mortgaged house.

Like Booker T. Washington, the freed slave and founder of Tuskegee Institute who emerged as a savvy politician, my mother believed in practical education. Nursing was her choice for me in an age when a girl's other career options were teacher and social worker. So, I did her bidding, gave up dreams of becoming the next Dorothy Dandridge or Lena Horne, and studied nursing for three years at Bellevue Hospital. While working as an operating room scrub nurse, I came closest to anything that even remotely might be considered activism. In April 1963, I wrote a scathing letter to Robert S. Bird, the national correspondent of the *New York Herald Tribune* critical of "Ten Negroes," his series of articles described by the paper as "a powerful, provocative portrait of today's Negroes."[2] Bird's journalism and his meeting and reporting of Negroes, brought him to see that the subjects of his reporting "seemed to be no different except as we all are different as individuals." I did not think that Bird was telling me or any Black person something that they did not already know, even if for him, this reporting "neutralized . . . the preconceptions and loaded overtones which looking on the Negro color had formerly cued off in my mind." The paper published my letter, along with my picture and the bold caption, "An Angry Woman."[3] In his conclusion, Bird said that his series had generated an "avalanche of mail." He wrote, "Much of it was praise from both Negroes and whites." Mine was not one of those. Here's how he described it, "One of the bitterest, angriest and most contemptuous letters—and one of the most literate—came from a woman."[4]

Four months later, on August 28, I went from writing letters to marching in the streets. I joined a busload of New Yorkers, organized by a local union for the trip to the nation's capital and the March on Washington for Jobs and Freedom. I was one of an estimated 250 thousand marchers, actually doing more standing around on the Mall than marching.

Just as my angry letter had made an impression on Bird and his enlightenment, which he made public in a newspaper, his reporting resonated in a different way with me—not fully at the time, but some years later, after I had become a journalist. I understood that journalists, like Bird, like me, are biased. We are products of our backgrounds, our experiences, our education—everything that makes us the unique Individuals we all are. And I understood that being a journalist was an opportunity, and an obligation to bring all of who I am to the work I do. Whether that work was in Houston, Albany, Albuquerque, or New York City. This insight would be the essential principle of my work moving along a career path that began with me in the role of "accidental anchorwoman."

In 1968 when WABC-TV *Eyewitness News* hired me, first as a vacation relief reporter, and then signed me to a regular contract. I spent eight years covering the gamut of local news in the nation's number one TV market. From my earliest assignment (reporting the beginning of construction on the World Trade Center Towers) to my last report (a half-hour profile of Gordon Parks, the groundbreaking photojournalist and filmmaker), my news career had mostly been that of a general assignment reporter. Meaning, I had no regular beat, no specialty based on expertise or experience, I was not primarily responsible for reporting and/or breaking stories about education, politics, police and so on. Instead, I simply showed up every day and got sent on whatever scheduled happenings or breaking news the assignment desk editor thought our station needed to cover—transit strike, busted water main, four alarm fire, drug bust, bank robbery, hostage taking, anti–Vietnam War protests, teacher strikes, women's lib demonstrations, Black Panther school breakfasts, fashion show, and more.

Over time, as I gained experience and showed interest in, and a willingness to take on other kinds of assignments, I served as co-anchor and associate producer of the Sunday evening news program. I cohosted *Like It Is,* a Black issues–oriented public affairs program, along with *AM New York,* an early morning news and information talk show.[5] Among our notable guests, Congresswoman Shirley Chisholm who was then campaigning to become US president (years later, I would interview her for a long article in *Good Housekeeping* magazine), and Ed Lewis a publisher of *Essence,* a new magazine for Black women. I hosted and reported for *People, Places, and Things,* a weekly magazine format features series; *Melba Tolliver's New York,* a one-off compilation of feature stories; and served as a featured reporter on the local Monday Night Football pregame show with sportscasters and former players, Frank Gifford and Don Meredith. With Howard Weinberg producing, I was also the reporter for *Consciousness Rising,* a program intended to translate some of the most commonly accepted feminist rhetoric into everyday reality as lived by everyday women.

In this same time frame, 1970–1971, I went to management with an idea for an ongoing series that I wanted to create and call *Profiles.* They gave the OK and I invited producer Howard Weinberg to team up with me. *Profiles* became a popular series of mini docs, ranging in length from five to twelve minutes and featuring people who gave our region its character, but who were not your typical newsmakers. Feminist poet Robin Morgan, the Pointer Sisters singing trio, the Brooklyn Atoms girls track club, poet Nikki Giovani and writer Ida Lewis in their startup of an international news magazine were among the mostly women—Black and white—I interviewed for the eighteen episodes.

I was proud of *Profiles*, personally and professionally. It reaffirmed my belief, and what I admit is my consciously arrived at personal and professional worldview, that everyday ordinary folks have stories to tell and deserve to tell them on TV where millions of people can learn something about someone or something they previously knew nothing about. I hoped each viewer would watch my segment and come away thinking or saying, "I didn't know that." Or "I never thought about it that way before." *Profiles* was a winner, but this program breathed its last when cigarette advertising was pulled from TV, resulting in budget cuts.

In 1973, the ABC TV network, created *Americans All,* a *Profiles*-like show for its national audience. "We wanted to try something more serious," said the vice president for documentaries in a December 14, 1973, *Washington Post* article.[6] Explaining the genesis of a programming alternative to the promotional time slot fillers that followed the Sunday night movies, he said, "and we decided on a vehicle that would not only share the contributions of minorities to the fabric of America, but give our minority employees a chance to research, produce, and handle something on their way to bigger things with the network." Four staffers, three of them Black females, were assigned to the program. On the list of subjects for the first year of the program, according to *Americans All* associate producer, Willie Kathryn Suggs, were eight Black topics or individuals, three Spanish-speaking people, and one American Indian. I served as the on-camera narrator-interviewer for films featuring Alvin Ailey, Black choreographer and founder of his American Dance Theatre; Roberto Mondragon, Chicano Lt. Governor of New Mexico; Tom Bradley, Black mayor of Los Angeles; and Brock Peters and Vinette Carrol, Black actors reading the works of Langston Hughes. Other films featured Harry Low, a Chinese American judge and political figure, and Norman Mineta, a Japanese American congressman, both Californians; and Vine Deloria, Standing Sioux theologian and author of *Custer Died for Your Sins.* Working on *Americans All* was for me a welcome opportunity to travel, interview, and learn from a variety of folks of different backgrounds and cultures. But unlike *Profiles*, they were not the everyday, ordinary folks I generally tended to cover.

In March 1973, more than four years before the National Women's Conference, I was the subject of a profile in the Sunday *New York Times*. It recounted my path from secretary to the article's description of me as a television superstar reporter. In 1967 I had been drafted as a last-minute substitute for the anchorwoman of *News With The Woman's Touch*, after Marlene Sanders and her on-air colleagues went on strike, leaving the three broadcast networks with several empty anchor chairs to fill. I would subsequently be branded a scab, a strikebreaker. I would also subsequently become the guinea pig or first trainee in an ABC TV News training program. A program devised in the wake of the Kerner Report and its stinging criticism of the news media's hiring practices with regard to Negroes. The article, headlined, "Melba, Toast of the Town," described me as "a new kind of celebrity," a television reporter seen by almost a million viewers in the intimate spaces of their homes every night.[7] Some of my comments stepped on a few toes. For instance, I said "that given a choice, I preferred reporting news to selling brassieres at Macy's." Yet hardly anyone even spoke to me about the article.

I slammed the copy-cat approach of TV news. News stations, with few exceptions, led with the same stories and aired the same stories, at the same point in their programs. I believed they showed little originality of content and little context for what they put on the air. I felt there was little or no connecting of the dots that would allow viewers to understand why certain news was relevant to their everyday lives. I struck back at executives who kept me off the air when I chose to stop chemically straightening my hair, deciding to wear it natural just days before going to cover Tricia Nixon's White House wedding. Though I later believed I was mistaken and gave credence to a gross generalization when I said what happened with my hair would not have been a problem had there been a Black in authority at the station. Kinky hair is not beautiful to *all* Black people. Not then. Not now. Of all the positive letters I received about my hair, only one said my hair was a disgrace. The writer identified himself as a Black man.

In that same article I said being Black in a field dominated by white men was a bigger problem for me than being a woman. At the time white men ran everything having to do with me and my work. Not white women. Despite having mixed feelings about the women's movement, I felt that the women's movement had made more progress in six years than Black folks had made since Reconstruction. "I see the women's movement as a white family quarrel." It made all the sense in the world to me that white women who are oppressed are oppressed by white men. White men who wield the power. White men who may be their own husbands, sons, brothers, cousins and so on. Power is the operative here. And those who use their power against those who have less of it, if they are so inclined. Furthermore, if white men oppress white women—and others—what role in all of this do the white mothers raising white children play? What values are they instilling in their white sons? What demands are the white women making of their white husbands? Their white uncles and cousins? To quote the white journalist, David K. Shipler, author of *A Country of Strangers: Blacks and Whites in America*, "Discussions of race are imprisoned by words."[8]

The New York Times article caught the attention of Ben Yablonky, director of the National Endowment for the Humanities Fellowship program for journalists at the University of Michigan in Ann Arbor. He thought I sounded like a woman who badly needed to take a break, and he invited me to apply for a fellowship. I replied, "Thanks. But no thanks." Two years passed and I wrote Mr. Yablonky again, asking if I might reconsider his invitation. He obliged, I applied and joined eleven other journalists—all of them newspaper people—all of us taking a year away from our jobs, and the stresses of deadlines and office politics to study anything—except journalism—that our hearts desired.

Against the advice I got from most people who said, "You're making a big mistake. A year off the air and people will forget all about you," I chose to take that risk and go off to Michigan. I was frustrated with journalism and with myself. I wasn't sure why I just knew I had expected more. And I also wanted to look into the racial divide as it revealed itself in American history and literature from the perspectives of a white majority and a Black minority. So, I signed up for two large survey classes representative of the white majority group, and in the Black studies department, I did history with Harold Cruse, author of the *Crisis of the Negro Intellectual*, and literature with novelist Gayle Jones, author of *Eva's Man* and whose editor was Toni Morrison. Although on the same university campus, the paths of these two tracks rarely crossed; it was as if they occupied two different universes. Kind of like the racial majority/minority divide I witnessed living my own everyday life.

Another opportunity, totally unforeseen, gave me—a Black woman reporter—a chance to collaborate with a white woman and the only untenured woman associate professor in Michigan's journalism department. She was looking to create a conference on women and discrimination, and I volunteered to help, not questioning if she was thinking only about white women and suggesting that she might also extend her interest to minorities. She liked the idea and in April 1977, a decade after President Johnson appointed the Kerner Commission to investigate the long hot summer of riots in more than three dozen American cities, Professor Marzolf and I directed Kerner Plus 10: Conference on Minorities and the Media.[9]

That year away was an important turning point for me personally and professionally. That period of study and reflection helped me see how the majority assume the power of definition, especially their definition of others. And the Kerner Conference inspired me to find more ways of including the voices and experiences of everyday people in my reporting. All of this was excellent preparation for covering Houston.

Before leaving New York, I had jumped stations, going from top-rated WABC *Eyewitness News*, to its closest rival and top-rated wannabe, WNBC *News Center 4*.[10] I had barely set foot in the new station when they sent me to cover New York's preliminary state meeting. I can't remember many details of that assignment except that it was in Albany and I had to hit the ground running. A photo of me taken by Diana Mara Henry caught me seated before a bank of manual typewriters, biting down hard on a pencil and probably wishing I had just a little more time to work on my story. Positive feedback on the state meeting convinced our newsroom bosses that Houston would be a big deal.

Once the decision was made to cover it, the field producer, Merle Rubine, a white woman, and I got on a plane to Houston and without much planning, got to work. She handled most of the logistics of getting our tapes to the NBC local affiliate for editing and air and checking in with the producers back at 30 Rock. I did the on-camera reporting and interviews, the standups and narration. We sometimes worked together and sometimes went our separate ways—and without walkie-talkies or cell phones, managed to stay in touch. She went after certain delegates for me to interview and I was scouting out information from various caucus meetings. We called it "crash and burn."

My stories over that weekend aired on both the early and late news. I mixed interviews with narrations explaining the most important and sometimes divisive policies and planks over scenes of caucuses and meetings. I sought to include everyday ordinary women as often as I could in the limited time, I had to find them inside the Coliseum. I also talked to women outside and not part of the conference and who opposed the feminist movement in general. The pieces ranged in length from two and a half to five minutes, less time than it takes to boil an egg. My enduring recollection of Houston is that I was surprised. I had never witnessed anything like it. I admit I am still surprised. I thought the personalities that drove the conference, and the words and actions that animated it, were evidence that I was watching, at the very least, the birth of a new national political party. And I often ask "why" it didn't happen.

Notes

1. "Melba Tolliver." *Notable Black American Women*, Gale, 1996. Biography in Context, link.galegroup.com/apps/doc/K1623000767/BIC1?u=dclib_main&xid=351792ee. Accessed October 14, 2017.

2. Robert S. Bird, "Ten Negroes," *New York Herald Tribune,* 1963.

3. Melba Tolliver, "An Angry Woman," *New York Herald Tribune*, April 1963.

4. "Ten Negroes" a series of articles by Robert S. Bird, Herald Tribune national correspondent, appeared April 30–May 12, 1963, in the *New York Herald Tribune.* Senator Jacob K Javits (R-NY) had the articles read into the "Congressional Record." Bird included both my letter and photo in his conclusion to the series.

5. "Melba Tolliver: Being Black, Female, City-bred," *New York Amsterdam News*, April 25, 1992.

6. John Carmody, "ABC's 'Americans All: American Shorts,'" *Washington Post*, December 14, 1973, D1. Accessed January 10, 2021.

7. Barbara Campbell, "Melba? She's the Toast of the Town," *New York Times*, February 18, 1973; "Never a Dull Moment for 'Girl Friday': Ex-Model Plays Role Behind TV Scenes," *New Pittsburgh Courier*, June 15, 1963, 18.

8. David K. Shipler, *A Country of Strangers: Blacks and Whites in America* (New York: Vintage Books, 1998).

9. Training programs for minorities were part of the response to the 1968 Kerner Commission report. Created in the wake of rioting in Watts, Chicago, Newark, and Detroit, the National Advisory Commission on Civil Disorders, as the Kerner Commission was officially known, the commission was tasked by President Johnson commission with understanding and preventing race riots. The commissions' wide-ranging recommendations included several targeted at the media itself. Increased coverage of the Black community and recruiting, training and promoting Black journalists were intended to counter journalism that looked at the world "with white men's eyes and a white perspective." National Advisory Commission on Civil Disorders, *Report of the National Advisory Commission on Civil Disorders* (New York: Bantam Books, 1968), 389. On Kerner Plus 10, see Marion Marzolf and Melba Tolliver, "Kerner Plus 10: Conference on Minorities and the Media," University of Michigan, April 22, 1977.

10. George Nelson, "ABC's Tolliver Returns; NBC Has Her," *New York Amsterdam News*, Aug 20, 1977.

19

Sharing a Precious Gift

Photographing the National Women's Conference

DIANA MARA HENRY

THE 1970S WERE THE DECADE when the greatest number of African Americans entered Congress and the decade when I photographed the politics that made history with them. As the official photographer for the National Women's Conference in Houston, I had access to some of the most influential women leaders of the time and of the century.[1] In Houston, I worked for Bella Abzug,[2] chair of the National Commission; Lee Novick, conference coordinator; the US State Department who contracted for my work; and Congress, that funded the commission. Through all these entities I was, ultimately, working for the American people. I took it as my job to make a record of the historic event and its participants.

Personal artistic considerations kept me from wanting to impose my personality or agenda in my photographs. The less visible I was, the more immediate the impact and the more truly the personalities of my subjects could be conveyed to the viewer.[3] I wanted *their* personality to be projected via my images of them; I thought *their* agenda should come through with minimal editorializing on my part. This is the difference between news and editorial photography, a distinction that is being lost today as most people do not read newspapers, which traditionally had separate news (fact) and editorial (opinion) pages.

I was trained as a newspaperwoman in the 1960s, at the same time I was learning photography. I tell people, "Harvard was my trade school." With the idea of learning a new skill, I set out to compete for the photography "board" of the student newspaper, *The Crimson,* in the winter/spring term of my sophomore year, 1967. I became a photo editor (not simply a photographer), just as others were never simply designated to be reporters or writers but either news editors or editorial page editors or feature editors. This glorification of our roles was intended to magnify our chances in the job market after college. *The Crimson* is where I learned the difference between news and editorial content; and where I learned the difference between the news photo that tells the story in one shot and a photo essay that shows several dimensions of the story. My coverage of the First National Women's Conference includes both.

. . .

After graduation, I moved to New York City. There, when I heard Bella Abzug's voice for the first time, my life changed. Her brash bellow was carried across the NYC night air by WBAI Pacifica radio, my constant companion in the darkroom, and it was unlike any female voice I had ever heard. She certainly didn't deliver her message with the quiet ladylike reserve my mother modeled and encouraged.[4] After hearing Bella's voice, I resolved to see this woman—and photograph her, of course. So, off I went to the Battery, at the south end of Manhattan, to photograph the press conference where she inveighed against the powers that had gerrymandered her district.

I was so excited to see Bella with handheld, hand-lettered signs behind her, some in Chinese lettering, some with NOW. slogans, that I dropped my lens. I crouched at her feet so as not to antagonize the male TV reporters whose legs I had wormed past to photograph her close up. Maybe my photograph of her, which she used for campaign posters, radiant against the backdrop of lower Manhattan's skyline, helped her win the next election in 1972—just as my photograph of Elizabeth Holtzman on the Brooklyn Bridge that same year helped Holtzman capture fifty-year veteran Emanuel Celler's Congressional seat.[5] I offered my photographs for free when I brought them in to Bella the first time, but she paid me for all my work after that, including photographing her airplane-hopping tour to upstate New York to promote her candidacy for US Senate in 1976.[6]

There had been, and would be, other assignments: one more exciting: James Brown in performance at Rikers Island House of Detention, photographed from onstage in 1973, at the behest of William Van Den Heuvel;[7] some more glamorous: Malcolm Forbes and family, at their balloon meets in Normandy, flown over in the Concorde and housed in his castle, in 1979 and 1980; assignments more radical: the Women's Pentagon Action, 1980;[8] and one more poignant: the campaigns of Congressman Allard Lowenstein and his funeral. But when I was hired as official photographer of the National Women's Conference—after only ten years of holding a camera and five years of doing so professionally—I knew this would be the biggest opportunity and probably the most historic assignment of my lifetime.

Figure 19.1. *a*, Bella Abzug in Battery Park, New York City, 1972; *b*, Elizabeth Holtzman at the Brooklyn Bridge, New York City, 1972. Diana Mara Henry Papers (PH 51). Special Collections and University Archives, University of Massachusetts Amherst Libraries. Copyright © Diana Mara Henry / dianamarahenry.com

First came the assignment from Bella to photograph the New York State Women's Meeting.[9] The flyer for the meeting read, "Drop those dishes . . . put your work aside . . . cover up your typewriter . . . for the first Federally-sponsored women's meeting ever held in NY State." I took the opportunity to create photography exhibits at the magnificent venue for the occasion, the Empire State Mall in Albany. So, in addition to photographing amazing women such as Ruby Dee and Vinie Burrows, Melba Tolliver and Mary Burke Nicholas, I created an exhibit of the work of E. Alice Austen and a slide show entitled, and featuring, the work of "Seventy Women Photographers of NY State."[10]

Turning my attention to the upcoming conference in Houston, I took the unusual step—for me, at the time—of strategizing. I was encouraged by Steven Louis Borns, another young "Concerned Photographer," as we styled ourselves when we flocked to the International Center of Photography to work for Cornell Capa and subject ourselves to his whims and ambitions.[11] In 1977, Steve and I were already attending American Society of Media Photographers events and arming ourselves with their professional guidelines. I used their assignment confirmation and delivery memos to ensure my copyright protection for the images of the NWC, all of which I also registered in 1978 at the US Copyright Office. Having taken these steps, I have been able to ward off the predations of many individuals and publishers over the years, from feminist icons to expensive purveyors of public-domain materials and heavy-hitting publishers.[12]

In order to travel to Houston, I had to get time off from teaching photography at the Convent of the Sacred Heart, a posh girl's school in Manhattan for students like Caroline Kennedy. The order of the nuns of the Sacred Heart had a convent in Houston, too; I was the grateful recipient of their hospitality. I only had to drive myself to and from the conference each day to catch a few hours of sleep.

For the work, I carried a navy canvas camera bag weighed down with two canon F-1 cameras (one for black-and-white film—Kodak's Tri-x, my favorite—and one for color slides) and several lenses, from my favorite, the 35mm, to the 135mm that was probably my longest lens.

I decided on the first day right there on the conference floor that I would have to stop smoking in order to have the strength and stamina to stay at the task, which was physically demanding. While other photographers came onto the floor of the conference for twenty minutes and then had to rotate out to give their pass to another, I, as "official photographer" with "total access" could stay there indefinitely. I could go from the stage to the corridors under the

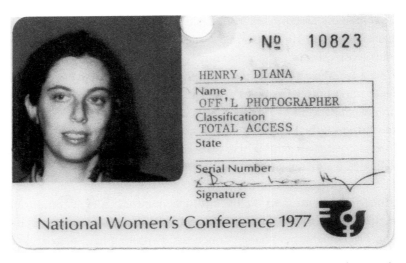

Figure 19.2. Diana Mara Henry's official identification for the National Women's Conference. Diana Mara Henry Papers (PH 51). Special Collections and University Archives, University of Massachusetts Amherst Libraries. Copyright © Diana Mara Henry / dianamarahenry.com

convention center, where the commissioners were brought on tour before the opening, to the hotel rooms where they met late at night to consider strategy for the next day's events.

At previous events, such as the Democratic National Convention at Miami Beach in 1972 and the demonstration for the use of the term Ms. at the *New York Times* in 1974, I hadn't stopped to ask for names of those I photographed. I am very glad indeed that Mim Kelber asked me to do so for this assignment. If anyone was to make a continuous record of the event and an attempt to photograph everyone there, I had the best chance and the greatest responsibility to do so. But I didn't get everyone's name, as much as I wanted to. There were simply too many people and too much happening.

I captured images at the NWC that many call "iconic," partially because they tell a story in one shot. These include the three First Ladies and Bella holding aloft the torch that was run from Seneca Falls to Houston;[13] women waving their bras; three women of different races and ethnicities holding the stars and stripes; Gloria Scott raising the gavel (Figure 3.1); Barbara Jordan signing autographs (Figure 12.2); a Gloria Steinem look-alike watching Gloria on a monitor; and my most published photograph, of the women leading the march into the convention center with Billie Jean King at one end and Betty Friedan at the other (Figure 2.1).

In between those moments, I had three days to complete an extended photo essay.[14] I was gifted with the delicious possibility of wandering into private spaces and sharing atmospheric details with posterity.[15] These include my photographs of women from the states or territories with their headdresses and outfits chosen to represent their heritage; women with their individually crafted statements such as the attorney with her calling card in the form of a rape whistle or the resentful delegate with her individually hand-lettered "Keep 'em in the closet" sign; Texas women, from First Lady "Lady Bird" Johnson to the delegates, with their "Viva La Mujer" buttons; former Black Panther Eldridge Cleaver pontificating about men being keepers of the sperm, Roman Catholic priests pontificating about who knows what; and women of all political persuasions at their needlecrafts.

Figure 19.3. Unknown delegate with a clear gaze, Brownie, and flashbulb. Diana Mara Henry Papers (PH 51). Special Collections and University Archives, University of Massachusetts Amherst Libraries. Copyright © Diana Mara Henry / dianamarahenry.com

Figure 19.4. Sergeants at Arms. Diana Mara Henry Papers (PH 51). Special Collections and University Archives, University of Massachusetts Amherst Libraries. Copyright © Diana Mara Henry / dianamarahenry.com

When I took photographs of women who were not particularly famous, I indulged my predilection to photograph those who were working at the conference.[16] When I was hired to photograph parties, I would always photograph the servers as well as the guests of honor. It just seemed right. My collection from Houston includes policewomen and bus drivers, signers for the deaf (men and women), people shooting the ID photos, sergeants at arms (Figure 19.4) and the amazingly competent conference organizer, Lee (now Rabbi Leah) Novick.[17] At one point I also took an hour off to photograph Phyllis Schlafly's press conference on the occasion of her organizing a huge "Pro-Family" counter-conference/rally in Houston that weekend.

When I returned to New York, I spent three days and nights processing the images. On the first day, I unrolled thirty-two rolls of film in the dark of my closet and placed them in canisters, into and out of which I poured chemicals into the kitchen sink, then water to wash them, before hanging them up to dry from the shower rod in my bathroom. On the second day, I made contact sheets of all the film strips to see tiny images of all the shots I had made, and the next day, I made forty or so enlargements. That's how photography was done in the first one hundred and fifty years of the medium, when images were created by the action of light reflected off the subject onto a light-sensitive silver coating on glass, film or paper, developed and fixed in chemical baths and washed in water to acquire lasting archival quality. Color processes are ephemeral, but the black and white paper prints I made could last as long as the pyramids, in the right climatic conditions—such as in the middle of the pyramids.

After I returned from Houston, my efforts to alert the press that I had images of the National Women's Conference were met with little interest except at the *Village Voice*, which published my photo of the women waving their bras on the front page on December 2, 1977, and *Viva* magazine, which in March 1978 published a collection of images and text titled "United we Stand, Scenes from the National Women's Conference by Diana Mara Henry." The "Editor's note" in the March issue included the following in their contributor profile: "Diana herself was a government major at Radcliffe—'Yucch,' she editorializes succinctly—but the background gave her entrée to a lot of smoke-filled rooms during recent political campaigns. Diana always seems to be the one in there snapping while other journalists are still outside banging on the door. We're glad to have her." That article may have spawned another, their June 1978 article by Eddie Adams, a renowned war photographer: "They Shoot Pictures, Don't They?" about women photojournalists, including myself.

My photograph of the women marching abreast to the conference became my best-known and most-published image, while the one of Coretta Scott King has sold most as a print. One of the delights of the last decade has been identifying, corresponding with, and in some cases meeting the women that I photographed so long ago, some of whom are in this book: Clara McLaughlin and her daughter Rinetta, my personal favorite of all the images (Figure 18.1); Freddie Groomes (Figure 5.1); and Michelle Cearcy, who along with Sylvia Ortiz and Peggy Kokernot Kaplan carried the torch for the last mile of the 2,600 mile relay from Seneca Falls to Houston for the opening of the conference (Figure 2.1). I have always insisted that the caption for that photograph include the names of all the women in it that I can identify: Billie Jean King, Susan B. Anthony, Bella Abzug, Sylvia Ortiz, Peggy Kokernot, Michelle Cearcy, and Betty Friedan.

My aspiration as I photographed women at the First National Women's Conference was to honor them, and my aspiration now is that you will too—by creating and doing for yourselves and others the way these brave women, and others before them, did for themselves, their children, and for you.

Notes

1. Conference badge # 10823 "Classification: Off'l Photographer / Total Access."

2. I was hired by Lee Novick, conference coordinator, to whom I wrote a letter of inquiry on 9/6/77 at the recommendation of Mim Kelber, Bella's writer and close associate. My negotiations with the State Department for the assignment went through Mim Kelber.

3. Examples of photographers who are very visible in their photographs: Annie Leibowitz, Cindy Sherman.

4. Although, with my father's help, my mother built a business around her talent and experience with design. She ruled the firm's 250 employees—and my father who was CFO—with benevolence and consideration.

5. Holtzman's own characterization of the role of my iconic photograph of her. https://www.youtube.com/watch?v=npp5IeAinV8&feature=youtu.be

6. http://www.nytimes.com/learning/general/onthisday/bday/0724.html

7. "Contact High: Shooting James Brown At Rikers: The stories behind Diana Mara Henry's iconic shots," by Vikki Tobak, 3/2/17, and http://www.dianamarahenry.com/JamesBrownatRikersIsland.htm

8. http://www.dianamarahenry.com/GracePaleybyDianaMaraHenry.htm

9. July 8–10, 1977, dates of the New York State Women's Meeting. See http://www.dianamarahenry.com/wotm/NYState_Women_s_Meeting.html .

10. http://www.dianamarahenry.com/DianaMaraHenryandtheAliceAustenHouse.htm

11. Kornel Friedmann (Cornell Capa), photographer and curator: born Budapest 1918; Director, International Center of Photography 1974–94; died 2008, promoted "images in which genuine human feeling predominates over commercial cynicism or disinterested formalism."

12. As a freelance photographer, I often photographed events under my own steam, "on spec." I was supported by no publication or network to photograph feminist events; only Congresswomen Bella Abzug and Liz Holtzman paid me. No one was hiring photographers, even freelancers, to cover feminist events; only photographer Bettye Lane and I could usually count on seeing each other there. I don't think it worked out much better for her than it did for me financially.

13. Published in Newsweek Books' *Best of Photojournalism 4* by the National Press Photographers Association/University of Missouri School of Journalism, ed. Edwin D. Bayrd Jr., p. 45. Mine was one of very few photographs chosen that was by a freelancer.

14. I shot thirty-two rolls of film, 36 or 37 frames each, for a total of 1,152 images. That's 384 per day; thus 32 per hour in a 12-hour day, for an average of one photo every 2 minutes.

15. This sense of a gift and the title of this essay were expressed by Melba Tolliver: "Thank you Diana for holding this precious gift," as recorded in the video from UMass Amherst: https://www.youtube.com/watch?v=npp5IeAinV8&feature=youtu.be.

16. See a similar sensibility in Robin Morgan, "A Brief Elegy For Four Women" op.cit. p. 148. "Too many sisters who would be willing to die defending a radical brother would on the other hand find it difficult, if not impossible, even to relate to the daily suffering of any woman in the secretarial pool."

17. I also picked up every piece of paper I could get my hands on, as I did for every event of the women's movement that I photographed. That ephemera (press releases, flyers, maps of the marches, brochures and invitations) and the collection of books, films, articles, and websites using my photographs that I always request a copy of, are, to my mind, as interesting and valuable as the photographic record I made. All are part of the Diana Mara Henry: Twentieth Century Photographer collection at the Du Bois Library, UMass Amherst: http://credo.library.umass.edu/search?q=diana%20mara%20henry&page=201&facets=

Contributors

LINDSAY AMARAL is an ACLS Leading Edge Fellow (F'22) working as a research manager with Hunger Free America in New York. She is the author of the dissertation "Too Poor to Eat: A Socio-Political History of Food Stamps in the United States from 1964–1996" and a *Washington Post* op-ed entitled Perspective, "Why Donald Trump's New Food Stamp Rule is About Cruelty, Not Responsibility."

RACHEL JESSICA DANIEL is director of the Center for Employee Enrichment and Development and professor of English at Massasoit Community College.

AMIRA ROSE DAVIS is assistant professor of history and African American studies at Penn State University and the author of *"Can't Eat a Medal": The Lives and Labors of Black Women Athletes in the Age of Jim Crow.*

JULIE DE CHANTAL is assistant professor of history at Georgia Southern University. She is the author of "Before Boston's Busing Crisis: Operation Exodus, Grassroots Organizing, and Motherhood, 1965–1967" in *Motherhood in Public and Political Life.*

CARLYN FERRARI is assistant professor of English at Seattle University.

JANINE FONDON is chair of Undergraduate Communications and assistant professor at Bay Path University. She is a contributing author of *The Power of Women: Celebrating Women From the 1600s to the Present Day* and coauthor of *The Practice of Power: Finding Success in a Diverse World.*

ZINGA A. FRASER is assistant professor of Africana studies at Brooklyn College and director of the Shirley Chisholm Project on Brooklyn Women's Activism. She is the author of *Shirley Chisholm In Her Own Words: Speeches and*

Writings and *Sister Outsider / Sister Insider : A Comparative Study of Shirley Chisholm and Barbara Jordan; Black Women's Politics in the Post–Civil Rights Era.*

JULIE A. GALLAGHER is assistant professor of history at Penn State Brandywine. She is the author of *Black Women and Politics in New York City* and coeditor of *Reshaping Women's History: Voices of Nontraditional Women's Historians.*

KELLY N. GILES, a PhD student in the Department of Sociology at the University of Massachusetts Amherst, is an emerging interdisciplinary scholar whose research interests are rooted in Sociology; Black Studies; Women, Gender, Sexuality Studies; Public Health; and Public History. Her doctoral research interrogates the intersections of race, gender, age/aging, and sexual and reproductive health, by exploring intraracial relationships and intergenerational dialogue among Black women during their mid-30s to mid-50s. This project examines Black women's ideas about sexual and reproductive health and health education and how it informs their relationship to self-care, intraracial community, civic engagement, and political activism.

DIANA MARA HENRY is a photographer whose historic work constitutes the Diana Mara Henry Twentieth Century Photographer Special Collection at the Du Bois Library at UMass Amherst and the Diana Mara Henry Collection at the Schlesinger Library at the Harvard Redcliffe Institute, and may be seen at her website, www.dianamarahenry.com.

KIRSTEN LENG is assistant professor of women, gender, and sexuality studies at the University of Massachusetts Amherst. She is the author of *Sexual Politics and Feminist Science: Women Sexologists in Germany, 1900–1933.*

DESTINEY LINKER is a doctoral candidate at the University of Massachusetts Amherst.

LAURA L. LOVETT is assistant professor of history at the University of Pittsburgh. She is the author of *With Her Fist Raised: Dorothy Pitman Hughes and the Transformative Power of Black Community Activism.*

JOHANNA M. ORTNER is instructor in the Department of History and the Women's, Gender, and Sexuality Studies Program at the University of Connecticut Stamford.

SABINA PECK obtained her PhD from the University of Leeds in 2018 and now works as a researcher outside of academia.

SARAH B. ROWLEY is assistant professor of history at DePauw University. She is the author of "Married Congresswomen and the New Breed of Political Husbands in 1970s Political Culture," published in *Suffrage at 100: Women in American Politics since 1920.*

CAMESHA SCRUGGS is a doctoral candidate in history at the University of Massachusetts Amherst.

MELBA TOLLIVER is a journalist who worked as a reporter and television news anchorperson in New York City.

MARCIA WALKER-MCWILLIAMS is executive director of the Black Metropolis Research Consortium. She is the author of *Reverend Addie Wyatt: Faith and the Fight for Labor, Gender and Racial Equality.*

CRYSTAL LYNN WEBSTER is assistant professor of history at the University of British Columbia. She is author of *Beyond the Boundaries of Childhood: African American Children in the Antebellum North.*

Index

Page numbers in italics refer to figures.